Romanian
Foreign Policy
Since 1965

Aurel Braun

Romanian Foreign Policy Since 1965

The Political and Military Limits of Autonomy

PRAEGER PUBLISHERS
Praeger Special Studies

New York   •   London   •   Sydney   •   Toronto

Library of Congress Cataloging in Publication Data

Braun, Aurel.
  Romanian policy since 1965.

  Bibliography: p.
  Includes index.
  1. Romania—Foreign relations. 2. Romania—Military
policy. 3. Russia—Military policy. I. Title.
DR267.B72   327.498   78-9516
ISBN 0-03-043471-8

PRAEGER SPECIAL STUDIES
383 Madison Avenue, New York, N.Y. 10017, U.S.A.

Published in the United States of America in 1978
by Praeger Publishers,
A Division of Holt, Rinehart and Winston, CBS, Inc.

89   038   987654321

Printed in the United States of America

to my parents

Preface

The Romanian government of Nicolae Ceausescu followed through with the foreign policy breakthroughs of Gheorghe Gheorghiu-Dej after the latter's death in 1965. At times Romanian deviations from Soviet foreign policy lines, though, appeared to be close to the breaking point of Moscow's tolerance. Romanian challenges, however, cannot be properly understood unless they are placed within the perspective of East European and, particularly, Soviet policy. This book is an attempt to use such a perspective to evaluate the political and military limits of autonomy for Romania.

Many people have given me their generous help. In writing this book I benefited greatly from the comments, criticisms, and suggestions of Mr. Philip Windsor of the London School of Economics, Professor John Gellner of York University, and Professor Bennett Kovrig of the University of Toronto. I also profited greatly from the special insights of Professors Richard Gregor and H. Gordon Skilling of the University of Toronto during the many discussions we had together on the subject. Special thanks are due to Professor Nils Orvik, the director of the Centre for International Relations at Queen's University, and especially to the Chairman of the Department of Political Science at the University of Western Ontario, Professor M. W. Westmacott, whose assistance and encouragement were instrumental in bringing about the completion of this book. As well, I wish to mention the aid given me by my brother Stefan. Without his probative questions and suggestions and patient criticisms of the first draft, the manuscript may not have seen completion until much later. I am, of course, solely responsible for any errors or omissions.

Finally, I wish to express thanks to Rochelle Weinberg, who deciphered my handwriting for the first draft, and Finny LaBrier, Wendy Skillings, and Faye Murphy, who patiently and expertly retyped all subsequent drafts.

Contents

Introduction

In the 1960s the image of monolithic Communism gave way to that of polycentrism, the term coined by the late Palmiro Togliatti to describe a multi-centered, more flexible type of Communism which rejected the existence of a directing center.[1] Some Western authors felt that in Eastern Europe itself the countries that had been under total Soviet domination were breaking away and ending Soviet hegemony in that part of the world.[2] The Soviet and Warsaw Pact intervention in Czechoslovakia in 1968, however, demonstrated that there was a limit to the amount of divergence the Moscow leadership was willing to tolerate. Romania, which beginning in the early 1960s had been at odds on numerous occasions with Soviet policy in formulating its own foreign policy, escaped the ultimate Soviet sanction of military occupation, thereby lending credence to a hypothesis that it had not breached the limits of divergence set by Moscow. This is not to say that only a breach of the limit could have acted as a brake on divergence among the East European states that up to the 1960s had been tightly controlled by Moscow. A breach of this limit, in our definition, would have brought a Soviet prohibition against the continuation of a certain policy by an East European state (and enforcement thereof). Lesser types of divergencies to the Soviet line would have brought warnings and political and/or economic sanctions. Attempts at intimidation through military intervention, or the threat or attempt of such intervention, would have been, respectively, the ultimate sanction or the ultimate deterrent.

We view these limits themselves as dynamic rather than static. They were not decided upon in Moscow in an abstract manner, but were subject to general policies and actions both in Moscow and in Bucharest. All of these elements, acting together, prevented a Soviet military intervention into Romania and could have allowed the latter to continue certain divergent policies by maintaining safe limits. In that sense these combinations of factors may be compared to a net-work of defenses. From Romania's point of view, those factors or elements that were determined in Moscow alone constituted passive defenses, while those originating in Bucharest were active defenses. The two, interacting in action-reaction syndromes, added new elements to the defense network. In turn the defense network would have had the potential to enlarge, to constrict, or to maintain the limits for Romanian divergence from Soviet policy.

While it may not be possible to ascertain the precise decision-making process of the Romanian and the Soviet leadership, we can gauge the broader policy aims of both deductively. Therefore, when we speak about limits we are alluding to tendencies in policy or vague parameters, not precise, clearly defined confining lines for Romanian foreign policy autonomy. Furthermore, in hypothesizing that various defenses defined the limits, we do not mean that a particular defense had an established weight in the calculation; rather we talk in terms of important defenses building a strong defense network.

We propose to use the term "autonomy" in analyzing Romanian foreign policy during this period because of certain advantages it has over the term "independence" in the study of East European states. In the first instance, we speak of the power or right to self-government and particularly the formulation of autochthonous policies, whereas "independence" would have connoted freedom from dependence upon others. In view of the fact that Romania has remained a member of both the Warsaw Pact and the Council of Mutual Economic Assistance (Comecon) and has reiterated its loyalty to and membership in the fourteen-state Socialist camp, we considered the term "independence" unsuitable for this study.

Instances of Romanian autonomy in foreign policy were numerous under the leadership of Ceausescu. In the period from 1964 to 1967 Romania refused to participate in Warsaw Pact maneuvers and unilaterally reduced induction periods for conscripts; in 1967 it became the first Soviet-bloc state* to establish diplomatic relations with the Federal Republic of Germany and the only bloc state not to break off diplomatic relations with Israel following the Six-Day War in June 1967; it criticized severely the Soviet and Warsaw Pact intervention into Czechoslovakia in 1968 and insisted on maintaining close and friendly ties with the Soviet Union's arch-rival, the People's Republic of China; and it sought and maintained close trade links with Western nations, becoming the first Soviet-bloc-state member of the International Monetary Fund and of the International Bank for Reconstruction and Development during 1972. In December 1972 the Romanian Grand National Assembly adopted an "all horizons" defense law, while in 1974 at the 11th Party Congress the Ceausescu leadership decided to restructure the Romanian Communist Party along novel lines. This—but a partial list of Romanian autonomous foreign policy moves—indicates that the Soviet Union could have had cause to reassert its control over Romanian foreign policy. The continuation of Romanian policies of autonomy gives a preliminary indication that due to her defensive network, it did not breach the limits of autonomy tolerated by the Soviet Union and thus it was able to avoid the Soviet prohibition and ultimate sanction of military intervention. In this study, therefore, we will attempt to analyze the various "defenses" which made up the network and their effectiveness individually and collectively in allowing this formulation of Romanian foreign policy autonomy in the political and military spheres.

For a number of reasons, there will be a restriction to the above two spheres of analysis to the considerable exclusion of the economic one. It is

---

*By "the Soviet-bloc states" we mean to include Poland, East Germany, Czechoslovakia, Hungary, Romania, and Bulgaria. After the early 1960s Albania had ceased, for all intents and purposes, to be a member of this bloc.

true that the origins of the Soviet-Romanian disputes are to be found in economic causes. Romania's quest to industrialize rapidly led it to disagree with Moscow's policies by the late 1950s. Neveretheless, a thorough analysis of the economic limits and "defenses" of Romanian foreign policy would require a knowledge of the science (or art) of economics that this writer does not possess, and a large, complex analysis that this limited study of foreign policy would have difficulty in encompassing within its framework. Therefore, the analysis of "economic defenses" will be restricted largely to the examination of Romanian actions and defenses in the institutional framework of Comecon. Second, we submit that Romania had fought her crucial economic battles under the leadership of Gheorghiu-Dej. In the Six-Year Plan of 1959, the latter set the Romanian economy on a firm course of rapid industrialization from which it refused to deviate despite Nikita Khrushchev's 1962 program of "Socialist division of labor."[3] By the time Romania issued the "Declaration of April 22, 1964," in which it stated its right to determine its own development,[4] and especially by the time of Ceausescu's succession to the position of Secretary General of the Romanian Workers Party on March 19, 1965, it would have been most difficult to reverse the direction of Romanian economic development. Thus, there was a momentum for domestic economic development as well as for an autonomous economic policy that would have carried Ceausescu along, rather than a gradual development that he could have shaped. In the period since 1965, then, autonomous decisions in economic policy should not have had as great an impact on the limits to autonomy as other factors over which Ceausescu had more control.

In the political and military spheres the seeds of foreign policy autonomy may have been sown by Gheorghiu-Dej, but even a preliminary examination of Romanian actions following his death shows that major moves were made after 1965, and that the figure of Ceausescu loomed large over these actions. The political-military limits acted jointly on Romanian foreign policy, but, for analytical purposes, we felt the need to make certain, rather artificial divisions to facilitate our study. The political sphere will be analyzed within a broad scope that will include the political-ideological elements, the institutional elements, and the legal elements. In the military sphere, we will focus on Moscow's requirement of military security and the limits of Romanian foreign policy inherent in that aim, together with an empirical check of Soviet military actions vis-a-vis Romania. Further, we will attempt to analyze the active Romanian military defenses for her policies.

NOTES

1. Quoted by Giorgio Galli in Walter Laquer and L. Labeds, eds., *Polycentrism: The New Factor in International Communism* (New York: Praeger, 1962), p. 127.

2. Ghita Ionescu, *The Breakup of the Soviet Empire in Eastern Europe* (Baltimore: Penguin Special, 1965).

3. *Le Monde* (Paris), June 19, 1962. Romanian Deputy Premier Aledandru Birladeanu voiced Romania's opposition to an excess of bloc centralization which would tend to curb considerably the rate of economic expansion.

4. *Lupta de Clasa* (Bucharest), April 1964, pp. 3-12. A monthly organ of the Central Committee of the Romanian Workers Party, after 1972 it became the biweekly *Era Socialista.*

Romanian Foreign Policy Since 1965

1

The Political-Ideological
Limits of Autonomy

The Soviet Union, despite its superpower status and need for geopolitical practicality, has not given up its commitment to the maintenance of ideological cohesion in the Soviet bloc. In fact, in the postwar era, as Leonard Schapiro has observed, it has feared that what it perceived as ideological laxity in certain bloc states in the 1950s and 1960s would have led to the breaking up of the bloc, or that the disintegration of Communist rule in a bloc state would have spread to the Soviet Union itself.[1] Therefore, a criterion for remaining within the limits of behavior tolerated by the Soviet Union from a bloc state was the satisfaction of the need for Soviet ideological security. If these Soviet needs were satisfied, a bloc state such as Romania would at least have had a chance to exercise some foreign policy autonomy because such assurance would have been a form of defense. In broader terms, the very evolution of Soviet policy toward the bloc indicated the criteria that Romania had to satisfy.

We therefore propose to look at the areas within the parameters of political-ideological defense that could have helped Romania pursue a policy of autonomy in foreign affairs without breaching the limits of autonomy. Both Soviet and Romanian policies and their interaction in the form of passive and active defenses worked cumulatively to provide a subnetwork of defenses. The six areas that we will attempt to analyze in this chapter are the Romanian Communist Party's (RCP) control in the country, the Ceausescu leadership's control of the party, Romanian style of diplomacy, Romanian bridge building to the West and the nonaligned world, the opportunities of the Sino-Soviet rift, and the effects of the 1976 Berlin conference and Eurocommunism.

In choosing these six headings, this chapter should be able to focus on the political-ideological challenges put forth by Romania in deviating from the Soviet line as well as the defenses it possessed in this area. The study of these

1

six sections on one chapter bears the caveat again that the separation is made for analytical purposes only. Romanian political-ideological defenses were connected with other defenses in the larger network, each possessing various weights of significance; and then, even this sum remains only part of the larger picture that the other chapters will fill in.

Political-ideological challenges to the Soviet Union offered by the Ceausescu leadership appeared to enjoy what was perceived in the West as elements of polycentrism. But ascribing more flexibility to the Soviet camp through this term of "multicentricity" does not explain sufficiently the potential passive defense that Soviet foreign policy could provide for Romania. Both Romanian foreign policy and the Soviet view of the bloc states since 1965 evolved through stages, and were heavily influenced by previous policies. Alongside analyzing the defense for Romania that Soviet policy itself could have provided, the historical perspective of Soviet policy, and thereby the importance of the Romanian challenges, should also be assessed.

Romanian foreign policy decisions under Ceausescu, such as insistence on the right to decide with whom Romania should not establish or maintain relations, or on the right to join various international organizations, or on the sole right to determine participation in military maneuvers and moves within the Soviet bloc, and the opposition to supranational planning were among the chief constituent factors through which Romania struck at the political-ideological cohesiveness of the Soviet bloc. This *maître chez nous* syndrome was not unique to Romania, for many policies similar to its were exhibited in one form or another by various bloc states in the postwar era. Soviet reaction to the Romanian and other bloc states's manifestations of foreign policy autonomy signified, however, what types of defenses Romania could find within Soviet policy and which of these political-ideological defenses could have been most effective in allowing Bucharest to continue these policies.

At the outset it is important to discern whether Soviet reaction to these Romanian actions indicates if the former interpreted these to be challenges. Indications are that this was the case. Moscow orchestrated the East European press, particularly that of East Germany (which needed little prodding at any rate), in rather vituperative attacks on Romania's decision to establish diplomatic relations with West Germany in 1967. Similarly, the Soviets vigorously attacked Romania's decision not to sever diplomatic relations with Israel in conformity with bloc action following the Six-Day War. Following the intervention in Czechoslovakia, the Soviet Union again decried the support that the Ceausescu leadership had offered to autonomous Czechoslovak policies promulgated by the reform leadership of Alexander Dubcek in 1968.[2]

Thus there appeared to be a certain degree of dichotomy in Soviet policy toward Romania during the period under study. While polycentric trends worked toward a greater acceptance by Moscow of some diversity in the policies of the bloc states, the ingrained Soviet desire for bloc cohesion and ideological uniformity made it look askance at moves of autonomy. Romania's policies, therefore, were viewed as a challenge; but the response to them, and the possible defenses they could activate, depended to an extent on Romanian precedents and on the evolutionary changes of Soviet policy toward Eastern Europe during the entire postwar era. It is, then, not a question of whether the Soviet leadership would have tolerated any challenges (for they were bound to tolerate some), but rather the type of challenge with which they would accommodate themselves.

The first factor that comes to view in this regard is that the Brezhnev-Kosygin leadership simply did not have the leverage that Joseph Stalin had in enforcing conformity within the Soviet bloc. It is not merely a question of the loss of certain formal channels of control (such as the withdrawal of Soviet troops from Romania after the 1958 agreement), for Romania was still bound to the Soviet Union by strong treaties. Rather it was a question of the new Soviet leadership having lost significant informal channels of control. The penetration of key bloc state governing organs by Soviet personnel, which had been a feature of Soviet control under Stalin and during much of the 1950s,[3] had largely ended in Romania by the time Ceausescu acquired power. Even more significant, the Brezhnev-Kosygin leadership did not have the awesome prestige that Stalin had enjoyed in the Soviet bloc. Of course, after Khrushchev's revelations of Stalin's tyranny and vicious personality cult at the 20th Party Congress, it was not possible for any Soviet leader to create a Stalin-like aura around himself. In concrete terms, Stalin's personal prestige acted as a means of constraining bloc state autonomy (with the notable exception of Yugoslavia) in the form of an "anticipated reaction." As Milovan Djilas has written, in the immediate postwar era leaders of the bloc states were so eager to ingratiate themselves with a legendary Stalin that they tried to foresee his wishes and to act on those assumptions.[4] In the late 1940s, for instance, Gheorghiu-Dej, the Secretary General of the Romanian Workers Party, proceeding under the assumption that he was following Stalin's wishes, supported an abortive plan by the Kremlin to join the East European People's Democracies to the Soviet Union.[5]

Moreover, as with any new leadership, that of Brezhnev-Kosygin required some time to acclimatize itself with power and to formulate its own policies toward the Soviet bloc. In view of the new leadership's criticism of Khrushchev's "harebrained" schemes and badly-thought-out decisions, it was likely and logical that they would have acted with some restraint toward the bloc in the first few years in power, thereby permitting the new Romanian leadership of Ceausescu a breathing space within which to consolidate itself. Indeed, during the period of 1965 to 1967 Ceausescu did just that—therein acquiring greater resiliency in resisting Soviet pressure.

Second, in the scheme of Soviet tolerance of diversity in the bloc, particularly that of foreign policy autonomy, precedents of Romanian autonomous moves were bound to have some substantive importance. Opinion among Western scholars varies as to the date when Romania first embarked on a course of foreign policy autonomy, from a commencement date of 1948 according to

Stephen Fischer-Galati,[6] to one as recent as 1962 according to Kenneth Jowitt.[7] Some differences with Moscow on Romanian economic development, as we stated earlier, were already evident in the late 1950s. But while there is disagreement as to the exact date, the general consensus appears to be that autonomy had commenced in certain forms under Ceausescu's predecessor.

In the early 1960s there were clear signs of a Romanian divergence from Soviet policy, which took the combined economic-political, as well as the purely political, form. The former appeared in the shape of an economic challenge in the refusal to go along with Khrushchev's 1962 plan for the "international division of labor," which would have stifled Romanian industrial development in favor of production of raw materials, and was again manifested in the open Romanian declaration of April 22, 1964, whereby Romania asserted its right to decide its own fate.[8] But this economic autonomy had political implications, for Gheorghiu-Dej turned to the West for economic aid. Bucharest concluded important trade agreements with Italy in 1961,* with France in 1963 and 1965,† with West German firms in 1965,[9] and signed a preliminary agreement in January 1965 with two American firms for the construction of a huge synthetic rubber and a large petroleum plant.[10] Overall, Romania's trade with the Socialist states fell from 73.6 percent of its total exchange in 1960 to 64.38 percent in 1965.[11]

This shift in the direction of Romanian trade struck at the economic dominance and control that Moscow exercised over Bucharest and in that sense it was a political move as well. By attenuating the stranglehold that the Soviet Union had over the Romanian economy and by denying Moscow the right to act as a directing center for the Socialist camp, Bucharest also blocked certain Soviet channels of control, and thereby enhanced Romania's defensive capacity to resist external pressures. Thus this precedent of autonomous action by the Gheorghiu-Dej regime could be of considerable help to its successor Nicolae Ceausescu.

Furthermore, the Romanians offered some clearly political challenges to Soviet desires for cohesion in the bloc under the leadership of Gheorghiu-Dej. In April 1963 the Romanian Foreign Ministry announced that it was dispatching an ambassador to Albania, thereby becoming the first Soviet-bloc country to resume diplomatic relations with the dissident Tirana leadership—at a time

---

*On June 5, 1961, a four-year trade agreement was signed which envisaged an increase of trade of 15 percent per annum between the two countries. *Scinteia* (organ of the Central Committee of the RCP) (Bucharest), June 7, 1961.

†On February 22, 1963, a three-year agreement was signed which provided for a 50 percent increase of trade between the two states. *Scinteia*, February 23, 1963. On February 8, 1965, France and Romania agreed to increase their trade by another 60 percent during 1965–1969 with the French extending long-term credits. *Times* (London), February 9, 1965.

when the Soviet Union and the other bloc states maintained their diplomatic boycott of this minuscule Balkan country.[12] On June 20, 1963, moreover, the Romanian Workers Party published a summary of the critical letter of June 14, 1963, of the Central Committee of the Communist Party of the Soviet Union on Sino-Soviet Relations—hitherto unpublished in the Soviet-bloc states. Michel Tatu, among other Western observers, believed that the publication of the letter was "a direct affront to Moscow's orders and an apparent conclusion on Romania's part that the Peking-Moscow breach offers room for maneuver."[13]

Again, concomitant with the political challenges, Gheorghiu-Dej erected some political defenses. By the 1960s he succeeded in entrenching the Communist party into Romanian society through a long process of what has been labeled "community building,"[14] especially in the sense that he could maintain power without external help. He had attained internal stability through orthodox Stalinist policies, and appeared to have a very firm control over the party apparatus. Thus, he could resist a considerable amount of Soviet pressure directed against his quest for foreign policy autonomy. And as has been seen, he did make a number of important assertions of autonomy in the conduct of Romanian foreign policy which constituted a breakthrough in Romania's unqualified postwar adherence to Soviet foreign policy directives. Moreover, Gheorghiu-Dej carried out his policy effectively both during the leadership of the mercurial Khrushchev and that of his successors Brezhnev and Kosygin until his death in March 1965. He therefore laid the foundation of foreign policy autonomy quite clearly for his designated heir, Ceausescu, thereby providing him with a valuable political defense.

The long-range evolution of Soviet foreign policy toward the bloc states in the postwar era, particularly in the political sphere, delineated further the political limits of Romanian foreign policy autonomy. For, while there are arguments as to the extent to which the Soviet Union was willing to tolerate diversity on the road to polycentrism, the Soviet and Warsaw Pact (WP or WTO) intervention in Czechoslovakia in 1968 demonstrated that Togliatti's concept of polycentrism had not been attained yet, and that there clearly was a limit to Soviet tolerance. Nevertheless, the evolution of Soviet policy should have reflected on the political defenses that Romania had and could build after 1965 and which in turn would allow her to stay within the limits of Moscow's patience.

Our main hypothesis in this area is that central to the evolution of Soviet policy was the security of the Moscow-molded Communist ideology in these bloc states. In practical terms, this meant the control of the Communist party in each bloc state. We will attempt, therefore, to assess briefly the validity of the hypothesis and how it would have tied in with the shape that Soviet policy took toward the bloc, and, by implication, toward Romania.

Soviet attitude toward Eastern Europe has evolved through a number of phases and even a cursory examination of this progression indicates periods of acceptance of some diversity and others demanding strict adherence to the

Moscow line. From the end of World War II to 1947 Moscow allowed a considerable amount of diversity among the states of Eastern Europe. This diversity was more apparent in domestic policies than in the area of external relations, but nevertheless there was diversity. Naturally there were a great many differences in the status of the Communist party and leadership in each East European state, ranging from that of Tito's in Yugoslavia, where the Yugoslav Communists had achieved power through their own volition, to that of the minute Romanian party, which had to rely totally on Soviet support. While Soviet leaders did not appear to have had a comprehensive master plan for the countries of Eastern Europe, they did seek the installation of a Communist-controlled government and the transformation of the economy to the Soviet mode of production at the earliest possible date in each Eastern European state. This in turn necessitated the tolerance of some local diversity, so that the various Communist parties went all out to enhance their position, to build and to maintain the apparatus of control, with Soviet acquiescence and even support.[15] The national Communist parties became quite preoccupied with their own domestic problems in this phase, known as "domesticism."[16]

In foreign policy, Tito saw the flow of power from the "particular" to the "general" in the Communist camp and along this plane he tended to identify the interests of world Communism with national-domestic Yugoslav interests.[17] In another instance, Romania and Hungary felt confident enough in their autonomy to clash openly at the Paris Peace Conference.[18]

Thus some relative autonomy among the East European states existed even under Stalin for a number of years. The main reason for this was expediency, particularly in moving rapidly the reparation payments from the East European states that had been allied with or occupied by Hitler, to the Soviet Union, as well as lack of sufficient Soviet preparation for a comprehensive plan for the region. The institution of the Communist Information Bureau (Cominform) at Szlarska Poreba in Sepember 1947 signalled an end to Soviet acquiescence to domesticism. But this attempt to consolidate the bloc, we submit, did not negate the fact that, under certain circumstances, even Stalin had been forced to accept some bloc-state autonomy in order to help Communist control in the bloc states.

Khrushchev, despite his rejection of the Georgi Malenkov "New Course," did tolerate a certain degree of autonomy from the Soviet-bloc states. In the case of Poland, the Evolutionist group, led by Wladyslaw Gomulka (and which stood for economic reform as well as for a less subordinate role before Moscow), succeeded in 1956 in ousting the Stalinist, or Natolin, faction. Moscow backed away from a military confrontation and accepted the change. In the next few years Poland significantly increased its economic ties with the West, particularly the United States, with Moscow's apparent acquiescence.[19] In the early 1960s Khrushchev again accommodated his policy toward the bloc states with Gheorghiu-Dej's resistance to economic specialization within the bloc. This acceptance was given rather grudgingly, but when it is considered that the bloc specialization that Gheorghiu-Dej stifled had been a cornerstone of the Soviet leader's policy toward Eastern Europe, the fact that he did not take strong enough measures to oust the Romanian leader demonstrated a remarkable degree of restraint.

The new leadership of Leonid Brezhnev and Alexei Kosygin revealed that it too was capable of tolerating a certain amount of diversity within the bloc. Besides a partial acceptance (in the sense that they did not intervene militarily) of Romanian foreign policy autonomy, they were prepared to acquiesce to a certain degree of ideological and institutional diversity in the bloc states. During the late 1960s and early 1970s, Moscow permitted Hungary a considerable measure of economic liberalization, in the sense of decentralizing economic decision making. Similarly, they reconciled themselves to the new economic measures (which to an extent reflected those in Hungary) introduced in Poland by the new leader, Eduard Gierek, following Gomulka's fall from power in 1970.

This short list depicting instances of Soviet acceptance of some domestic and foreign policy diversity in the Soviet bloc is not intended to show an evolution toward a real acceptance of diversity, for indeed this was not the case. Stalin tolerated some diversity during 1945 to 1947 because of the circumstances extant, rather than as a result of consciously formulating a policy that tolerated diversity. The Soviet bloc after 1964 did not enjoy Togliatti's envisioned polycentrism, but it is evident that the Soviet leaders were not prepared to clamp down on all manifestations of autonomy. There was a certain restraining mechanism within their policy which acted frequently to protect some of the autonomous moves of bloc states. This negation of tendencies toward an unbridled Soviet interventionism, in turn, were bound to act as a defense for Romanian foreign policy autonomy.

On the other hand, Soviet foreign policy was also characterized by a number of retrenchments in the tolerance of even minimal bloc diversity under all the major leaders. Stalin ordered the formation of Cominform in 1947 to ensure bloc cohesion, and, after 1948, employed all the covert means at his disposal in an endeavor to destroy the dissident Tito leadership in Yugoslavia. Khrushchev in turn resorted to the use of military force in his drive to crush the dissident regime of Imre Nagy in Hungary during 1956, and just weeks earlier had attempted to intimidate, with military might, the Evolutionists and Gomulka in Poland. The most glaring example of Soviet demands for bloc-state adherence to the Soviet policy line under the Brezhnev-Kosygin leadership came in August 1968, when Soviet military power was utilized to stop the "democratization" process of the Dubcek-Svoboda leadership in Czechoslovakia.

Instances of Soviet tolerance and rejection of diversity, however, did not occur as mere anomalies; there were rather substantive links between them. Therefore, in this chapter we will attempt to highlight the political determining factors in some of the main crisis points such as East Germany in 1953, Hungary and Poland in 1956, and Czechoslovakia in 1968, and attempt to evaluate the role of the maintenance of the security of Communism in a bloc state within Soviet calculations of their own security.

In Poland, Khrushchev recognized the dangers of autonomy—domestic and in foreign policy—that the leadership of Gomulka posed to Soviet hegemony over the bloc. But of the various countervailing factors, the political-ideological ones must have weighed heavily on the former's thinking. The Gomulka leadership endeavored to convince Moscow during the Warsaw negotiations that domestic concessions would actually fortify Socialism in Poland. The commitment of the Gomulka leadership to Marxism-Leninism was resolute and, moreover, perceived to be so by the Soviet leadership.[20] Furthermore, the new Polish leadership was united and clearly in control of the party as well as the country. On the other hand, in the case of the German Democratic Republic (G.D.R.) in 1953, Hungary in 1956, and Czechoslovakia in 1968—all instances of Soviet military intervention—Moscow detected, or at least it professed it detected, a disintegration of the Communist system in the bloc state.

In the G.D.R. Moscow claimed that the rising of the workers constituted an attack on the Socialist system, inspired by "American Imperialist plots" as well as by "fascist provocateurs."[21] In the case of Hungary, the Soviet leadership alleged late in October 1956 that counterrevolutionary elements were threatening the "foundation of Socialist order."[22] And it is true that after October 24, 1956, Hungary moved rapidly toward a pluralistic system. Premier Imre Nagy appointed several prominent non-Communists to his cabinet, and he helped to achieve the restoration of a multiparty system on October 30, 1956. Within the next two days Nagy announced Hungary's withdrawal from the Warsaw Pact, proclaimed the country's neutrality, and rejected allegiance to the Soviet camp.[23] These external policies of Hungary further reinforced the Soviet Union's view that Communism was disintegrating in that bloc state.

While the situation in Czechoslovakia in 1968 was not analogous to that of Hungary in 1956, Moscow did perceive great danger to Communist control. Dubcek's programs of "democratization" involved the abolishment of the vestiges of Stalinist blanket suppression of all dissent and substituted for it a policy of tolerating more open criticism of the party and of placing greater emphasis on raising the standard of living. None of this entailed a relinquishing of the dominant power of the Communist party, nor was there a change in form under Dubcek. But the burst of pluralistic opinions in the publications of the country, and even some rather abstract discussions expressing an intention to give some of the former bourgeois parties a very limited role, worried the Soviet leaders. An argument has since been advanced by some Czechoslovak emigres that the reforms in fact strengthened the Czechoslovak Communist Party as it gained genuine national support, but the Soviet leadership instead perceived a disintegration of Communist control.[24] Thus, in the case of Czechoslovakia, a key catalyst for Soviet response consisted of a possible Soviet misperception of the reforms under Dubcek. It is, however, this Soviet perception—whether accurate or not—that at least partially prompted Soviet reaction, and, therefore, it ap-

role of ideology denied ?

peared that it was imperative to reassure the Soviets of the survival of Communist control in that state by the Communist party. Dubcek's failure to project the correct image to Moscow should of course have been a warning to a state like Romania, which was pursuing an autonomous foreign policy.

Thus the evolution of Soviet policy toward the bloc states was not linear. Nevertheless a greater tolerance of diversity under Brezhnev and Kosygin, as compared to the very brief expedience-induced acceptances of some diversity under Stalin, indicates that the development could not be justifiably classified as cyclical either, despite several retrenchments in Soviet tolerance. While, as the events in Czechoslovakia showed, the Soviet leaders were not prepared to accept true pluralism or polycentrism in the bloc, the movement in that direction was at least latently teleological. That in turn should have provided a more optimistic prognosis for the development of Romanian foreign policy autonomy. The Soviet leadership also demonstrated that they were not interventionist "by nature," and that they acted only if they felt their vital interests were threatened. Power has been increasingly a matter of peacefully managing interdependent relationships. On the other hand, when these interests were menaced beyond peaceful redemption, they moved quickly and decisively to suppress the perceived threat. And the threat of the disintegration of the Communist rule in a bloc state—in fact, the loss of control by the local Communist party acted as a key impetus for Soviet restriction of autonomous action by the bloc state whenever such a danger was perceived by Moscow. The reassurance of the Soviet Union by a bloc state of the security of the Communist rule domestically, both in fact and appearance, should in turn have had many of the properties of a true corollary, and acted as a powerful defense within the defense network of a bloc state. Therefore, if Romania was to successfully pursue an autonomous foreign policy under Ceausescu, it was imperative to it that it avail itself as fully as possible of the defense that satisfaction of Soviet needs of Communist ideological security within a bloc state provided.

PARTY CONTROL IN ROMANIA

Control by the Communist party in a bloc state, in this manner, inferred stability in Soviet eyes, and stability in turn enhanced the national power of the bloc state. As Hans Morgenthau has asserted, moreover, in his classic work *Politics Among Nations,*[25] internal stability in any state is one of the key sources of national power. Romania needed to place its foreign policies on the solid foundation of internal stability, which in terms of bloc politics meant control by the RCP. Since the RCP would have to have both exercised and demonstrated this control in order to satisfy the Soviet Union, we propose to analyze the party control through a threefold perspective: first, the theoretical commitment to party control; second, the political-practical commitment; and third, the cultural manifestation of party control.

Back in 1966, the RCP theoretician Ilie Radulescu, writing in *Lupta de Clasa*, equated the party with the state:

> In the social classes and categories of the country there are no antagonistic interests . . . and in the interest of the people, the state organized the building of Socialism, the rational evaluation of the national resources, the scope of the development of the country and the raising of the standard of living.[26]

But even this lack of "antagonistic interests" in a Socialist Romania was not to be taken to mean that the Romanian theoreticians held that there were no contradictions left in society, since this could have been interpreted as a cause for the relaxation of party control.

Since in Marxist terminology Romania remained absorbed in the dialectic of building Socialism, the role of the party had to be specified. Perhaps the most interesting work done on this question was that of the important Romanian scholar Mihail Cernea in his book *Dialectica Construiri Socialismului*,[27] and was further elaborated upon by another RCP theoretician in 1972, Radu Florian.[28] Both Cernea and Florian held the view that contradictions were to continue under Socialism, but that they would be of a different character. Cernea divided contradictions into antagonistic and nonantagonistic types,[29] while Florian utilized a tripartite division of contradictions into those of the antagonistic type, those involving qualitative differentiation representing relations between interdependent elements, and those in the relations of interdependent elements of the same quantity among which there existed some unidentical properties.[30] While both theorists, then, claimed a nonantagonistic type of contradiction for the Socialist phase in the development of a state, they clearly postulated the notion that contradictions did not disappear at a particular stage, but merely took on a different form.

These contradictions, then, would still have to be resolved. Since both authors felt that disagreements among the terms of nonantagonistic contradictions were highly unlikely to become generalized in a manner necessitating a qualitative change, but that, instead, these would have been identified, localized, resolved, and in certain cases foreseen and avoided,[31] there would have to have been an important subjective factor (the party) to achieve this. In fact, Cernea did assign the party a key role in the development of society and of the Socialist conscience of the people:

> The conscious intervention imprimates such organization and configuration on the process and the forms of Socialist work until they generate certain determinate effects in the sphere of the conscience and assure on the whole the amplification of the educative betterment of the workers.[32]

The Czechoslovak leadership of Dubcek also assigned an important role to the Communist party, but this was not sufficient for the Soviet Union. Thus

the contention of Romanian theoreticians that the party was to be of importance—even of vital importance—would not have been an effective defense unless
the role assigned to the party even at the theoretical level ensured the kind of
dominance it enjoyed in the Soviet Union. Petru Berar and Ioan Mitran, writing
in *Lupta de Clasa*,[33] appeared to go a long way in reassuring the Soviet Union of
this. They contended that the social mission of the subjective factor (that is,
the party) could not be enclosed in rigid forms of an administrative nature, for
that, in their opinion, would inevitably lead to stagnation or tension, both of
which would be harmful to the development of Socialism. Nor could, in their
view, the role of the party be diminished to simple ideological influencing of
the masses, because this would have resulted in "a line of spontaneous social
development with negative consequences for the progress of the new order."[34]
Thus these two RCP theoreticians exhibited the same distrust of spontaneity in
the development of the Socialist system that Lenin had. And not only did Berar
and Mitran reject spontaneity and any attenuation of the party's controlling
role, but they went on to argue that the role of the party in society would be
augmented with the increasing complexity of life, instead of withering away.
This, in their opinion, was both a theoretical and practical necessity.[35] Romanian theoreticians maintained this view of the central role of the Communist
party during the mid-1970s with remarkable consistency. One of the most important Romanian theoreticians, Professor Ioan Ceterchi, Chairman of the
Legislative Council, wrote in 1975 that the Communist party represented the
core around which the entire society was gravitating, " . . . it fulfills the role of
vital center from which radiates the energy securing the operation of the whole
gearing of the socialist social system."[36]

It was Ceausescu himself who best summed up the approach of the Romanian theoreticians on the role of the party and on the preservation of the
Communist system in the country. At the plenary meeting of the Central Committee of the Romanian Communist Party on June 29, 1977, he stated that
the role of the party must be strengthened in the country's economic and
social life and all party members must act to intensify the growth of the leading
role of the party in all sectors of society.[37]

At the empirical-political level, the Romanians sought to ensure the
security of Communist rule through specifically planned acts to maintain or
fortify the control of the RCP. The 1965 constitution, which was adopted under
Ceausescu, clearly affirmed in Article 3 that "the leading political force of the
whole of society is the Romanian Communist Party."[38] This was reconfirmed
through the six major amendments to the constitution since.[39] The editorial in
Lupta de Clasa claimed subsequently that the inclusion of the article on the
role of the party was a principal foresight of the new constitution and a recognition of the party as the foremost instrument for the realization of the political,
economic, and cultural tasks made increasingly complex by the advancement of
society.[40]

During the period under study, the control of the party in Romania appears to have been maintained without any indication of laxity. Certainly there were no reforms that relaxed party control over the life of the country on the scale of Hungary in 1956 or Czechoslovakia in 1968, or even that of Poland in 1956 and 1970. The new Penal and Penal Procedure Codes which came into force on January 1, 1969,[41] were designed to rectify some of the abuses of civil liberties that occurred under Gheorghiu-Dej, but they did not in any way weaken the control of the party over society.[42] There is evidence, on the other hand, that on a number of occasions, almost invariably following certain gestures of foreign policy autonomy, there was a tightening of party control over life in Romania. It is not clear whether the main impetus for such action was concern by Ceausescu to prevent events from getting out of control or whether it was a result of attempts to attenuate Soviet apprehensions at crisis points in regard to Romanian ideological commitment, or both, but the timing should have aided the RCP in controlling the country and in conveying the existence of this control to Moscow.

Following the establishment of diplomatic relations with West Germany in January 1967, Ceausescu intensified his emphasis on the control of the party over Romanian life and declared that, "In the development of Socialist democracy, the growing role of the Communist party as a dynamic force, as the leader of the people in ensuring the forward movement of the whole society, is affirmed."[43] The May editorial of *Lupta de Clasa*, picking up on Ceausescu's theme, indicated that a tightening of the party organization, membership, and national control was indeed taking place. It emphasized that the leadership capacity of the party was based on the structure of the party and "the moral quality of the Communists, their professional and technical scientific competence, their ideological preparation."[44] Furthermore, the editorial warned that there had to be constant vigilance against residual bourgeois ideological influences in the country which were being stimulated by some domestic and external reactionary forces. As such, in its view, there had to be closer guarding of party and state secrets, as well as increased criticism and self-criticism.[45]

In the wake of Romanian refusal to sever diplomatic relations with Israel in line with bloc policy, the June 1967 editorial of *Lupta de Clasa* announced more concrete measures for improving the party organization. It proclaimed that higher standards were being applied for party membership, with the result that 85 percent of the activists of the party apparently had graduated from higher party schools. At the time the editorial revealed that in the previous year 85 party secretaries of regional and city committees had been fired for not succeeding in their tasks, while 240 directors, chief engineers, and chief accountants of national enterprises were replaced because of incompetence. The party activists, in the editorial's view, fulfilled their duties only when they brought success to the party's political lines, and when they ensured the practical application of the decisions and directives of the party.[46] Those who failed to achieve this would suffer the consequences. Later in the year, at its national conference, the RCP announced measures for further strengthening party control of the country under the guise of increasing administrative efficiency. Ceausescu declared that in order to simplify work and to allow for greater individual responsibility, one individual would deal with any issue at both party and state levels.[47]

The Soviet and Warsaw Pact intervention in Czechoslovakia in August 1968 was greeted as a crisis for Romania by the Ceausescu leadership. He told a mass rally of 100,000 people gathered in front of the Palace of the Republic in Bucharest that there was complete unity between the party and the people, and full support for the party's policies.[48] He then proceeded to take concrete measures to achieve this unity—which in effect meant party control. In October 1968 the Central Committee of the RCP announced, at the conclusion of a two-day meeting in Bucharest, its decision to establish the Socialist Unity Front, which would be comprised of a mass participation organization under party control and guidance, and which in turn was to coordinate the activities of other organizations such as trade unions and youth groups. The election of Nicolae Ceausescu as president of the Front and that of Premier Ion Gheorghe Maurer as the first vice-president merely served to reinforce the impression that the Front was another device for stronger party control.

During 1971, when the Soviet Union showed its displeasure with Ceausescu's visit to China in June by conducting military maneuvers along Romania's borders, the Bucharest leadership again tightened party control. On July 7, 1971, the RCP Executive Committee endorsed unanimously Ceausescu's proposals to combat "foreign influence, cosmopolitanism and parasitism" in Romanian life.* Later, in the fall, speaking before the party Plenum, Ceausescu called for intensified discipline and self-criticism as well as for a buttressing of the party's role in all areas of the economy, in education, and in culture.[50] Thus, the Soviet government could be reassured that Romanian contacts with her arch-enemy China would not result in any weakening of Romanian commitment to Communism.

As the Romanians were discussing the new "all-horizons" Defense Law that was to be adopted later in December 1972, Ceausescu renewed his call for tighter discipline in the nation's labor force, for limits on the number of people allowed to go into "nonproductive" careers such as the arts, and for a reshaping of the system to provide more workers and fewer intellectuals.[51] Equally significant was his emphasis during the same speech on the necessity of maintaining the party as the leading political force in all the domains of activity in the entire country.

At the Central Committee Plenum held during March 25 and 26, 1974, the Romanians made important changes both in the governmental and the party structure. Ceausescu's powers were increased through the creation of the new

---

*By "cosmopolitanism" Ceausescu meant the attraction to Western ideas and material goods, while "parasitism" referred to young adults who lived off their parents.[49]

post of President of the Republic and by his appointment as Commander-in-Chief of the Armed Forces following the closing of the meeting. The party changes, however, were even more significant. Following the course of innovation which Ceausescu had begun at the national party congress in 1972, the party decided to abolish the permanent presidium in favor of a permanent bureau to be mainly made up of ex-officio members responsible to the party's executive committee, not its central committee. This was in violation of the previous party statutes. As well, it was decided to change the name of the Executive Committee to the Political Executive Committee and it was enlarged considerably. The permanent bureau, which was to have consisted of 14 or 15 ex-officio members, had only five members—the President and four of his closest advisors who had been promoted over more senior party leaders. This permanent bureau was expanded in 1977 to nine members, the additional members including the President's wife and Cornel Burtica, rumored to be his brother-in-law.[52]

These changes in the party structure were viewed as rather dangerous for Romania by Western observers, because it was felt that any move by the Romanians to set themselves up as independent ideological spokesmen would be faced with sharp Soviet reaction.[53] Romania, however, had always been very careful to indicate that her policies were restricted to the conditions extant there and that they were not to serve as models for other states. Therefore, the danger of contamination from any Romanian ideological innovation was rather limited, and the Soviet Union recognized this factor. Just as important, these reforms in Romania did not endanger the position of the Romanian Communist Party within Romanian society. Therefore, any Western alarm regarding the consequences of these actions by Romania underestimated the importance that the Soviet Union attached to the substance of Communist control in the state, as opposed to the form, which may not have been preferred by Moscow but which nevertheless would be tolerated if the substance of control was maintained. The Romanians were very careful to prove at this stage that, indeed, the substance of control was maintained. The editorial in *Era Socialista* on August 15, 1974, underlined the fact that the RCP had been and was going to continue to exercise an ever-increasing role in the entire political life of Romania and that "it had affirmed itself with power in crucial moments for the destiny of the country as the national political *force* for the protection of the national interests of the entire people." Therefore, the challenge that the Romanians offered to the Soviet Union was limited and it was compensated for by proof of the continuance of the maintenance of Communist control in the country.

Lastly, during the conference of the European Communist Party in East Berlin during June 1976, the Romanian leader again reiterated the autonomous stance that Romania had been pursuing in its foreign policy formulations. It was time to again prove to the Soviet Union that foreign policy deviation did not mean a lessening of party control. Ceausescu, speaking to the Armed Forces, reiterated his and the party's intention of maintaining their position in Romanian life: ". . . we can say that at the Berlin conference it was powerfully demonstrated that Communist and Workers parties have an ever-increasing role to play in the life of each nation."[54] The party in Romania would adhere to this precise principle of control.

Thus Romanian policies on party control should have gone a long way in reassuring the Soviet Union of Bucharest's maintenance of domestic ideological orthodoxy, despite foreign policy initiatives at which Moscow looked on askance. By reinforcing party control over the country at crisis periods and by strengthening the party organization, the Romanians demonstrated that they were not about to let things get out of hand as happened in Hungary in 1956 and Czechoslovakia in 1968. Even stress on Romanian nationalism did not attenuate the RCP's total control over the country's life. Fischer-Galati himself, who gave the most benign Western reading to a collection of Ceausescu's speeches that this writer has seen, admitted that intellectual expression was not allowed to endanger the party's control.[55]

The Soviet Union, therefore, should have been well contented by Romanian actions and demonstrations of the security of Communism in Romanian actions and demonstrations of the security of Communism in Romania; and perhaps it was. On the other hand Soviet conduct toward Eastern Europe, while often characterized by restraint, was not noted for exhibiting strong Soviet ideological security. As such, it would be difficult to construct even an hypothetical case of excess zeal by a bloc state in reassuring the Soviet Union of the health of Communism in that particular bloc nation. By going beyond the measures discussed, Romania then would have helped its case, even if marginally, and thereby built a stronger defense for an autonomous foreign policy.

The available evidence suggests that Romania took such "excess" measures as a result of a combination of Ceausescu's desire to strengthen his personalized style of rule, as well as an intention to provide a demonstration for the Soviet Union. The most significant of these measures started with a "mini-Cultural Revolution" in 1971, following Ceausescu's return from the Orient, and continued into 1972.

Cultural laxity, especially in a view of the political connotations that it assumed following the actions of the Petofi and Crooked Circle clubs in Hungary and Poland respectively during 1956, as well as through the activities of the Czechoslovak intellectual organizations during 1968 in pushing for reform, was recognized for its "inherent" dangers by the Romanian leadership. At the November 1971 RCP Plenum, the delegates took it upon themselves to define the Socialist function of culture in order to set the limits of intellectual activity. In their definition, culture was to be primarily a dialectical reflection of the position of scientific materialism of social life.[56] This amounted to, in what Ceausescu later explained in less ideological language, a duty by artists and writers to show the benefits of the Socialist way of life.

Perhaps the clearest elaboration of the Romanian leadership's view was made by the then "cultural watchdog" Dumitru Popescu, a member of the Executive of the Central Committee of the RCP. In an article that appeared in

Lupta de Clasa in 1972, he delineated the "duties" of culture.[57] Among these, he saw those of reflecting the "objective" truths of life, of contributing to the decoding of the contradictions of the Socialist order, of suggesting methods of solution, and of mobilizing all energies for the attainment of the Socialist ideal. Even more significant, he stated that the artist must not place himself in a position where he acts as a defender of the "old order," for he would not be allowed to be a "brake on social development":

> The social function of literature and art presuppose a contribution to the correction of public morals, for the sanity of society. The "grotesque" is the reverse of the humanity of Socialism. The major subject of the talent of the artist and writer today is the Socialist hero, for his is the most original and interesting artistic personality— the man in the full metamorphosis of Communist thought and action . . . also both the Socialist and Romanian aspirations must be communicated in art.[58]

These restrictions on intellectual expression suggest that Romania was still at the level of Stalin's Socialist Realism. By 1974, the Romanian position on restrictions on various cultural activities eased somewhat. Following the meeting of the Plenum of the Central Committee in March 1974, certain constraints were eased on the press and the editors were made responsible for censoring their own publications.[59] This amelioration of censorship, however, was rather short lived. Following the writers' conference in June 1976, new restrictions became increasingly evident in all manifestations in the cultural realm. Such hard liners as writer Mihai Beniuc and a member of the editorial board of *Era Socialista*, Gheorghe Stroia, rushed into print with articles demanding that culture and education be placed firmly within the work of dialectic materialism, that art must not contain any "antihumanist" elements, and moreover that there should be a link between art and the social and national evolution of society.[60] Burtica, who was in charge of culture, showed some flexibility prior to the conference in June 1976 but he increasingly displayed the same hard line as his predecessor. The very few dissident writers in Romania were pushed out of the writers' union, and one in particular, Paul Goma, finally had to leave the country when he was unwilling to bend along with the new restrictions.

That these restrictions came from the higher level was made clear by Ceausescu's speech before the Plenum of the Central Committee of the Romanian Communist Party in June 1977. He announced that new regulations would be introduced in the entire cultural and educational activities in the country. He admitted some self-criticism and then went on to state that from then on, in all publications, control would be placed in the hands of the party, away from the previous press committees, and so on. The party activists would be in control and they would be individually responsible for all that appeared in print. Particularly, Ceausescu reiterated some of the criticisms of Titus Popovici, one of the cultural hard-line moguls, whereby he (Ceausescu) stated that it was inadmissible that books that were rejected by some of the national publishers could appear through some regional presses. He declared, "We do not have—I am repeating, for I don't know the how-manyeth time—more than one single philosophy in Romania: dialectical, historical materialism. . . . We cannot make any sort of concession about our philosophy of the world and life."[61] He reiterated this hard line on culture and education during the national conference of the RCP held during December 7–9, 1977, when he called for intensified work in the cultural/educational field in order to raise the Socialist consciousness of the masses.[62] The Romanian Communist Party's position on culture, particularly after 1976, indicated a posture of rigidity on intellectual expression that went beyond ensuring the control of the party, to the point of stifling any manifestations of diversity or of deviation from a central policy. As such, Romanian policy was among the most restrictive in the bloc, and in several ways more so than that of the Soviet Union, where by 1977 some limited artistic diversity was permitted. The cultural control imposed by the RCP, then, should have appeared to the Soviet leadership as the "icing" on the Romanian commitment to orthodox Communism.

It may be argued quite fairly that these measures to tighten party control may have alienated a large part of the Romanian population. Since there were no free elections it is difficult to assess the support that the Romanian people felt for the Communist Party. Membership in the party itself increased substantially under Ceausescu, but this could well have resulted from the fact that career advancement required such membership. What these measures did accomplish was to deny any opposition the opportunity to organize. Therefore, while many Romanians—perhaps the vast majority—resented Ceausescu's government, they had to acquiesce to it. In that sense the rule of Communism was secure in Romania.

The willingness of the population to support the government against an external threat was affected by a number of factors. First, there had been historically a considerable amount of anti-Russian feeling in Romania, going back to the Czars. The loss of Bessarabia only aggravated these feelings. Second, the Ceausescu leadership deliberately cultivated these feelings through a de-Russification program. Third, in case of external threat people generally rally around their own government even though they may not have supported it before. Despite Stalin's ruthless repression in the 1930s, the majority of the Soviet people rallied around him against the Nazis and fought determinedly.

In sum, Romania possessed a formidable defense which should have enlarged, or in the very least maintained the limits of foreign policy autonomy for it. The tripartite demonstration of party control through theoretical, political-practical, and cultural commitments to that end should have relieved any Soviet insecurity about the endurance of Communism in Romania.

THE CONTROL OF THE PARTY BY THE CEAUSESCU LEADERSHIP

It is axiomatic that a state would find it easier to intervene in the internal affairs of a neighboring state, or to apply pressure against it, if the latter did not possess a united leadership. The true corollary of this should help provide stability for the leadership of the state in two senses. First of all, the leader would have a greater chance of survival and continuity in his position, and second, he could use the unity of support to dismiss or rotate subordinates in order to carry out his policies more efficiently and to resist pressure, especially external ones, effectively.

In the Soviet bloc, the possibility of the utilization by the Soviet Union of various factions in a local party to secure its own objectives is more than hypothetical. Under Stalin it constituted one of the informal links exploited for the application of pressure throughout the bloc. There is considerable evidence that the Soviet Union had endeavored to employ this tactic in Romania in 1967. Victor Zorza alleged in the May 10, 1967, *Guardian* that the Soviet leaders, in order to arrest Romania's autonomous policies, were prepared to plot the overthrow of its national Communist leadership. An attempt had been made to assemble an alternative to the Ceausescu leadership, Zorza claimed, and the Soviet leadership had found some willing collaborators inside the highest party leadership, but nevertheless failed to achieve their objective. Ceausescu's May 7, 1967, speech corroborates much of Zorza's hypothesis:

> In discussions we had with the representatives of a fraternal party, we discussed the problem of whether it is admissible for a member of the party, without the approval, and over the head of the leadership, to establish links with the representative of the other party, to participate in actions against the line of his own party. The answer is clearly no. Proletarian internationalism demands that there be principal relations of co-operation and help between Communist parties. These relations have to unfold in an organized framework, party to party leadership. The attempts of one party to establish relations with members or groups from another party outside of the organized framework constitutes a transgression of the principle of proletarian internationalism. Any party has a right to ensure its own political-organizational unity.[63]

In June 1967, Alexandre Draghici, a member of the RCP presidium and a putative opponent of the drift away from the Soviet Union, was removed from the presidium, ostensibly for being responsible for some of the secret police excesses during Gheorghiu-Dej's regime.

Thus Ceausescu's grip on the party leadership was a vital variable in the "defense" network. When he succeeded Gheorghiu-Dej as Secretary General, he was succeeding a man who had full and absolute power. His relationship with Gheorghiu-Dej reflected a kind of "dauphin" complex, in which the latter wanted Ceausescu to succeed him, and the succession was quiescent and balanced. Since Ceausescu was obscure, the old guard believed that a real collective leadership would follow. In fact, Ceausescu initially did emphasize the collectivity of the Romanian leadership in the nature of a troika composed of himself, President Chivu Stoica, and Premier Gheorghe Maurer; the real troika, however, consisted of Ceausescu and two of his supporters, Paul Niculescu-Mizil and Ilie Verdet. By late 1965, moreover, Ceausescu had conducted an extensive reshuffle and had quietly removed many of the old guard, though Deputy Premier Emil Bodnaras and Deputy Premier Gheorghe Apostol remained.[64] But following the December 1967 party congress, Chivu Stoica "offered" the presidency of the Council of State to Ceausescu, while both potential rivals, Emil Bodnaras and Gheorghe Apostol, were demoted.[65] By the end of 1967, Ceausescu appeared to be fully in command, his control being powerful enough to survive the Czechoslovak crisis.

In the post-Czechoslovak period, Ceausescu demonstrated that he had an unseverable grip on the party leadership. Between 1968 and 1971, in a game of musical chairs, he shifted about or replaced the entire higher party leadership. On December 17, 1968, Radio Bucharest announced that the Communist party's Central Committee had accepted the resignation of three members of the party's Executive Committee, and had elected Petre Lupu, Manea Manescu, and Gheorghe Stoica to replace them. In fact the Romanian leader has removed, for "reasons of health," three members of the Executive Committee and replaced them with personalities known to be his supporters.[66] By placing his own men in the highest positions Ceausescu also fulfilled one of the key rules of power, namely to link the fates of his subordinates with his.

The Romanian leader demonstrated considerable acumen and imagination in maintaining his hold on power. Following the denunciation by K.F. Katushev, the chief Soviet delegate to the Tenth RCP Congress (August 6-12, 1969), of "attempts by Western governments to use the perfidious tactic of "bridge building" to undermine the cohesion of the Socialist countries of Eastern Europe," Ceausescu had himself reelected Secretary General of the RCP by an unanimous vote of the Congress—instead of just by the Central Committee—thereby further shielding himself against Soviet attacks.[67] Following his controversial visit to the United States in 1973 Ceausescu had the Executive Committee pass a resolution approving his visit.[68] Ceausescu also made certain that the increase in his power was institutionalized in the Constitution of the state. The Constitution was modified in 1974 following the changes already made by Ceausescu in the structure of the Romanian Communist Party and the role of the President of the Republic was enhanced and a printed oath was included.[69]

By the end of 1971, Ceausescu had replaced all of the party secretaries except himself. When Ceausescu was nominated for, and approved as, the head of the new Supreme Council for Economic Development at the national conference of the RCP in July 1972,[70] he acquired a more direct role in the administration of the country's economy and further strengthened his position. At the conference, it was also decided to expand the Central Committee from 165 to 185 full members, and from 115 to 135 alternate members (thereby bringing in more of Ceausescu's supporters), with Elena Ceausescu, wife of the President, being named a permanent member of the Central Committee—the first wife of an East European to achieve such high party rank.[71] During 1974, when Ceausescu reorganized the Communist party and created the permanent bureau to replace the presidium, he ensured that the other four members were people who owed their positions entirely to him. When the permanent bureau was enlarged in 1977 to nine members, Ceausescu again made certain that the new members were loyal to him. One of them was his wife, Elena, who thus became the most powerful woman in the Communist world, and the other new member was Cornel Burtica.

Thus, Ceausescu had been able to attain a degree of control unsurpassed in the Soviet bloc. The personality cult that the Napoleon-sized Ceausescu had fashioned for himself has left many an egotistical leader envious. Almost every issue of the official party paper *Scinteia* following January 1967 has carried a large front-page picture of Ceausescu, and a substantial part of daily television broadcasts have been devoted to the coverage of the President's activities. Ceausescu's control of the party has been virtually Maoesque.

With the success of Ceausescu in resisting Soviet pressure to his leadership and his ability to continue his quest for an autonomous policy with the support of his subordinates, Romania's defensive capacity for such a policy was increased. In depriving the Soviet Union of an alternate leadership or a fifth column, Romania also circumvented one of the levers of control that the Soviet Union had over bloc states during Stalin's rule. To this extent, then, Romania enlarged the limits for foreign policy autonomy.

THE ROMANIAN STYLE OF DIPLOMACY

It is interesting to note that while there have been disputes on whether diplomacy is an art or a science, there appears to be a general consensus that it is still relevant to effective national policies. The history of Romanian diplomacy is a rich and proud one. From long centuries of Turkish domination the Romanians have learned the finer points of diplomacy, of maneuvering among larger powers, of extracting every particle of autonomy from close-knit control, and of taking advantage of all of the Byzantine intrigues that Turkish control spawned. Romanian diplomacy has been characterized by what one may call a sense of "good timing." This type of diplomatic ability, so characteristic of past great Romanian statesmen such as N. Titulescu or N. Iorga and of past Romanian governments, has apparently been inherited by the Communist regime. As in the historic past, the manner and form of Romanian action under Ceausescu on the international arena could also have acted as a form of defense for Romanian autonomy. The chief elements of the manner and form of action may be characterized for our purposes as the signal, the quality of leadership, and the manner of "attack"—with each one of them contributing to the diplomatic defense.

Among the dominant factors leading to international conflict is the misperception of what an opponent is doing or is planning to do. Misreading of the "signal" of the opponent is very common because of the difficulty of separating the signal (the actual sign of what is happening) from mere "noise." In a delicate situation of near conflict it is essential for the weaker power to ensure that the right signal reaches the opponent to reassure him that there is no cause for alarm. In other words Romania has had to be on guard to ensure that Moscow received the correct signal—that things were under control—that Romania was not acting rashly.

In an analysis of the crisis points in Romanian foreign policy it becomes quite clear just how adept the Romanians have been at conveying the right signal. For example, six months before the establishment of diplomatic relations with West Germany, Romania had concluded an accord under which West Germany allowed the Romanian mission in Frankfurt to distribute visas and process passports while a similar right was granted to the West German trade mission in Bucharest in effect there was a de facto exchange of consular rights.[72] The East Germans and Moscow had enough time to try to dissuade Romania, they did try, and for this reason there was no surprise. Similarly, in the case of the Six-Day War, Romania conveyed early-warning signals to Moscow that it would not condemn Israel when, one month before the war, Ceausescu cautioned that he could not support the policy of a state that wished to destroy another state (that is, Egypt).

Six days before the intervention into Czechoslovakia, with the entire party secretariat gathered around him, Ceausescu sent out signals in a speech on the "unity between the people and the army":

> The Romanian army has a long tradition of fighting for the liberty of the Romanian people from the old days of Decebal, Mircea the Old . . . to the shoulder to shoulder fight with the Soviets against Nazi Germany. There have been some mistakes in the past in relations between Socialist states—that is why we must make sure that relations will be on the basis of the principles of Marxism-Leninism and Socialist Internationalism. In the years of the construction of Socialism, the state and the party have formed a new type of army which knows of no other interests than to serve the nation without bounds, an army devoted without bounds to the cause of Socialism and peace—the unafraid guardian of the independence and liberty of the fatherland.[73]

The warning was repeated after the intervention into Czechoslovakia, when before a crowd of 100,000, Ceausescu declared:

> We have decided today to form armed Patriotic Guards, made up of
> workers, peasants, intellectuals, all defenders of our Socialist native
> land. . . . We answer all; the whole Romanian people will not permit
> anyone to tread on the territory of our native land.[74]

The signal was unmistakable—though short range: Romania would fight in the
event of a Soviet attack.

Romanian opposition to bloc negotiations at the European Security talks
in 1972 was again signaled well in advance. As far back as 1970, Nicolae Ecobescu
and D. I. Mazilu wrote in an article published in *Lupta de Clasa* that a European
security conference would have to begin with the assurance of equal rights of
initiative, participation, proposition, and suggestion, so that the conference
would be a collective work of all the participating states and reflect as closely as
possible the effort of all states in finding and in ensuring the international
guarantees.[75] Prior to the June 1976 Berlin conference of the European Communist Parties the Romanians again signaled their autonomous stance well in
advance. Constantin Florea, the deputy chief editor of *Era Socialista*, wrote
that Romania had full participation rights in international affairs and that they
would also stress relations with the nonaligned states.[76] Thus, the Romanians
almost invariably attempted to send out a sharp and clear signal to notify
Moscow of their future conduct. Often, of course, this had to be in a form of
echo sounding, waiting for the reaction of Moscow or other bloc members to
proposed Romanian actions. But this, too, extended the time for conflict resolution and, in the delicate actions necessary in maintaining the autonomy of
foreign policy within the Soviet bloc, this manner of signaling could represent
an important tool of defense.

The quality and effectiveness of a country's diplomacy is also dependent
on the diplomatic skills of the leader. Ceausescu, during the period under study,
proved that Romania had a considerable asset in the field of diplomacy by
having him as leader. His skill may be illustrated briefly by his keynote address
to the 10th Party Congress in August 1969. He publicly condemned "imperialism" but without saying which imperialism he was referring to; he did not refer
to Nixon's visit in a five-hour speech, but praised Soviet space exploits in the
same breath as the "great victory of the Apollo space mission"; and finally he
reiterated Romania's loyalty to the Warsaw Pact, without mentioning, however,
that it did not take part in the intervention into Czechoslovakia.[77]

In peaceful conflict resolution is it similarly important not to have sharp,
direct (nonphysical) attacks among the parties. It has been a common tendency
in Communist propoganda techniques to utilize quotations from prominent
foreign scholars to enforce a Socialist or Communist viewpoint. Romania, however, has reduced this technique to an art form in its attempts at maintaining its
foreign policy autonomy. In calling for the elimination of military blocs, for
example, they referred to "that well-known military-political doctrinary," Henry
Kissinger, to show that military blocs such as the North Atlantic Treaty Organi-

zation (NATO) do not function well and thus, by implication, that the Warsaw Pact could not function properly either.[78] In attacking encroachments on Romanian sovereignty, the Romanians frequently used Hans Morgenthau as the straw man by repeatedly lambasting his ideas of limited sovereignty. (Incidentally, Soviet scholars had been just as busy denouncing Morgenthau's ideas.) This oblique mode of attack is especially valuable when the potential enemy possesses such overwhelming military strength as the Soviet Union.

Finally, Romania used a diplomatic technique that may best be described as a variation on the "Mutt and Jeff" routine.* Designed to confuse the opponent as to what faction in the prospective victim state should be encouraged and which should be suppressed, it deliberately obfuscates the signals. In the summer of 1967, Ceausescu appeared vulnerable: He had just recognized West Germany; he was maintaining good relations with Israel and had conducted a "house cleaning" within the party organization. Yet on May 7, he obliquely denounced the abortive Soviet attempts at changing the Romanian party leadership.[79] His premier, Gheorghe Maurer, however, took the soft line the following day, and declared that the friendship between Romania and the Soviet Union would continue because the two countries were linked by common systems and aims.

In his July 24, 1967 speech before the Grand National Assembly, Ceausescu took the soft line and was very conciliatory toward the Soviet Union. The next day, however, Maurer took the hard line against the Soviet Union, and implied that Moscow was applying pressure on bloc countries in defiance of international Socialist morality.[80] Since Maurer was Ceausescu's man, it should be reasonable to conclude that the whole act was staged to relieve Soviet pressure on the party leadership by presenting a less clearly identifiable target.

Thus, the manner and form of conducting foreign affairs can be a valuable active tool of defense for a small nation. Used skillfully, it can have coordinated Romania's other active defenses and thereby helped plug gaps which may have existed in Romania's defense network. It also enhanced worldwide Romanian prestige and visibility. Her very success in pursuing certain autonomous foreign policies would tend to indicate that her diplomacy did enjoy fulfillment as an element of defense.

BRIDGE BUILDING TO THE WEST AND THE NONALIGNED WORLD

Among elements of national power are those of natural resources[81] and Romania was reasonably well endowed with such resources, including the key

---

*A technique of police interrogation used in North America on occasion to break down the resistance of a crime suspect and get him to confess. Two officers alternate in interviewing the prisoner with one being excessively harsh, while the other is exceedingly compassionate. The prisoner is supposed to become disoriented and confess.

energy resources of oil and natural gas. However, as a country undergoes industrialization, it develops an increasing need for exchanging goods with other countries and, in the early growth stages, for importing vast amounts of capital, thus making self-sufficiency virtually impossible. Yet dependence on trade, especially when trade is concentrated in a limited number of exchange markets, renders the developing country particularly vulnerable to foreign economic pressures. In 1960, Romanian trade with the Socialist nations constituted 73.6 percent of its total external exchange, and trade with the Soviet Union itself stood at 40.5 percent of the total volume. Shifting trade to the West, however, carried the danger that the very act of opening lines to the capitalist states could have been viewed by the Soviet Union as an unacceptable provocation. By the time of his death in 1965, though, Gheorghiu-Dej was able to reduce Romania's trade with the Socialist world to 64.38 percent, thereby decreasing dependence on that particular source of exchange.[82] But perhaps just as significantly, he had effected a qualitative change in trade. By opening up economic "bridges" to the West he had achieved a breakthrough. New credit sources and, very significantly, alternate sources for materials pivotal to Romanian economic growth had been located. Alternate sources of capital and materials coupled with a considerable wealth of natural resources could pose a considerable defense against economic pressures.

In neutralizing, by a considerable degree, the Soviet powers of economic pressure, Gheorghiu-Dej blocked off Moscow's channels of political control and in that sense his economic bridge building to the West was a form of political defense. Ceausescu, exploiting this valuable precedent, could enlarge the economic bridges and build political ones as well.

Despite the precedents, there was continued danger. The Soviet Union could have been so provoked by these moves that it would have augmented pressure against Romania to an increasingly higher level in order to stop the latter from pursuing the offending policies. And, if these failed, it could have attempted direct military intervention. Romania, therefore, had to be careful to ensure that links with the West did not appear as direct provocations to the Soviet Union, and this had been partly achieved through the skill of its diplomacy. Bucharest also had to ensure that bridge building was gradual and in coordination with its other passive and active defenses so that it would not breach the limits for foreign policy autonomy.

Success for the Ceausescu government in preserving the links established by Gheorghiu-Dej and in building further economic and political ones suggested benefits on two planes. First, as under Gheorghiu-Dej, Romania could resist more effectively further politically motivated Soviet economic pressure and thereby prosecute more easily autonomous policies, both domestically and externally. The effectiveness of Romanian defenses, of course, could be measured by its ability to pursue its own foreign (or domestic) policies despite Soviet opposition and pressures. Second, by establishing political bridges to the West through nonideological leadership links—in addition to the economic links—the

Romanians could exploit these contacts for the purposes of exercising counter-vailing pressures against the Soviet Union. While the power of Western countries to influence the Soviet Union in the policies toward bloc states was very limited, because of Moscow's sensitivity to any outside interference in intrabloc affairs, the Kremlin's desire for better relations with the West in the late 1960s and during the 1970s provided the latter with some leverage. And as scant as this leverage may have been, Romania could tap some of its power and thereby add another small element to its defense network.

Qualitative change in trade, however, is as important as the quantitative aspect. With rapid industrial growth, Romania needed to import increasingly larger quantities of iron ore for its steel mills and oil to keep its refineries operating at full capacity. The logical source for both of these strategic resources was the Soviet Union, which apparently did not hesitate to use these goods as a lever for pressuring Romania to conform to Soviet policies. Some indication of Soviet pressure was given in an article in *Lupta de Clasa* by Professor R. Moldovan, an alternate member of the Romanian Academy. He suggested that Romania wished to enhance the efficiency of Comecon by improving the finalization of accords, contracts, or understandings in which there would be "firm obligations for the partners involved in the respective action," as well as by creating ways and means of ensuring the fulfillment of the reciprocal obligations that had been assumed.[83]

Romania thus had to seek alternate sources of supply. It looked to the West and the Third World. In February 1968, Romania and Iran signed a $235 million trade agreement, which covered Iranian oil exports to Romania and Romanian machinery exports to Iran.[84] On September 2, 1969, another trade agreement was concluded with Iran, totaling $80 million, whereby Iran was to furnish crude oil and other raw materials. Further, on October 13, 1969, Ceausescu visited India and with the occasion of the visit, signed a one-year trade pact as well as a five-year technical cooperation accord whereby India was to supply Romania with 22 million tons of iron ore in exchange for 10 Romanian-built bulk-carrier ships.[85] And, taken over a perspective of several years, Romanian trade with the West appeared to maintain a steady rhythm. In September 1966, the Renault Corporation of France announced that it had reached an agreement with the Romanian foreign trade organization, Industrial Export, to build an $83 million automobile factory at Pitesti, Romania.[86] On April 15, 1967, Romania and Israel signed an economic agreement to increase overall trade from $3 million to $40 million per annum.[87] This trend continued when, on December 22, 1969, Romania and West Germany signed a long-term economic and technical cooperation agreement for the period 1970–74, and a trade agreement for the year 1970; while on January 9, 1970, Romania signed a long-term trade agreement with France for 1970–74 which envisaged a doubling of trade between the two countries.[88]

As significant as trade had been with the West, it was not more significant than Romania's attempts to build credit reservoirs in the West for its developing economy. It sought Most-Favored-Nation (MFN) trade status and credits in the United States and, following his visit to the United States in October 1970, President Ceausescu began to speak of joint ventures with Western countries roughly along the lines of the initial Yugoslav proposals of 1967. The President's ideas were put in more concrete terms on March 17, 1971, when a law on foreign trade and economic and technoscientific cooperation was enacted, providing for the establishment of joint enterprises in industry, agriculture, construction, and some services. Although Romanian law did not permit private ownership of production facilities, the new law stated the Romanian government's agreement to guarantee capital investments, to permit repatriation of profits in hard currency (without a reinvestment provision), and to allow eventual capital repatriation. Foreign capital investment was limited to 49 percent of total requirements, but the division of profits was an item of negotiation whereby, in a priority industry, a Western corporation could obtain a higher share than 49 percent.[89]

The 1971–75 Romanian Five-Year Plan illustrates the significance of foreign credits to Romania. It called for a 470-billion-lei capital investment, estimated to be worth about $21 billion in U.S. terms by the Romanian economic counsellor to the United States, and it was predicated on acquiring 14 percent of this investment ($3 billion) from the West.[90] As a result, several joint ventures were established between Western partners and Romania, in third countries. These embodied a wide variety of projects with the relative ownership positions of the two parties varying from corporation to corporation. A significant measure in helping the creation of such ventures was taken in January 1971, when a Franco-Romanian bank, owned 50-50 by Romania and a consortium of French banks, was established in Paris with a capitalization of 20 million francs. One of the key purposes of the bank was the financing of joint transactions with Romania.[91] In May 1971 the first joint U.S.–Romanian corporation was established with the company Romanda Corp., to be owned 50-50 by the Romanian state agency Terra, and by Robert B. Anderson & Co. Ltd., New York, with the primary purpose of developing ventures in which Romania would obtain an equity position. And in September 1971 Rodeco, a similar organization, was established in West Germany.[92]

Romania also made vigorous attempts to break through Western trade barriers and in November 1971 it became the 80th member of the General Agreement on Trade and Tariffs (GATT). In his conference with French Foreign Minister Maurice Schumann, Corneliu Manescu, his Romanian counterpart, asked that his country be allowed to benefit from the preferential (duty-free) treatment that the European Common Market had granted to developing nations, and Schumann promised to help.[93] In March 1972, President Nixon signed an executive order authorizing the U.S. Overseas Private Investment Corporation to extend its loan and investment program to Romania and Yugoslavia, the first two Communist countries to obtain this official trade and investment incentive.[94] Furthermore, on December 15, 1972, Romania became the first East European bloc country to join the International Monetary Fund and the International Bank for Reconstruction and Development,[95] and in 1975 it received MFN status in the United States.

While Romania had been successful in shifting its trade away from Comecon to the extent that by 1976 it conducted a lesser percentage of its trade with fellow Socialist states than any of the others, its success in redirecting its trade to the non-Communist world during the 1970s enjoyed only mixed success. The rather rosy predictions for Romanian trade growth with the industrialized West floundered in the 1970s. This was due largely to two factors: the Romanian economic inefficiency and the oil crisis. In the first instance, despite rapid industrial growth, Romania remained the most industrially backward country in Eastern Europe. Its industrial growth had been largely labor intensive, characterized by very inefficient and technologically unsophisticated production. Despite lower prices, its goods simply were unable to compete on the Western market. By 1971, as a result, Romania had run up the largest deficit of the Soviet-bloc states in its trade with the industrial West ($1.8 billion)[96] and by 1975 its deficit with the industrial West surpassed $3 billion, ranking it just below Poland and the G.D.R.[97]

Using the two most common methods of measuring the burden of foreign debt, namely, relating the size of the debt to the volume of the export to the West, and second, measuring the cost of servicing the debt, Romania is in a very poor position vis-a-vis the West. Its total trade in 1976 was only slightly over $10 billion, and within Eastern Europe itself this was the second lowest total volume of trade and by far the lowest per-capita volume of trade.[98] Remedying the situation has been very difficult for Romania. As we stated earlier, it has sought trade concessions from the West, particularly from the European community, on the basis of being a "developing country" and it sought the MFN status from the United States. Even in 1977 it was complaining that Western restrictions on trade inhibited the growth of Romanian exports to the West.[99] The granting by the U.S. of MFN status to Romania did increase the volume of trade between those two countries and Romania hoped that by 1980 trade would reach $1 billion. However, the gap in the trade between the two countries during 1974 reached a record of $408 million in favor of the United States.[100] Nevertheless, this is still a low dollar level of trade, and, even more important, it was estimated that as late as 1974, of Romanian exports to the West, machinery and industrial equipment comprised only 5 percent of the total.[101] There have even been allegations in the West that Romania, in its eagerness to increase its industrial exports to the West, has been guilty of dumping. An investigation was commenced in Britain to determine whether Romania was in fact dumping chipboard exports.[102]

Romania's second problem has been the supply of energy. Romania is not a very large producer of coal and since 1970 it has been a net importer of a larger and larger proportion of its oil requirements, hitting the level of 8.475 million tons in 1976.[103] Since the West is a net importer of oil and Romania could not go back to purchasing oil from the Soviet Union for political reasons, it had to turn to the Arab world, and Iran. Because of its economic difficulties in earning hard currency, Romania had to seek barter trade with countries where it could sell its low-quality but very inexpensive goods in exchange for raw materials. The Arabs and the Third World possessed oil and other raw materials that it needed and the latter particularly could use the inexpensive Romanian industrial goods. The necessary shift was reflected in the changes in Romanian trade during the 1970s. While its trade with the industrial West declined as a percentage of its total, its exchanges with the Third World and the Arabs increased dramatically from 6.89 percent in 1970 to 18.3 percent in 1976, inclusive of trade with the Arab states, which itself increased from 2.8 percent in 1970 to 8.9 percent in 1976.[104]

In the case of the Arab states Romania was willing to pay the political price for closer relations. It recognized the Palestine Liberation Organization (PLO) as sole representative of the Palestinian people and allowed them to set up a sumptuous "embassy" in Bucharest. It voted closely with the Arab States at the UN is condemning Israeli occupation of land and in 1976 it stopped shipping Iranian oil across Israel's oil pipeline and decided to abide by the Arab boycott of Israeli companies. As a result, on September 14, 1976, the Commissioner General of the Arab boycott announced that all Romanian enterprises were to be removed from the Arab blacklist.[105] Thus while Romania managed to improve its relations with the Arab states and aid its own economy, it was at the same time able to remove an irritant in Soviet-Romanian relationships through the cooling of Romanian-Israeli relations. Therefore, in shifting its trade away from the Soviet bloc Romania increased its defenses by making itself less susceptible to economic pressures; but in the 1970s this protection will increasingly have to come from the Third World and the Arab states, where their largest increase in trade was occurring, rather than in the trade with the West.

The Institutional Limitations of Comecon

These Romanian actions and contacts with the non-Communist world, then, had the potential to provide significant defenses if they did not provoke the Soviet Union into unacceptable retaliation. Bucharest had to be careful not to pose uncontainable institutional challenges and, in essence, autonomous Romanian economic policies were tied in significantly with the impact they had on the Comecon and the importance the Soviet Union attached to that institution.

J. M. Montias defined economic nationalism in Eastern Europe as any "commercial policy tending to harm the economic interests of a group of countries or 'bloc,' for the sake of pursuing some domestic goal."[106] But to assess the "harm" that Romanian pursuit of domestic goals effectuated, we must assess the goals of the group, in this case the Soviet-led institution of Comecon. Yet, even the most cursory examination of Comecon indicates that it cannot be analyzed as a mere economic institution, for political considerations have been essential throughout its evolution.

The very institution of Comecon, established in 1949, was predicated on political factors. It was conceived of as a propaganda device to counter the Marshall Plan and it was activated in response to the European Common Market (EEC).[107] Until the mid-1950s it remained dormant, and even subsequently there were only three major attempts to infuse it with important supranational planning and integrative functions, in 1962, 1971, and 1975. Some measures were taken in the latter part of the 1950s to strengthen Comecon, such as the establishment of 12 standing committees in 1956, a treaty on multilateral settlements in 1957, and the adoption of a formal charter in 1959, which provided each member with a veto power,[108] but it nevertheless remained an ad hoc type of organization.

It was only in 1962, when the "Basic Principles of International Socialist Division of Labor" were ratified and the Executive Committee, composed of the deputy premiers of the member states, was established,[109] that Comecon really gravitated toward consolidation. There had been an increasing number of joint projects before 1962, such as 2,500-mile oil pipeline to Eastern Europe begun in 1959,[110] and the commencement of work on a giant electricity grid linking the Soviet Union with all the other members.[111] And some of the more perceptive Western observers noticed a move toward specialization.[112] But it was only in 1962 that Khrushchev put forth his program officially. While previously Comecon lacked effectiveness because of a weak executive, the lack of rational prices, ineffective incentives to specialization, and tendencies toward autarkic development coupled with bilateralism in trade, the 1962 plans would have provided for both a strong executive as well as for specialization. The plan represented both economic and political goals for Khrushchev, because, in addition to increasing economic efficiency, it would also have reinforced Soviet political control over the bloc.

For Romania, however, the plan meant a setback both economically and politically, as it would have stifled the nascent industrialization and nationalism under Gheorghiu-Dej. While there may have been some opposition to the plan by other Comecon members, in view of the likelihood, as Michael Kaser has said, that the move for consolidation overreached itself,[113] it was largely due to Romania's strong objections to a central planning body (supranationality), backed by her veto power, that supranationality and multilaterality was dropped. By mid-1963 Comecon officials declared that "bilateral consultations create the best preconditions for multilateral plan coordination in the Comecon framework."[114] Romania, then, had succeeded in maintaining Comecon as a loose association which at best gave the Soviets some legitimacy in pressing for a high level of trade among all members. Moreover, the political victory coupled with the value of the precedent ensured that future Romanian economic links with the West in the 1960s could not be said to attack directly Soviet institutional authority.

Thus Ceausescu's maintenance of bridges to the West, necessitated by the economic needs of industrialization and the political ones of nationalism, may have displeased Moscow, but should not have been considered as an attack on Soviet institutional rights, for Comecon remained a weak organization which lagged as a tool of Soviet control over Eastern Europe behind others, such as bilateral ties and threats of intervention. Though there was some progress after 1963—such as the creation of the International Bank for Economic Cooperation and the transfer rouble (which had only limited transferability), as well as the signing of scientific-technical cooperation agreements in the decade of the 1960s—these brought minor improvements in intra-Comecon trade because of a lack of a supranational controlling body. This weakness, however, allowed for flexibility, and Romanian challenges could be contained, again virtually by definition, for they would not have struck at vital Soviet institutional interest.

In line with this flexibility, the Soviet Union demonstrated that despite displeasure at Romanian autonomous policies, which meant bridge building to the West, it could tolerate many of these policies. During May 1966 *Pravda* reprinted a lengthy speech by Ceausescu in which the latter reemphasized his determination to continue rapid industrialization[115] (which in effect meant maintaining links with the West for technological and capital imports). Later the paper reported that a mid-May meeting between Brezhnev and Ceausescu, held in Bucharest, took place in a "warm" and friendly atmosphere.[116]

The Soviets also showed that they could contain Romania by excluding it from certain decisions. It was not invited to the Dresden Comecon meeting of top political and economic leaders in March 1968, which took cognizance of the increasingly political nature of the organization in view of events in Czechoslovakia, or to that in Bratislava later in the year. Despite the fact that Romania was absenting itself more frequently from routine Comecon meetings, it objected to decisions being made in its absence, and generally to any move which smacked of supranationalism.[117] It could make such a challenge even in the late 1960s because there was no clear Soviet consensus as to how Comecon should be developing, but only on its general goals. On the other hand, Moscow could contain or even exclude certain members, such as Albania, and invite to membership non-European states, such as Mongolia in 1962 and Cuba in 1972.[118]

It was in 1971 that Comecon endeavored to introduce a new "comprehensive program" during the 25th Session, held in Bucharest. While the Soviet Union had previously pressed for more supranational planning, especially after the 24th Comecon Council Session in May 1970,[119] and made some progress toward integration through the utilization of some joint companies such as Intermetal and Interchim, and the new Institute for Economic Problems of World Socialist Systems, it viewed economic integration as just one facet of a broader integrative framework that was on its face ideological and political, and as a result it still did not have a comprehensive plan until 1971. In the "comprehensive program" of 1971 the Kremlin favored the development of supranational planning as a framework for close coordination of national plans, but even at this point there were no concrete steps (the plan only spoke of joint forecasting and planning on a voluntary basis). Rather, the communique stated that the implementation of the plan required conclusion of further agreements.[120] The section concerned with monetary reforms provided only for the formulation of an agreed methodology in 1971 and the introduction of new exchange rates during 1972 and 1974, but true convertibility, as opposed to convertibility among the national currencies and the rouble, was relegated to the distant future. Even limited convertibility had the late implementation date of 1980. In stressing voluntarism in participation, the program also appeared to arrest the use of the veto power, and thereby allow interested states to effect joint cooperation. By depriving states of the veto power, it became possible to contain more easily a Romanian challenge, for instance, but as a partial balance, nonparticipants were given the right to link into a joint project at any time. Finally, the plan should have allayed some Romanian fears through its vigorous assertion that economic integration would not be accompanied by the creation of supranational organs.

The diplomatic opportunities that Comecon provided should not be over-looked. As long as the organization did not demand strict, unquestioning adher-ence to a central policy it could act as a forum for conflict resolution. Romania, as well as other members, could offer criticism with some immunity, for the institution could accommodate compromise.

Thus the program had at once a look of great compromise and of very narrow scope, quite unlike the ambitious plan put forth by Khrushchev in 1962. There were objective and subjective causes for this. Objectively, it reflected the difficulty of coordinating economic reform in the bloc, and the technical prob-lems of rationalizing the currency system. Subjectively, though, it was a con-frontation between those who favored supranational planning and those who wanted to create a common Socialist market that would have allowed a degree of competition among enterprises across national frontiers within a framework of indicative planning. The Soviet Union favored the first proposition, but Romania, which opposed supranationality politically as well as economically, was not the main force lined up against the Soviet position (as it had been in 1962), and certainly it was no great proponent of the second position. Rather it was Hungary, Poland, and Czechoslovakia before 1968, who had pressed for a Socialist common market.[121]

Czechoslovakia, who had been an original member of GATT, wanted to tie in domestic reform with reform of Comecon before the intervention,[122] but fell in line with Moscow afterward. It was, in fact, Hungary who exerted the main pressure for reform. As far back as 1967, Hungarian planners stressed the need to adapt Comecon institutions to the principles of market Socialism.[123] In 1968, the Hungarian Deputy Prime Minister and Chief Representative to Comecon, Antal Apro, warned against isolation from the world economy and argued that closer Comecon integration necessitated a common currency.[124] Common currency would in effect have meant decentralization of decision making and more political autonomy for the member states. Later in the year

Apro criticized Comecon and advocated a more flexible framework that, concomitant with the principle of voluntarism, would preserve national sovereignty over economic policy and reform.[125] Reszo Nyers, the chief architect of the Hungarian economic reforms (New Economic Mechanism), also rejected joint Comecon planning in favor of national independence, and while he admitted the necessity for integration he insisted on voluntarism, flexible foreign trade, and on increased Comecon currency convertibility.[126]

Hungary continued its challenge into the 1970s, attesting to the fact that Romania was not unique in some of its autonomous policies and in financial dealings with the West. In 1970 Budapest floated two loans through banks in London and South America.[127] As late as January 1971 the Hungarians did not change their aims and advocated modernization of the financial, trade, and price systems; integration through multilateralism and convertibility; and more specifically they called for more flexible trade quotas, elasticity in export-import prices, and partial convertibility to gold and free currencies.[128] Like Romania, Hungary also tried to develop contacts with the EEC and other international agencies.[129] While overall Hungarian activities during the 1970s may have quieted down as had those of Poland and other states because of a greater dependence on the Soviet Union, they and not Romania remained the spearhead for the institutional reform of Comecon. As an indication of this, during 1972 there were some attacks in the Soviet press on Hungarian "bourgeois nationalism,"[130] the first such attacks since 1956.

While Romania was not the leader of the institutional attack on Comecon despite its general opposition to supranationality, its bridge building to the West represented a significant deviation from Soviet policy, so it did make a number of concessions and some of these are worth mentioning at this point. Following the intervention into Czechoslovakia, Romania became a little more placid in opposing supranational integration and began to attend Comecon meetings regularly. In January 1969 Ion Fintinaru wrote in a large front-page *Scinteia* article that in the sphere of external economic links of Romania, the central place for collaboration was destined to be retained by the Socialist states.[131] The next year, Romania consented to participate in Interchim and work more closely with Intermetal, another joint Comecon institution, while in January 1971 it agreed to join the new Comecon investment bank.[132] It joined the bank despite its opposition during the previous four months to a provision in the charter that called for majority decision making in return for a face-saving formula that promised "respect for the sovereignty of all member countries."[133] This particular concession may have indicated that Romanian economic difficulties plus the economic might of the Soviet Union were drawing Romania closer to Comecon, as was the case generally in Eastern Europe.

Romania went even further to reassure the Soviet Union of participation in Comecon projects by repeatedly publicizing the many examples of its past participation and by announcing its intention, in 1971, to participate in joint investments in Soviet iron-ore mining as well as its willingness to cooperate in a long string of Comecon industrial and agricultural projects.[134] During 1972 Ceausescu reiterated his support for Comecon and for the integration plan adopted by the 25th session in Bucharest in 1971.[135] In this manner its policies resulted in a mixture of gains and some concessions.

There were a number of other factors which up to 1973 would have helped safeguard Romanian autonomy within Comecon. The real per-capita income and the national income of the East European states grew at a higher rate than in the Soviet Union. In fact the East European states derived increased benefits from their association with the Soviet Union. Large energy and raw-material exports to Eastern Europe forced the Soviet Union to forego larger purchases from Western countries of machinery and other commodities unavailable in the bloc states. Moreover, the Soviet Union sold these raw materials at prices below those in the world market. In this sense the Soviet Union was paying an increasingly steeper price for the dependence of the East European states. In a cost-benefit or a liability-asset analysis done by some scholars in the West, it has been shown that Eastern Europe as a whole had been an economic liability to the Soviet Union.[136] Some East European countries such as Bulgaria benefited greatly from their association with the Soviet Union both through the availability of a market where goods of a quality unacceptable in Western industrialized countries were salable and from large infusions of capital and of loans. The Soviet Union's main concern was control over the bloc states and the economic loss was a trade-off. Therefore, if the Soviet Union was able to maintain an acceptable level of political control over Romania without having to accept the economic losses entailed in this type of control in other parts of Eastern Europe, then a Romanian economic disassociation from the Soviet bloc constituted a much lesser challenge. Furthermore, as the indebtedness of the Comecon countries increased vis-a-vis the West to a level of over $45 billion by the end of 1976,[137] neither the Soviet Union nor the other East European states would have been anxious, from an economic point of view at least, to grant credit to Romania in order to induce greater integration of that country's economy within Comecon. Therefore there were sound economic reasons for the Soviet tolerance of Romanian challenges to Comecon.

The 1973 oil crisis changed the picture somewhat. The drastic increase in world oil prices meant that the Soviet Union was suffering tremendous economic loss by selling oil at preset prices. The economies of the East European states including Romania were particularly hard hit by the increases in the prices of Western manufactured imports. Therefore, economic integration in Comecon began to make much greater economic sense than before. In 1975 the Soviet Union renegotiated intra-Comecon foreign trade prices retroactively to January 1, 1975. The price of oil was increased, though not to the world level. Hungary, the first country with which the Soviet Union renegotiated prices, revealed the provisions for the changes in the party daily *Nepszabadsag*, issue of February 23, 1975. They included an increase of 2.3 times more than the 1974 price level for Soviet oil, but this was still only two thirds the present price of oil. The price of Hungarian goods exported to the Soviet Union was to increase as well but at a lower percent. As a result Hungary's burden in its trade with the Soviet Union would be increased. Nevertheless, this would still not fully compensate the Soviet Union for the loss that it incurred by not selling the oil on the world markets. But throughout Eastern Europe, all the Comecon states were extremely hard hit by the oil crisis. As a result they all had more modest growth targets for the five years, from 1976 to 1980. Romania was the first to embark upon conservation measures. Nevertheless, the burden of oil and high-priced Western machinery imports affected the Romanian economy as well and pushed it closer to the East European states.

The Soviet Union had always been willing to shoulder the economic burden of the Soviet bloc because of the political advantages. The relationship could not be assessed purely in economic terms. The Soviet leaders were conditioned to perceive integration as both feasible and desirable. The methods employed by Brezhnev may have differed from those of Khrushchev in that integration for the former was to come from below, beginning with the selective coordination of various economically feasible aspects of the bloc economies, as opposed to the latter's integration from above, but the intention for both has been eventual integration. The economic developments following the oil crisis and the readjustments in the Soviet process for exports of raw materials made such integration more feasible because the East European states became more dependent upon the Soviet Union as their economies stagnated and their vulnerability increased. This dependence would continue in the future even if the Soviet Union became a net importer of oil. Moscow would remain the largest supplier of other raw materials for the bloc and remain the largest market for the industrial goods produced by the bloc states. The Soviet Union would still find the East European states an economic liability because the latter were not going to pay full world prices for Soviet raw materials, but these price readjustments would make the burden smaller.

Therefore, in 1975 the Soviet Union began to press very hard for integration in the Soviet bloc. At the 29th plenary session of Comecon held in Budapest June 24–26, the Agreed Plan for Multilateral Integration Measures was adopted. This plan was more detailed than ever before regarding coordinated economic plans as well as a series of multilateral integration measures aimed at the completion of the comprehensive program approved in July 1971. It was hailed by the Soviet Union as a great achievement on the road to integration.[138] The Soviet Union tried to maintain momentum in 1976 and pressed for further integration at the Comecon meeting in East Berlin July 7–9. However, the final communique did avoid the sensitive term "joint planning."[139]

Romania reacted to these moves toward integration in typical fashion. It combined denunciations of integration with certain substantive concessions. Economic collaboration, in its opinion, was to be geared toward redressing the imbalance in the level of development of the various Socialist states. It denied that the complex program, or any other program of Comecon, was designed to set up supranational bodies or that they were to infringe on the essential and inalienable attributes of the national sovereignty of each state.[140] Ceausescu, speaking in an interview in July 1976 following the Berlin Comecon meeting, stated that Romania based collaboration in Comecon on the equality of states with restriction to the spheres in which each state was interested, and he emphasized that respect for the principles of leadership of each party in government of the national economy was to be maintained.[141]

On the other hand Romanian collaboration with the bloc states in Comecon remained at a high level and, though it declined from the 1960s as a percentage of total trade, it was a much lesser decline than the trade with the Soviet Union.[142] For the period of 1976-80, total volume of Romanian trade was designed to grow between 72 to 80 percent, compared to 1971 to 1975.[143] But Romanian trade with Poland was to increase almost threefold for this period,[144] and by 172 percent with East Germany.[145] While trade with the Soviet Union was to increase by 70 percent[146] and with Hungary only by 60 percent,[147] overall Romanian trade with Comecon then should increase slightly as a percentage of the total.

Despite the increased momentum for integration, Romania benefited from the fact that most of the Soviet bloc states (the exceptions being Bulgaria and, to a much lesser extent, the G.D.R.) still did not envision a submerging of national identities or sovereignties in an integration movement in Eastern Europe. The Hungarian delegation, for instance, at the 1976 meeting of Comecon stated that comprehensive reforms were still needed and that the organization was not moving quickly enough toward its stated goal of making its unit of account, the "transferrable rouble" fully convertible into Western currencies. Moreover, the Hungarians stated that integration, in their opinion, excluded the setting up of supranational planning bodies as well as any interference in the way members ran their own economies.[148] It was reported that even the East Germans were apparently cool toward any greater deepening of Socialist economic integration for the time being.[149] Therefore, the Romanians again were not the sole challengers to Comecon and in fact the type of challenge that the Hungarians offered had more serious economic implications (through the suggestion of decentralization) perhaps than the Romanian challenge. As such the prospect of Comecon becoming a rigid integrative framework still remained remote in the latter half of the 1970s.

Therefore, Romania benefited from the fact that Comecon never became a tightly knit organization, an attack upon which would have meant striking at direct Soviet institutional interests. Following Khrushchev's failure to give it supranational authority in 1962, Comecon developed as a forum for multilateral consultations as well as for shaping some limited spheres of cooperation. Because of this limited scope, Romanian bridge building to the West could remain an isolated posture while the other members could work closely together—in essence the Romanian challenge could be contained. The very nature of Comecon thus provided a passive, though after 1973 perhaps a slightly weakened, defense for Romanian foreign policy autonomy.

The Political Balance Sheet

Romania, in fact, achieved more in its link with the West than a relative immunity from Soviet economic pressures. Together with its breakthrough in trade (first achieved by Gheorghiu-Dej), Romania acquired some powerful friends in the West. De Gaulle, who visited Romania in May 1968, called on Bucharest to set an example of friendly cooperation with France and to work toward the "union of our continent."[150] Having a leader who was as influential as De Gaulle was in Moscow must have been an asset for Romania during the Czechoslovak crisis. When Willy Brandt, then West Germany's foreign minister, declared after the invasion of Czechoslovakia that he could not exclude the possibility of a Soviet invasion of Romania, this may well have served to deprive the Soviet leadership of any element of surprise or of the ability to present a fait accompli to the West, if they indeed were ever contemplating such a move. Nixon's visit to Romania in 1969 and President Ford's visit during August 1975 served to demonstrate to the Soviet Union that the United States was not prepared completely to abandon Romania to the Soviet influence and, moreover, that an intervention into Romania would put very severe strains on the new Soviet-American relations of detente.

Western attitudes toward Romania, however, were affected by the West German *Ostpolitik* and Soviet-American detente. *Ostpolitik* ended the diplomatic isolation of East Germany and this partial reconciliation of the two Germanys made contacts between the East European and West European states more natural and more frequent. The Soviet-American detente, while posing both dangers and opportunities to the East European states, also allowed for more frequent contacts with the West. Romania lost thereby its uniqueness in the bloc as other states increased their trade and cultural contacts with the West. While the ratio of the other East European states' trade with the West is not as high as that of Romania in absolute terms, both Poland and East Germany have a much larger dollar value trade with Western Europe and the industrialized Western world than Romania. The East European states—Hungary in particular—have also embarked on various joint enterprises and other forms of cooperation. Therefore, Romania lost some of its attraction to the West as a bridge to the other East European states. With the waning of the novelty of these types of contacts there has followed a certain weakening of the attachment of the Western world to a seemingly independent Romania, and this perhaps was best reflected in the so-called "Sonnenfeldt doctrine" and in President Carter's world trip during December 1977, when he chose to visit Poland but not Romania.

As far back as 1975, however, the Romanian regime sought consciously and perhaps instinctively to compensate for this weakening in its defense by seeking alternate ties with the Third World and nonaligned nations. Ceausescu, speaking before the Grand National Assembly, said that Romania was linked with developing states through "common aspirations for progress and prosperity . . . to the decision to act for the abolition of the old imperialist politics of inequality, for utilizations of real equality and of reciprocally advantageous collaboration among nations."[151] By 1976 he had visited over thirty of the nonaligned states and received as many of the leaders of these states as visitors. Commercial exchange with these countries grew phenomenally from 4 percent in 1960 to 18 percent of the total in 1976, and it is projected to grow to 30 percent by 1980.[152] After persistent courting of these nonaligned states, Romania succeeded in being admitted to the Group of 77 in February 1976.[153] Bucharest stressed that collaboration with these nonaligned states was in no way a contradiction with Romania's membership in the Warsaw pact. For while Romania was a Socialist state, it was also a state *in the course of development*. Therefore, in some ways Romania was acting in the classic manner of a state in danger. Such a state would seek as many formal or tacit allies as possible in order to ensure that any attempt by another state to intervene into its affairs, to invade it physically, or to intimidate it resulted in the largest possible worldwide shock waves. In this way, Romania would compensate for any loss in leverage that may have occurred in its relationships with the West through relations with the Third World states, who now comprised the majority of the UN General Assembly, and who were most vociferous in seeking protection of national rights and sovereignty.

To reiterate our earlier point, it is not suggested in the least that friendly Western and Third World attitudes toward or concern for Romania would have acted as a full deterrent to Soviet intevention. It is inferred, rather, that in weighing the utility versus the disutility of such an action, the Soviet leaders would have had to consider the strain that such an intervention would place on their relations with the West and the Third World and the above should suggest to them that there would be severe strain. If the rest of Romania's defenses created a fine balance between the "go" and "no go" decision of the Soviet Union in an invasion, the former's quest for good relations with the West and the Third World could have acted as a significant defensive factor on its behalf.

EFFECTS OF THE SINO-SOVIET RIFT

The mere existence of another major center of Communist ideology imposed a certain limitation on Moscow's claim to the position of sole ideological arbiter. China's opposition to Soviet ideological hegemony, moreover, was bound to affect the freedom of political-ideological maneuvers in the Soviet bloc.

No bloc country, however, has been more aware than Romania of the possibilities for autonomous action that the Sino-Soviet rift afforded. When a Romanian delegation traveled to Moscow in 1960, ostensibly to attempt to effect a reconciliation between the two Communist giants, a popular Romanian joke contended that their delegation just wanted to make sure that the two dis-

Tends to create ties to support this

puting sides were sufficiently implacable and preoccupied with themselves to leave Romania alone. If the dispute continued, actual contacts with China could have helped provide an additional counterweight to Soviet pressures.

On the other hand, while the Sino-Soviet dispute may have offered greater opportunity for diversity in policy formulation for a bloc state, contacts with or support for the People's Republic of China also presented serious dangers. The Soviet Union waged a worldwide ideological contest with China and therefore it was hypersensitive to any Chinese penetration into what it regarded as its exclusive domain—the Soviet bloc states. Chinese success in building close links with Albania without this resulting in Soviet military intervention in the latter cannot be considered a guide, for that remote, minuscule Balkan state held little political, economic, or military significance for Moscow. Romania, however, bordered on the Soviet Union with a territory the size of West Germany's and a population of 20 million, so that its shift to the Chinese orbit would have signified to Moscow an extremely dangerous breach of Soviet-bloc control.

If Romania was, therefore, to maintain close links with China, or if it was to defend Peking at Moscow-led meetings of Communist parties, it had to make certain that it did not provoke the Soviet Union. Along this line, Romania had to employ all its diplomatic skills to give the appearance of a balance and to convey to Moscow that expressions of friendship for China did not denote a lessening of friendship for the Soviet Union. More than just giving an appearance of balance, Romania was restricted with regard to the actual types of contact it could maintain with China before facing unacceptable Soviet retaliation. For instance, it appears highly unlikely that Moscow would have tolerated any sizable Chinese military presence in Romania. Thus, in order for Romania to receive full benefits from the Sino-Soviet rift, it had to ensure that the very establishment and maintenance of links with China did not provoke unbearable pressure from Moscow.

It should be pointed out that the breakthrough in Sino-Romanian relations had already occurred during the rule of Gheorghiu-Dej. In attempting to play the honest broker between the Soviet Union and the Chinese, Romania was able to express certain views while playing the two parties off against each other. Indeed, the so-called "Independence Declaration" by Romania on April 22, 1964, was ostensibly a denunciation of the "polemics" between the two Communist giants. While assigning the blame for the continuation of open polemics to China, the Romanians declared that they would continue their policy of rapid development of heavy industries and would refuse to participate in the Socialist division of labor. This "tradition" was carried on by Ceausescu, again under the guise of playing the honest broker, and the reductio ad absurdum of this image projection manifested itself in the manner of reporting Sino-Soviet disputes. An example of this was given in the September 13, 1968, issue of *Scinteia*. Romania had no comment on the latest Sino-Soviet border dispute, but printed the Soviet version side by side with the Chinese version, giving each fourteen and a half lines—and this thereafter became the standard Romanian way of reporting Sino-Soviet disputes.

Contact between the two nations, however, did bring very visible and tangible benefits to both Romania and the People's Republic of China. Gheorghiu-Dej went to great lengths to cultivate Chinese friendship, and in December 1963 China and Romania signed a trade accord providing for the Romanian export of petroleum and chemicals in exchange for minerals and rolled steel. The *Guardian* declared that, "no single commodity among those supplied by Russia to China in the past (and now curtailed) is of greater importance than oil."[154] It is interesting then to note that the new Chinese ambassador to Romania was a former minister of the oil industry. Moreover, on July 10, 1964, the *Christian Science Monitor* reported that, "news from Peking indicates that China would try to increase its purchases of Romanian oil because there have been drastic cuts in imports of Soviet oil."

Under the leadership of Ceausescu, trade with China again brought Romania considerable benefit. The trade agreement that was signed with China on February 14, 1967, not only provided for increased trade, but also for Chinese deliveries of badly needed iron ore for the vast new steel mills at Galati, Romania.[155] China again came to the rescue of Romania in 1970. *The Economist* reported that after Poland and the Soviet Union reneged on coke deliveries for Romania's steel industry, China "earned high marks for jumping in with emergency shipments and then backed this up with the biggest contribution for flood relief from any quarter."[156] The July 1971 editorial of *Lupta de Clasa* expressed Romania's gratitude.[157] The Chinese loan mentioned by *Lupta de Clasa* was of great significance to Romania in view of the colossal damage caused by the 1970 floods and of the refusal of the Soviet Union to supply credit. Thus, China had readily come to the rescue of Romania in a number of serious economic crises and, as a result of vast loans, by 1972 had a considerable financial stake in the latter country.

In the political field, as well, China had been just as ready to aid Romania and this aid was particularly helpful and visible during instances of Soviet pressure on Romania. Following Brezhnev's speech in Bratislava at the Czecho-slovak Party Congress on May 31, 1966 (and following Ceausescu's May 7, 1966, speech calling for the elimination of military blocs), in which Brezhnev called for greater unity and cohesion in the Socialist system, it must have been of considerable comfort to the Romanians to have Chou En-lai declare during his visit to Romania that "the Chinese people resolutely support your just struggle."[158] During the Czechoslovak crisis, China provided some much-needed moral support for Romania, even if it could not do much else, by again promising to support the Romanian "struggles for independence."

Romanian-Chinese relations during the 1970s in particular were determined by the degree of mutual interdependence. This in turn was affected by Sino-Soviet relations, by the Chinese need for Romania as a window to the world, and by the benefits of Chinese-Romanian economic relations. In the first instance, in order for Romania to be able to continue to play or attempt to play its role of honest broker, there could not be a settlement of the Sino-Soviet dispute. In this area at least Romania should have had no major concern. The Soviet Union has continued to attempt to isolate China both ideologically and, perhaps even as important, militarily. Moscow has attempted to establish an Asian collective security system that would isolate China, but it has not been very successful in this continuing aim.[159] The Sino-Soviet border has continued to be the most heavily militarized in the world, with national minorities on both sides and in some cases with the national homeland of these people being cut by artificial lines resulting from military and political considerations.[160] The new Peking leadership that took over upon the death of Mao shows no greater inclination to forego territorial or ideological claims against the Soviet Union. Therefore, a solution to the Sino-Soviet conflict is not apparent in the short term and Romania could in the forseeable future continue its previous role.

China's relations with the Western world have greatly affected its need for Romania as a window to the world. Romania, of course, continued to lend a certain ideological support to China—for instance in 1974 it worked to defuse a Soviet intention to denounce China—but this had a lesser value for Peking than in the 1960s. In the 1970s China made its peace with a large part of the world, it became a member of the United Nations, and it accepted a visit of President Nixon. Therefore, China in the 1970s had direct links with the Western world and did not need an intermediary. Its prestige increased in the Third World and it increased greatly with the nonruling Communist parties of Europe, again lessening Romania's value as intermediary. This weakening of dependence on Romania was perhaps demonstrated by Chou En-lai's statement in 1971 to a Yugoslav newspaper—but intended for Romania—that "distant waters do not quench local fires."

As far as Romania's economic relations with China were concerned, this also had to undergo changes. For one thing, Romania became an importer of oil while China discovered large sources of oil itself which made it self-sufficient and even allowed it to export a limited quantity in exchange for badly needed hard currency. Romania had to look to the Arab world and Iran to satisfy its energy needs. With China's improving relations with the West it sought purchases from these countries as did Romania, and both laid great stress on Third World markets. The trade between the two countries stagnated in the mid-1970s, with China occupying only the eighth place in Romania's total trade.[161] Both countries continued to recognize the importance of the relationship, but it appears that both relegated this relationship to a considerably lower level than in the 1960s.

Therefore, it appears that in the 1960s Romania was able to negotiate successfully the difficult path of establishing and maintaining firm links with China in the face of Soviet displeasure through the skillful use of diplomacy, through efforts at balance, and through maintenance of the links within a limited area of contact. By overcoming the danger that links with China caused,

Romania was able to enjoy the benefits of improved defense. Sino-Romanian trade in the 1960s, especially with emergency shipments of raw materials by the Chinese, attenuated the force of Soviet economic pressures against Romania, as did Chinese financial aid to the Romanian economy. In the 1970s, however, both countries began to recognize that while they could help each other (both China and Romania constantly reiterated ideological support for each other and this was important to morale), they would play a lesser role in each other's policies and defenses. Romania as usual, therefore, sought to compensate for the weakening of this particular defense by building defenses in other areas.

THE BERLIN CONFERENCE AND EUROCOMMUNISM

In its desire to maintain an autonomous foreign policy during the 1970s Romania looked both to gatherings of Communist parties and to Eurocommunism as an alternative and a defense supplemental to that of China. The Berlin conference where 29 European parties gathered in June 1976 provided a convenient forum for Bucharest to express and defend foreign policy autonomy. Likewise, Eurocommunism, if handled with care, could provide a similar defense. In the case of the East Berlin Conference, the Soviet Union had to make a serious concession in order to be able to gather the various Communist parties together and to get them to sign a joint declaration. This declaration made no mention of *proletarian internationalism*—the key phrase used by the Soviet Union in its doctrine of enforcing hegemony over the Socialist bloc. From Romania's point of view, what was extremely significant in this joint declaration was that the main opposition to any sort of assertion by the Soviet Union that Moscow continued to be the guiding center for world Communism, was provided by Joseph Tito and by the leaders of the West European Communist parties, with Ceausescu cast in a minor, supporting role. The Italian leaders' contention that there could be no leading party or state and that the theoretical development of Marxism required many different contributions from various sources fitted in well with Romania's policies, but the main burden of forcing the Soviet Union to admit to this was carried by others. Romania took great advantage of this declaration and President Ceausescu stated, following the conference, that the East Berlin meeting marked a "fundamental change in the Communist workers movement in which there does not and cannot exist a guiding center."[162]

In dealing with Eurocommunism (the particular form of Communism envisioned by certain of the West European parties), Romania was faced with similar problems as in its dealings with China. The Soviet Union was extremely sensitive to the contention of the Western European parties that they could create a specific form of Communism. The Soviet member of the Politboro, Boris Ponomarev, who was also the Secretary of the Central Committee in charge of relations with nonruling parties, wrote in a long article in 1976 that

Eurocommunism was not acceptable to the Soviet Union and therefore he rejected its precepts.[163] Moscow as well had denounced on several occasions the leader of the Spanish Communist party. Nevertheless, the Soviets maintained their contacts with the Eurocommunists because they wanted to keep their options open and because a total break would have entailed either opposition or, at the very least, serious reservations from some of the East European parties, particularly the Polish and Hungarian ones, who were interested in countering a one-sided integration into the Soviet-dominated Eastern system.[164] In maintaining open lines of communication with the Eurocommunists, however, Moscow looked for certain desiderata as outlined by Ponomarev[165] in his articles, including the dictum that the Eurocommunists must refrain from trying to impose their own concepts on the Soviet Union and its European allies. Moscow viewed the latter as an attempt to turn backward a development stage of Communism. In all of its contacts with the leaders of the West European Communist parties, Romania had been very careful to ensure that agreement between them referred to international relations and not to any changes in Romania's Stalinist domestic system. In joint statements with the leaders of Western parties, Romania emphasized its own interpretation of the Berlin conference that the relations of equality were to apply to all of the Communist states and not to the relations between a Soviet bloc on the one hand and the rest of the Communist states on the other side.

Within these limits the Romanians carefully cultivated their relationships with the leaders of the Western Communist parties. Both Santiago Carillo and Enrico Berlinguer visited Romania frequently at the invitation of Ceausescu. Invariably they were given sumptuous and enthusiastic welcomes. Their statements on the rights of sovereignty were always widely publicized throughout the Romanian press. During Berlinguer's visit to Romania at Ceausescu's invitation in January 1977, the two leaders issued a joint communique which stated that there was complete agreement on foreign policy and the absolute right of each party to decide its own course.[166] As well, they stated that they were fully agreed on the need for Communist parties to collaborate with Socialist, social democratic, and Christian democratic parties in order to create a new international order. This was a reassertion of Romania's autonomous stance, particularly following the conciliatory moves it had made toward the Soviet Union in the wake of Brezhnev's November 1976 visit. But again this assertion was made through a seemingly innocuous instrument.

Romania during the 1970s proceeded quickly to take advantage of the defenses offered by the Berlin conference and by the support it could gather from the Western European Communist parties. As the Chinese defense weakened, the defense of having influential West European parties concern themselves deeply with Romania's fate increased. While the threat of denunciation by the West European parties would not deter the Soviet Union from military intervention if it felt that its vital interests were irretrievably threatened, in a good many lesser cases of friction, it would have been affected by the opinions of these Western parties, particularly that of Italy, which may well achieve power in the future.

It appears, therefore, in the period since 1965 that Romania maintained and in certain cases enhanced an important set of political-ideological defenses. The effectiveness of these defenses was shown by the ability of the Ceausescu government to pursue continuously an autonomous policy in the face of Soviet disapproval and, on occasion, outright opposition.

A brief analysis of Soviet policy toward the bloc states in the postwar era demonstrates that it was not geared toward random intervention and, in the case of actual military intervention, Moscow often acted *in extremis*. This in itself constituted a passive defense and an opportunity for Romania to look for causative factors for Soviet intervention. Among such key causative factors— perhaps the main one—we found to have been the quest of the Soviet Union for ideological security in the bloc through the assurance of power for Moscow-style Communism in the bloc states. In practical terms this meant the security of the rule of the Communist party in a bloc state. Success in maintaining party control and in demonstrating such control to Moscow therefore constituted a very significant defense for a bloc state, permitting it to pursue some autonomous policies in other areas.

The Romanian Communist Party maintained strong control over the life of the country and gave ample demonstration of this control particularly at times of crisis and through a very strict direction of intellectual expression. This should have gone to a considerable length in reassuring the Soviet Union that Romania's pursuit of an autonomous foreign policy did not mean the lessening of domestic ideological commitment or a debilitation of party control.

Ceausescu himself demonstrated that he was able to maintain strong control over the party machinery, thereby eliminating an additional channel of informal control previously (before 1967) available to the Soviet Union: namely, influence over leadership changes. By being able to fill the presidium and later the permanent bureau with his own men and by rotating them frequently enough so that they would not be able to acquire a power base of their own from which to challenge him—in case any of them developed a desire for the top post—Ceausescu made himself less susceptible to Soviet pressures. To the above defenses, we must add that of Romanian diplomatic skills. Ceausescu and his leadership were careful to present disagreement with the Soviet Union as obliquely and as innocuously as possible. In addition, Ceausescu and his top subordinates strove to present to the Soviet Union as small a target as possible in the face of potential and actual Soviet pressure.

In building bridges to the West and in maintaining strong links with the Soviet Union's Communist arch-rival, China, and with the leaders of Eurocommunism, Romania faced a considerable danger of provoking Soviet retaliation for such autonomous foreign policies. Nevertheless, through the careful utilization of domestic skills and of defenses that were available, Romania succeeded in holding Soviet actions to a limited range of pressures which could be resisted by prior defenses and by the additional ones resulting from these links. And, these links did help increase Romanian resistance capacity to economic pressures as well as providing a source of countervailing Western, Third World, Chinese, and "Eurocommunist" political pressures vis-a-vis the Soviet Union. By giving Romania a greater opportunity for political maneuvering, these ties again constituted a significant part of its political defense network.

Romania thus proved the effectiveness of these (and other) political defenses by its ability to continue to pursue an autonomous foreign policy despite Soviet opposition. It may have made occasional small retrenchments, and the effectiveness of these political defenses fluctuated marginally at crisis points through the interaction of various causative factors, but it appears clear that the limits for foreign policy autonomy were kept sufficiently wide to allow Romania to maneuver with a substantive safety margin. Thus Romania's political defenses achieved their purpose, but again we must return to our initial proposition that it was a network of defenses which determined the limits of Romanian foreign policy, with political defenses only forming a part of this network and therefore being responsible only in part for the Romanian success. In order to round out the picture we therefore propose to attempt to analyze next the political/legal and the military defenses.

NOTES

1. Leonard Schapiro, "Totalitarianism in Foreign Policy" in K. London, ed., *The Soviet Impact on World Politics* (New York: Hawthorn Books, 1974), p. 16.

2. *Pravda* (Moscow), August 25, 1968, p. 1. It denounced the support for "political adventures from Prague" in Bucharest.

3. A. Braun, "The Evolution of the Warsaw Pact," *Canadian Defence Quarterly*, Winter 1973-74, pp. 29-30.

4. Milovan Djilas, *Conversations with Stalin* (London: Rupert, Hart, Davis, 1962), pp. 3-5.

5. Ibid., p. 160.

6. Stephen Fischer-Galati, *The New Romania* (Cambridge, Mass.: MIT Press, 1967), p. 197.

7. Kenneth Jowitt, *Revolutionary Breakthrough and National Development: The Case of Romania 1944-1965* (Berkeley: University of California Press, 1971), p. 199.

8. *Lupta de Clasa*, April 1964, pp. 3-12.

9. *Scinteia*, July 17, 1965.

10. New York *Times*, January 5, 1965.

11. *Statistical Pocket Book of the Socialist Republic of Romania* (Bucharest: CSB, 1971), pp. 330-47.

12. *Christian Science Monitor* (Boston), June 26, 1963.

13. *Le Monde*, June 25, 1963.

14. Jowitt, op. cit., pp. 114-30.

15. Ghita Ionescu, *The Politics of the European Communist States* (London: Weidenfeld and Nicholson, 1967), p. 4. "Apparat" is used here in the broader sense than party apparat. Ionescu mentioned eight apparats, for instance. The party apparat in this sense is not in full control of the country and of society but is subject to checks from other apparats.

16. Zbignew Brzezinski, *The Soviet Bloc: Unity and Conflict* (Cambridge: Harvard University Press, 1967), p. 53.

17. Ibid., pp. 55–62.

18. Imre Nagy, *On Communism* (London: Thames and Hudson, 1957), p. 239.

19. J. J. Brady, "The Political Implications of Polish/American Economic Relations Between 1957 and 1964" (Doctoral dissertation, University of London, 1967), pp. 188–92.

20. Brzezinski, op. cit., pp. 280–300.

21. Stefan Brant, *The East German Rising* (London: Thames and Hudson, 1955), p. 151.

22. *Pravda*, October 28, 1956.

23. Brzezinski, op. cit., pp. 231–8.

24. *Times* (London), November 13, 1968.

25. Hans Morgenthau, *Politics Among Nations* (New York: Alfred A. Knopf, 1967), pp. 129–35.

26. Ilie Radulescu, "Rolul conducator al statului nostru socialist," *Lupta de Clasa*, March 1966, p. 12.

27. Mihail Cernea, *Dialectica Construiri Socialismului* (Bucharest: Editura Stiintifica, 1964).

28. Radu Florian, "Cu Privire la Contradictiile Societatii Socialiste," *Lupta de Clasa*, May 1972, p. 47.

29. Cernea, op. cit., p. 17.

30. Florian, op. cit., pp. 47–9.

31. Cernea, op. cit., p. 184.

32. Ibid., p. 290.

33. Petru Berar and Ioan Mitran, "The Unity of Theory and Practice in the Party Activity," *Lupta de Clasa*, June 1971, p. 3.

34. Ibid., p. 11.

35. Ibid.

36. Ioan Ceterchi, *Socialist Democracy* (Bucharest: Meridiane Publishing House, 1975), p. 50.

37. Nicolae Ceausescu, *Cuvintare la plenara Comitetului Central al Partidului Comunist Roman, 29 Iunie 1977* (Bucharest: Editura Politica, 1977), p. 18, 24.

38. *Constitution of the Socialist Republic of Romania* (Bucharest: Meridiane Publishing House, 1969), p. 3.

39. *Constitution of the Socialist Republic of Romania* (Bucharest: Meridiane Publishing, 1975), p. 5, 32.

40. *Lupta de Clasa*, September 1965, p. 10–11.

41. *Codul de Procedura Penela 1969 Buletinul Oficial al R.S.R.* No. 145–416, 1969 and *Codul Penal al R.S.R.* (Bucharest: Editura Politica, 1968).

42. For the limits of the new codes see Michael Cismerescu, in *Radio Free Europe Research Report, Rumania*, January 24, 1969.

43. *Lupta de Clasa*, May 1967, p. 5.

44. Ibid., p. 6.

45. Ibid., pp. 3–14.

46. *Lupta de Clasa*, June 1967, pp. 3–11.

47. *Scinteia*, December 9, 1967.

48. *Scinteia*, August 22, 1968.

49. *Guardian* (London), July 8, 1971.

50. *Scinteia*, November 5, 1971.

51. New York *Times*, August 6, 1972.

52. *Scinteia*, January 26, 1977.

53. Kenneth Jowitt, "Political Enervation in Rumania" *Survey*, Autumn 1974, p. 150.

54. Nicolae Ceausescu, *Scinteia*, October 3, 1976.

55. Stephen Fischer-Galati, "The Socialist Republic of Rumania" in P.A. Toma, ed., *The Changing Face of Communism in Eastern Europe* (Tucson: University of Arizona Press, 1970), p. 31. The speeches referred to were published as N. Ceausescu, *Romania pe Drumul Desavirsirii Constructiei Socialiste* (Bucharest: Editura Politica, 1968).

56. *Lupta de Clasa*, November 1971.

57. Dumitru Popescu, "Implications of the Party's Ideological Program in the Literary Output," *Lupta de Clasa*, February 1972, pp. 18–21.

58. Ibid., p. 22.

59. New York *Times*, March 30, 1974.

60. Mihai Beniuc, "Politica si Literatura," *Romania Literara* (Bucharest), July 15, 1976; Gheorghe Stroia, "Arta, ideologie, politica," *Era Socialista* (bimonthly of Central Committee of the RCP), August 15, 1976, pp. 8–10.

61. Nicolae Ceausescu, *Cuvintare la plenara . . . ,* op. cit., p. 25.

62. *Romania Literara*, December 8, 1977, p. 8.

63. *Scinteia*, May 8, 1967.

64. *Washington Post*, December 23, 1965.

65. Emil Lendvai, *Eagles in Cobwebs* (New York: Praeger, 1965), p. 96.

66. *Le Figaro* (Paris), December 19, 1968.

67. *Scinteia*, August 13, 1969.

68. *Era Socialista*, December 24, 1973, p. 3.

69. *Constitution of the R.S.R.*, (Bucharest: Editura Meridiane, 1975), p. 19.

70. *Financial Times* (London), July 21, 1972.

71. *Guardian*, July 22, 1972.

72. *Times* (London), June 18, 1966.

73. *Scinteia*, August 15, 1966.

74. *Scinteia*, August 22, 1968.

75. Nicolae Ecobescu and D. I. Mazilu, "Securitatea and Colaborarea in Europe," *Lupta de Clasa*, June 1970, p. 12.

76. C. Florea, "Principiile Fundamentale ale politicii externe a Republicii Socialiste Romane," *Era Socialista*, March 6, 1976, pp. 31–2.

77. *Scinteia*, August 7, 1969.

78. I. Fintinaru, "The NATO Crisis," *Lupta de Clasa*, February 1965, p. 67.

79. *Scinteia*, May 8, 1967.

80. *Scinteia*, July 25, 1967.

81. Morgenthau, op. cit., pp. 110–12.

82. *Statistical Pocket Book of the Socialist Republic of Romania*, op. cit., pp. 330–47.

83. R. Moldovan, "Co-operarea economica intre statela socialiste," *Lupta de Clasa*, April 1970, p. 24.

84. New York *Times*, February 4, 1968.

85. *East Europe* (New York), November-December 1969, p. 62.

86. *Scinteia*, September 24, 1966.

87. *Scinteia*, August 16, 1967.

88. *Die Welt* (Hamburg), January 12, 1970.

89. A. S. Kretschmar and R. Floor, *The Potential of Joint Ventures in Eastern Europe* (New York: Praeger, 1972), p. 116.

90. Ibid., p. 112.

91. Ibid., p. 118.

92. Ibid.

93. *Le Monde*, November 18, 1971.

94. *Scinteia*, March 9, 1972.

95. *Scinteia*, November 17, 1972.

96. Edwin M. Snell, "Eastern Europe's Trade and Payments with the Industrial West," U.S. Congress, Joint Economic Committee, *Reorientation and Commercial Relations of the Economies of Eastern Europe* (Washington, D.C.: U.S. Government Printing Office, 1974), pp. 682-724.

97. M. Campbell and D. Lascelles, "Comecon," *Financial Times* (London), July 29, 1975.

98. *Anuarul Statistic al R.S.R.*, 1977, pp. 592-3.

99. Costin Kiritescu "Promovarea unor relatii economice largi, nestinjenite si stabile," *Revista Economica* (Bucharest), November 25, 1977, p. 25-6.

100. *Journal of Commerce* (U.S.), August 23, 1976.

101. *Foreign Trade*, No. 1 (New Delhi), January 1976.

102. *Times* (London), January 29, 1977.

103. *Anuarul*, 1977, op. cit., p. 439.

104. Ibid., pp. 422-9.

105. New York *Times*, September 15, 1976.

106. J. M. Montias, "Economic Nationalism in Eastern Europe," *Journal of International Affairs* vol. 20, no. 1, 1966, p. 61.

107. Henry Schaefer, "What Role Comecon," *Radio Free Europe Research: Economics*, April 1970, p. 2.

108. Ibid., pp. 4-5.

109. *Sunday Times* (London), July 15, 1962.

110. *Times* (London), September 28, 1959.

111. *Times* (London), September 26, 1961.

112. Isaac Deutscher, "Communism's Common Market," *The New Statesman* (London), July 11, 1959, p. 37.

113. Michael Kaser, *Comecon: Integration Problems of the Planned Economies* (London: Oxford University Press for Royal Institute for International Affairs [RIIA], 1965), p. 93.

114. Schaefer, op. cit., p. 5.

115. *Pravda*, May 8, 1966, p. 8.

116. *Pravda*, May 14, 1966, p. 1.

117. Gh. Constantinescu, "The Historical Function of Relations Between Socialist Countries," *Viata Economica* (Bucharest), November 29, 1968.

118. *Soviet News* (Press Department, Soviet Embassy, London), July 18, 1972, p. 234.

119. *Nepszabadsag* (Hungarian Communist Party daily, Budapest), November 20, 1970.

120. *Scinteia*, July 30, 1971.

121. Schaefer, op. cit., p. 8.

122. M. Kaser, "The European Economic Reforms and Foreign Trade," *World Today* (London), December 1967, p. 519.

123. Joszef Bognar (former Foreign Trade Minister), "Principles of Foreign Trade in the New Economic Mechanism," *The New Hungarian Quarterly* (Budapest), no. 26, 1967, p. 156.

124. Antal Apro, *Radio Budapest*, September 20, 1968.

125. Antal Apro, "The Correlations of the National and International Interests in the Economic Cooperation of the Socialist Countries," *Tarsadalmi Szemle* (Budapest), December 1968.

126. Rezso Nyers, "Questions of Principle and Practice in Socialist Economic Integration," *Nepszabadsag*, January 23, 1969.

127. *Le Monde*, July 15, 1970.

128. Peter Valyi, "Financial Co-operation within CMEA," *The New Hungarian Quarterly*, Summer 1970, pp. 49-53.

129. "The Economic Situation in the East," Nato Economic Directives (Brussels), no. 3, September 1972, p. 3.

130. *International Herald Tribune* (Paris), April 10, 1972.

131. *Scinteia*, January 19, 1969.

132. *Scinteia*, January 13, 1971.

133. *Financial Times* (London), February 17, 1971.

134. *Scinteia* August 12, 1971.

135. *Scinteia*, December 11, 1972.

136. Paul Marer, "Has Eastern Europe Become a Liability to the Soviet Union?" in C. Gati, ed., *The International Politics of Eastern Europe* (New York: Praeger, 1976), pp. 61-2.

137. *Times* (London), April 1, 1977.

138. *Pravda*, July 9, 1975.

139. *Scinteia*, July 10, 1976.

140. Nicolae Ecobescu and Sergiu Celac, *Socialist Romania in International Relations* (Bucharest: Meridiane Publishing House, 1975), p. 54.

141. *Scinteia*, July 24, 1976.

142. *Anuarul*, 1977, op. cit., pp. 422-9.

143. *Directives of the Eleventh Congress* (Bucharest: Meridiane Publishing House, 1975), p. 58.

144. *Lumea* (foreign affairs weekly, Bucharest), May 26, 1977, p. 2.

145. *Lumea*, June 9, 1977, p. 1.

146. *Lumea*, February 3, 1977, p. 9.

147. *Lumea*, June 23, 1977, p. 1.

148. *Times* (London), July 6, 1976.

149. Ibid.

150. *Le Monde*, May 16, 1968.

151. Nicolae Ceausescu, *Expunere la Mare Adunare Nationala cu privire la marele realizari ale poporului Roman . . . 18 Decembrie 1975* (Bucharest: Editura Politica, 1975), p. 21.

152. *Anuarul* 1977, op. cit., pp. 422-9.

153. *Lumea*, August 12, 1976, p. 4.

154. *Guardian* (Manchester), October 26, 1963.

155. *Scinteia* February 15, 1967.

156. *Economist*, July 25, 1970.

157. *Lupta de Clasa*, July 1971, p. 3.

158. *Scinteia*, June 17, 1966.

159. Arnold Horlick, *The Soviet Union's Asian Collective Security Proposal: A Club in Search of Members*, P-5195 (Santa Monica: Rand Corporation, 1974), p. 19.

160. Lowell Tillett, "The National Minorities Factor in the Sino-Soviet Dispute," *Orbis*, Summer 1977, p. 291.

161. *Anuarul*, 1977, op. cit., p. 422-9.

162. *Tribuna Romana* (Bucharest), July 15, 1976, p. 7.

163. *Financial Times* (London), August 5, 1976.

164. See Heinz Timmerman, "Eurocommunism: Moscow's Reaction," *World Today*, October 1977, p. 380.

165. Boris Ponomarev "The International Significance of the Twenty-Fifth CPSU Congress," *World Marxist Review* (Prague), May 5, 1976, p. 2.

166. *Lumea*, January 13, 1977; and *Times* (London), January 8, 1977.

2

Romanian Defenses
in International Law

Bucharest attempted to extend its political defenses through the utilization of the principles of international law. For the Soviet Union demonstrated
repeatedly through the extensive legal justifications it formulated for interventions in Eastern Europe that, while it was not deterred solely by legal arguments,
it was not immune to them. Romanian success in maintaining or enlarging the
limits for foreign policy autonomy through legal pleas depended on both active
and passive defenses. The latter consisted of the protection afforded by the
Soviet concept of international law and particularly its view of sovereignty. The
active defenses reposed in Romania's ability to formulate arguments in international law which would best justify her position internationally, while taking
advantage of defenses inherent in the Soviet position.

On September 26, 1968, *Pravda* declared that, "a Socialist state that is in
a system with other states constituting a Socialist commonwealth, cannot be
free of the common interest of that commonwealth." This, in the wake of the
Soviet intervention in Czechoslovakia, represented the core of the "Brezhnev
Doctrine" of limited sovereignty. Brezhnev personally reiterated this principle
on November 12, 1968, in a speech at the Fifth Congress of the Polish United
Workers Party, in Warsaw. He stated *inter alia*:

> When the internal and external forces hostile to Socialism seek to
> turn back the development of any Socialist country, to restore the
> capitalist order, when a threat emerges to the cause of Socialism in
> that country, a threat to the security of the Socialist commonwealth*

---

*While the use of the term "commonwealth" dating back to the 1950s was an at-
tempt to liken the interrelationship of the Socialist states to that of the members of the

49

as a whole, this is no longer a matter only for the people of the country in question, but is also a common problem which is a matter of concern for all Socialist countries.[1]

He later denied the existence of such a doctrine in a speech he made in Belgrade in 1971[2] but this denial was met with skepticism in the West, for the position of sovereignty in the Socialist bloc is still not entirely clear.

Yet the concept of sovereignty was not only crucial to the policies of the smaller Socialist states such as Romania, which tried to maintain their autonomy, but it also represented a key element of international law. Sovereignty in ordinary usage is understood to be a state of independence from internal or external authority. This cannot, however, explain the use of the concept of sovereignty in relations among the Soviet-bloc states and the evolution of "Socialist international law."

"Sovereignty" itself incorporates the phenomenon of the nation-state. In the Socialist context, the qualities of this phenomenon are determined by ideology and by the tactical necessities of Soviet or of dependent-state foreign policy formulation. In terms of ideological development, Marxism-Leninism has gone through a number of phases regarding the viability and the future of the nation-state. Moreover, its notion of the nation-state has been subjected to the polycentric pull that saw Poland denounce the Soviet intervention in Hungary in 1956, and Romania vehemently oppose the Soviet intervention in Czechoslovakia in 1968. Soviet support for universal class struggle, in turn, has had to compete with Soviet support of national liberation (and sovereignty) in the emerging nations of the Third World. Nevertheless, the continuity of the nation state remains crucial to the viability of the entire concept of sovereignty.

In the areas dominated by the Soviet Union, we have seen another dichotomy: the Soviets imposed real derogations of sovereignty on these countries but respected their sovereignty in formal terms and were committed to a belief in the general validity of the concept. A secondary problem also interposes itself at this stage, namely the increased frequency of Soviet references to "people's sovereignty." The quandary is whether in Eastern Europe there could have been a divergence between the people or the nation, and the nation-state. The answer was crucial in the Prague intervention of 1968 and remained so for Romania.

Modern industrial development creates a considerable degree of interdependence among states, and the Socialist countries have recognized this. Indeed, the Soviet Union has been pressing for closer cooperation in Eastern Europe and for rationalization of production. But ever closer cooperation, moving toward supranational integration, was seen as a threat to individual sovereignty by some of the Socialist states. The conflict between sovereignty and possible supra-

---

British Commonwealth, it is in essence a corruption of the term and did not denote the same type of free association.

national integration (that is, a process of interpenetration of different aspects of a state's autonomy) extended to the common Socialist-bloc institutions such as Comecon, the Warsaw Pact, and to regional cooperations as a whole.

Finally, in this chapter, we are concerned with the purpose for which the concept of sovereignty is used. Soviet jurist G.I. Tunkin has stated that the principles of Socialist international law (of which sovereignty is still a part) cannot be compared to general international law in terminology.[3] In his view, the purpose for which they are applied determines their character. Romania, for instance, has used the term "sovereignty" to resist Socialist supranational planning. It is, therefore, the purpose of this chapter to analyze not only variations in the Socialist view of sovereignty, but also to ascertain whether a country such as Romania could use the concept as a defense for its autonomy in the face of the might of the Soviet Union.

Could Romania adopt the Soviet theoretical position on international law and sovereignty to justify policies at variance with those of the Soviet Union?

THE ENDURANCE OF THE NATION-STATE

The eventual withering away of the nation-state has been one of the chief assumptions of Marxist doctrine. For the question of sovereignty, however, it is essential to determine when this process will take place so that short- and long-range policies can be formulated. Ralph Miliband feels that orthodox Marxism anticipated that after the revolution a state of considerable duration would remain, though it would begin immediately to wither away.[4] Before the 1917 revolution, Lenin also analyzed the postrevolutionary state in *The State and Revolution*. He wrote that:

> Once the revolution is completed and the dictatorship of the proletariat established, after a time, more or less long, but the variable depending on the circumstances, the decline of the state would commence. What would decline would be the *Proletarian half-state or the transitional type of state.*[5]

Thus, Lenin went further than Marx and stated that following the revolution, the state would not only begin to wither away but would already be in a high state of decomposition. While there would still be a revolutionary power in existence, it would not be exercised by the state in the usual manner. Lenin notes that, "it is a state nevertheless," but "in the shape of armed workers who proceed to form a militia involving the entire population."[6] The proletariat would govern but not dominate. The bureaucracy would be drastically reduced in size and would remain utterly restrained by direct popular supervision backed up by the power of instant revocability, while the other key institution, the army, would be abolished. Finally, the "rotten parliamentarism of bourgeois society would be replaced by the Soviets."[7] Therefore, at this stage Lenin considered the class struggle the most important part of the transition to Communism. State sovereignty seemed only incidental to him. Nor did he give much consideration, at this point, to national liberation or equality among states.

The State and Revolution raised a great many problems. The dictatorship of the proletariat is inconceivable without some degree of political articulation and leadership, which in turn implies political organization. Nor did Lenin clarify in this work what the relationship would be between the proletariat, whose dictatorship the revolution is deemed to establish, and the vanguard party, which educates, leads, directs, and organizes. By 1919 Lenin did, however, say:

> Yes, the dictatorship of one party. We stand upon it and cannot depart from this ground, since this is the party which in the course of the decades has won for itself the position of the vanguard of the whole factory, and industrial proletariat.[8]

Thus by 1919 he asserted the exclusive guidance of the party in a national-state. Furthermore, Lenin held that the attempt to distinguish between the dictatorship of the class and the dictatorship of the party was "an unbelievable and inextricable confusion of thought."[9] By 1921, as Robert V. Daniels notes, Lenin bluntly asserted that, "the dictatorship of the proletariat is impossible except through the Communist Party" (that is, the state organ).[10] Thus, *The State and Revolution* seems to be something of an aberration in Lenin's work, for he held out for state supremacy after the revolution. Not only that, but he would not admit to any possible dichotomy between the state, controlled by the Communist party, and the interests of the proletariat. It is also significant to note that from the very beginning Soviet doctrine was made quite flexible in order to comply with the "objective realities." In the wake of the failure of the revolution to spread to Western Europe and faced with the complexities of governing a vast state, Lenin could change his view on the state and class struggle, or at the very least reorganize his priorities.

Stalin placed heavy emphasis on the continuation of the state. Whereas one may claim that Lenin's postrevolutionary stance on the state was a tactical move, based on certain more general theoretical assumptions, a move influenced by events in Western Europe, Stalin's position had a sturdier theoretical framework. The latter believed that the role of the state in Socialist nation-state must be that of an indispensable tool for the acceleration of "inevitable" historical trends and that this positive role of the state deserved serious recognition in Soviet ideological perspectives.[11] Stalin placed a growing reliance on state institutions and the administrative structure. In the wake of World War II, the Soviet state was glorified as an almost co-equal of the Communist Party of the Soviet Union and any undermining of the state was said to harm Socialism.

The endurance and the significance of the state under Socialism has continued to be recognized in the post-Stalin era. Both Khrushchev and Brezhnev have repeatedly stressed that the state continues to perform an essential function under Socialism and that it is to continue yet for a considerable period of time. Despite the so-called Brezhnev Doctrine, the current Soviet leader has admitted to the formal sovereign rights of states and considers international relations as still dominated by a state-centric system.

In Romania the continuance of the major role of the state appears to have had an even greater amount of support in ideological-juridical thinking than in the Soviet Union. Already, in 1965 Ceausescu declared that:

> Our experience, as that of the other Socialist states, shows that the power of the state is—and will be for a long time—the principal instrument for the realization of the political-economic and cultural tasks which are made more and more complex by the advancement of society. . . . The attributes of the state as organizer of the national economy, of scientific and cultural activities and in all domains of social life is growing considerably.[12]

Thus Ceausescu not only rejected any immediate withering away of the state but rather claimed that in the immediate future the role of the state would be augmented.

Romanian political theoreticians and jurists have enlarged on this theory of the continuity of the state system. RCP theoretician Ilie Radulescu wrote that Marxism-Leninism itself assumes that the state, as well as the nation, would endure for a long time to come. In this vein, he claimed that the Socialist state, while comprising part of the superstructure, was in a continuous process of change and perfection.[13] He asserted that:

> The elimination of the capitalist ownership of the means of production and placing of relations of production on the basis of socialist property, creates an objective base of the rapid development of the economy, making it even more necessary for organized state intervention in overseeing the direction of the planning of the economic activities.[14]

Therefore, he concluded that "reality" demonstrated the justice of the thesis that the development of the forces of production and that of the Socialist leadership were "unitary in all the domains of activity and in the scope of harmonious development of the whole society."[15] As his argument was supposed to be based on the two most solid bases possible in Socialism—Marxism-Leninism and "objective reality"—it should have been rather difficult for the Soviet Union to refute.

V. Duculescu, writing in the RCP theoretical journal *Era Socialista*, claimed that the Socialist revolution in fact helped to increase the significance of the sovereign state and that of its growing participation in international life. The state, he maintained, was the main subject of all rights and obligations arising out of international judicial relations:

> It [the state] expresses the sovereign will of the nation which has created it, exercises the right of self-determination and is not conditioned by the will of other judicial subjects such as international organizations constituted by agreement of the sovereign state.[16]

Constantin Vlad, a member of the Romanian Academy of Social Sciences, continued in the building of the theory of the endurance and importance of the state in his book *Essays on Nation.*[17] He held that the current historical period was characterized by the "phenomenon of the nation." (He largely identified the nation with the nation-state.) Moreover, as trends toward national independence increased in the world, the nation-state, in his view, became more significant as a new type of "human community"—it became part of the framework of international relations.[18] This change, he claimed, had largely resulted from the presence of Socialist nations in the world, which in his view represent a higher stage in the development of the nation in the form of a "community." The tenacity with which Vlad espoused the virtues of the nation-state is perhaps best illustrated by the fact that in this book he quoted Stalin on the definition of the nation.[19] Thus, Vlad did not leave the slightest doubt that he believed that the nation-state was a lasting institution.

In the mid-1970s Romanian writings continued to emphasize the role of the nation-state. Ioan Ceterchi, then Secretary General of the Association for the Study of Political Science, and a law professor, wrote that the growth in the role of the state, particularly in the weight of its functions, was a characteristic of the present epoch.[20] In 1976 a very important book was published in Romania on the Socialist state in the present epoch with the main political and legal theorists of the country contributing to it. The thrust of the book was that the role of the state was growing and that the state and party roles would develop hand in hand and would continue to be important for the defense of sovereignty, which in turn represented the will of the people.[21] Finally, Ceausescu joined in the fray when in a major speech he attacked those philosophers and theorists who claimed that the nation under Socialism no longer had a future and that the policy of defending national independence was a violation of Marxism-Leninism. In fact, Ceausescu claimed that Lenin himself concluded, and was correct in doing so, that those who did not defend their right to freedom and independence deserved to be slaves.[22]

There was little disagreement between Soviet and Romanian views that the existence of the nation-state was justified. Writers and politicians from both states praised the development of the Socialist state and acknowledged its prolonged endurance. And this component—that the withering away of the state was not about to take place in the immediate future—made the concept of the nation-state rest on a continuingly solid basis. As such, its key element, sovereignty, had to be an important determinant in relations among Socialist states, especially in the view of the Romanians.

Nevertheless, the repetitiveness and frequency of Romanian pronouncements on the endurance of the state are particularly striking when it is remembered that the Soviet Union itself held for the endurance of the state. As such, it is reasonable to suppose that Romanian pronouncements on the state were part of a larger strategy which benefited by constant repetition of one of its basic props. It should also become apparent that while Radulescu, Duculescu, Vlad, and Ceterchi seemed to talk about the same repetitive position on the state ad nauseam, there were slight variations in their analyses that allowed them, cumulatively, to cover the entire spectrum of the evolution of the state. Thus they touched on the role of the state in classic Marxist-Leninist doctrine, in the transition from capitalism to Socialism, in the Socialist epoch, in relation to "objective" domestic and international realities. As such the Romanians fortified strongly a key component in their theory of relations among Socialist states. Before we begin analyzing this problem of Socialist relations, however, there is a secondary query that will have to be looked at briefly: the conundrum of whether under Socialism there can be a divergence between the state, and the nation or the people.

THE STATE OR THE PEOPLE

Most Soviet political writing and comments made scant admission of the possibility of a discrepancy between the aims of the people or the nation in a Socialist state and the aims of the state. Indeed, in formal official doctrine there was supposed to have been an "organic unity" between the two. On closer examination, however, the picture shifts and the possibility of a difference between the Soviet-bloc states and the Soviet-bloc peoples becomes increasingly evident.

Soviet jurists of the "Tunkin School" listed three subordinate principles of proletarian internationalism:

> 1) Respect for the sovereignty of Socialist states on the basis of which peoples exercise the right to self-determination; 2) Noninterference in the internal affairs of another state, which reflects respect for the national peculiarities and expectations of each people; 3) Full equality of Socialist states which reflects the Marxist-Leninist thesis of the equality of nations and of workers' parties.[23]

Evidently, then, all of these principles were made subject to the will of the "people," who supposedly represented the ideal of true proletarian internationalism. Should a situation arise where the "people" in a Socialist state would accuse their own governmental leadership of pursuing policies that were incompatible with proletarian internationalism and ask for the assistance of fellow

Socialist states, then such assistance might be rendered, for it may even be reasoned that Socialist states were under an obligation to do so.[24]

The Soviet Union used this argument during its intervention in Hungary in 1956 and Czechoslovakia in 1968. Despite the fact that 40 Czechoslovak party members were alleged to have asked for such "aid," the doctrine of "intervention by invitation" crumbled somewhat when the entire Czechoslovak government and Communist party promptly denied such an invitation. Nevertheless, the differentiation of the people from the state (that is, the governing organs) in a Socialist country presented a danger to the smaller East European state seeking to preserve its autonomy. Whereas Socialism in official Soviet doctrine was supposed to provide an organic unity between the state and the people or nation, a differentiation between the two amounts to "turning the wheels of history backwards."

In Romania, RCP theoretician Ilie Radulescu denied the existence of any dichotomy between the state and the nation.[25] He felt that as a result of the victory of Socialism society acquired a homogenous character. Similarly, Vlad, in his book on the nation,[26] appears to arrive at the same view, although his book tends to be ambiguous in its terminology at times. (Generally, he uses the term "nation-state" interchangeably with "nation.") Nevertheless, the picture does emerge from his book that an organic relation does exist between the nation (people) and the totality of social life, on the one hand, and the essential characteristics of this form of human community, on the other hand. Since Socialism, in his view, lacks class antagonisms the result is the creation of a Socialist culture common to all. As such, Socialist nationalism, he maintains, is different from Western nationalism in that, "it involves and promotes noble and advanced ideas."[27] Therefore, in his view, the nation continues on a higher state, throughout epochs of peoples developments. It evolves, as a whole, as an ethical social community.

Thus, whereas in his reference to bourgeois states Vlad indicates the existence of a divergence between state and the nation or people, in his discussion of Socialism this becomes increasingly blurred and eventually eliminated. While he states that the appearance of nations and the formation of nation-states occurred at the same time and in deep interconnection, he holds that it is the Socialist nation-state which effects the appearance of the "community of state."[28] In other words, under Socialism the nation-state as a feature of the nation turns into a community of the nation's political life—"an integrating force."[29] Moreover, the working class, he claims, further asserts itself as the most advanced social force in society. As such, there cannot be a contradiction between the nation and the state under Socialism, if one follows Vlad's reasoning. Ceterchi holds, in the same vein, that class has been eliminated and the state possesses a workers's character reflecting the unbreakable consensus between people and the state.[30]

The above view is, in turn, antithetical to the Soviet theories of intervention in Socialist states, supposedly on behalf of the people and against the governing organs of the state. As such, the divergence in Soviet and Romanian views is quite significant in the understanding of Romanian views on sovereignty.

SOCIALIST VIEWS ON INTERSTATE RELATIONS IN PERSPECTIVE

While the Brezhnev Doctrine may have disturbed certain contemporary views of the Soviet attitude toward international relations and law, many of the elements of the present attitude have long been entrenched in Soviet policy. During the period when the Soviet Union was the only Socialist state (with the exception of a totally dependent People's Republic of Mongolia), the question of external national sovereignty was significantly less important than in the post World War II era, when several European states came under Soviet dominion. Nevertheless, Lenin's ideas on relations between Socialist states and the Comintern's view on national rights versus the class struggle deserve a brief examination for the light they shed on the contemporary problem of these concepts.

While Lenin rose to the defense of the Soviet state, he still condemned nationalism as one of the many subterfuges designed to obscure the development of the class struggle and to destroy the "international sense of solidarity of the proletariat."[31] He wrote that:

> To be an internationalist, a person must not only think of his own nation, but put above it the interests of all . . . fight against petty national narrowness, isolationism, for the awareness of the whole and the universal, for the deference of private interests to general interests.[32]

Of course it is true that tactically this internationalism was to extend only to the non-Soviet Communist parties for the time being, as Lenin felt that in the immediate postrevolutionary era it was the duty of the world Communist parties to build the Socialist center, which merely happened to be in Moscow at this stage.

This Moscow-centered internationalism was one of the key principles in the formation of the Communist International (Comintern) on March 2, 1919. At the first meeting in Moscow, the leaders agreed to structure the organization on the basis of a political, ideological, and territorial entity whose interests would transcend those of its various national units. There was to be a central organ with the function of "subordinating the interests of the movement in each country to the common interest of the international revolution."[33] Class struggle was clearly to have precedence over national liberation, but it was to be a class struggle directed from Moscow. Since the leaders claimed that the nation was an outmoded institution, national decision making would have to be eliminated. In the "worldwide Soviet Republic" decisions would be made by the Comintern.[34]

The centralized form of decision making by the Russian Communist Party in the Soviet Union was to be followed worldwide by the Comintern. The 1919 Hungarian revolution illustrates this pattern. When Bela Kun established a Hungarian revolutionary regime (composed of Socialists and Communists), Lenin called on him (and Kun accepted) to ensure that the regime would be Communist instead of Social Democratic, while Grigori Zinoviev also notified Kun that the Executive Committee of the Comintern expected him and the revolutionaries to establish a Communist party which would clearly give the regime an orthodox Communist program.[35] By accepting the orders from the Comintern, Kun thereby recognized it as the retainer of a higher sovereignty than that of any national revolutionary government.

It may, of course, be justifiably argued that the Bolsheviks anticipated the spread of the revolution to Western Europe and with it an ensuing shift of the center. Nevertheless, as William Korey has stated, the Bolsheviks saw the Comintern as the focal point of power and their belief in its supranational authority (an aspect which Romania has repeatedly criticized in the 1960s and 1970s) continued well after all the revolutionary waves in Western Europe abated.[36]

Even more salient, the Comintern also fostered the belief that the "Socialist commonwealth" had the moral right to engage in military intervention in the furtherance of the world Socialist revolution. Zinoviev, who was the acknowledged expert on intraparty relations, had stated frequently that the Red Army should help if there was a Communist revolution in the Western European countries and that it would be ready to help established Communist regimes.* The Comintern's Executive Committee promised to send help to Kun's regime in Hungary, but the Red Army, although alerted, could not cross the Ukraine because of the White forces present there.[38] After this failure to save Kun, Zinoviev advocated intervention into Germany if France became Communist. This built-in rationale for military intervention was accepted and the hegemony of the Russian Communist party over other parties was never questioned in the Comintern during its existence to 1943. Thus, the sovereignty of nation-states was clearly not a prime concern of the Soviet party theoreticians at this stage of Soviet policy development.

It should be mentioned, however, that there were some Soviet jurists who were concerned with the norms of international law and sovereignty. The eminent jurist E. B. Pashukanis did conclude in the 1920s that the Soviet Union could and did utilize generally accepted norms of international law in conducting its relations with foreign states. In doing so, he postulated that it imbued them with a new Socialist content. He was, nevertheless, handicapped in having to explain how a principle of law applied simultaneously by the USSR and a

---

*Zinoviev wrote that the military intervention is to be judged by the criterion of whether it serves the forces of capitalism or those of Socialism.[37]

capitalist state could become Socialist when only one of the parties was Socialist. This was a particularly sensitive problem because of the Marxist concept of law as an instrument of a ruling class. Pashukanis was vigorously attacked for his view on international law and sovereignty and in the 1930s he was imprisoned partly because of a "weakly based philosophical position on form and content."[39]

After World War II, with the emergence of several Socialist states, gradual polycentrism became virtually inevitable. In 1966 Brezhnev himself (as had his predecessor Khrushchev) acknowledged that each party should have the right to solve the problems facing it in its own way.[40] Nevertheless, the preservation of the Soviet state power and the promotion of its security, which was even more accented by the Stalinist principle of "Socialism in one state" still characterized Soviet foreign policy. When in 1968 the Soviets felt that there was an ideological threat from Czechoslovakia, they immediately resorted to Zinoviev's dictum of using force to protect the "Socialist commonwealth."

Nevertheless, in the immediate postwar era Soviet dominance was so overwhelming and Stalin's prestige was so supreme in the newly emerging Socialist bloc that Soviet leadership was not questioned (with the notable exception of the Yugoslav break in 1948). Concern for state sovereignty was peripheral, and the Soviets were proposing various schemes for integration in Eastern Europe with the fairly sanguine approval of the leaders of these states, including, as we have seen, that of Gheorghiu-Dej of Romania. Milovan Djilas in his book *Conversations with Stalin* is convinced that the Soviet leaders were already toying with the idea of reorganizing the Soviet Union by joining to it the "People's Democracies." The Ukraine, according to this plan, would have been joined with Hungary and Romania, Byelorussia would have been joined with Poland and Czechoslovakia, while the Balkan states would have been joined with Russia.[41] Furthermore, the Balkan Union scheme planned by Tito and Dimitrov was also originally encouraged by the Kremlin. An analysis of the reasons for the failure of these schemes is outside the scope of this chapter, but what is germane here is the lack of Soviet consideration of national sovereignty and its emphasis instead on Soviet security or, viewed in a very benign light, their concern for the class struggle. Romania's acquiescence to real derogations of its sovereignty at this time illustrates the Soviet bloc's view on international relations immediately after the war. *The shifting perspectives of both Romanian and Soviet policy implies the existence of considerable flexibility.*

Another ingredient that sheds some light on the more recent Soviet concepts of sovereignty and international law is manifested in the peculiarly Soviet problem of "double sovereignty": the sovereignty of the USSR (the federation) and that of its member republics. Soviet jurist B. L. Manelis wrote a text on the subject in 1964 in which he attempted to reconcile the two.[42] In his view the federation was sovereign because the attributes of sovereignty were attached to it at its provenance in 1922 and not delegated to it by the member Republics. The Republics in turn, Manelis reasoned, did not lose their sovereignty by entering the federation but retained their full sovereign rights. This retention, on the other hand, did not exclude the existence of the complete sovereignty of the federation. Manelis explained this apparent paradox by stating first that the sovereignty of the federation and that of its members were in organic unity and, second, by referring to Lenin's declaration that the Republics preserved their independence on entering the Union—a fact reflected by the provision in the USSR Constitution concerning the right of the Republics to secede. It is a fact that in 1977 both Byelorussia and the Ukraine were members of the United Nations.

Though the above argument may be confusing, it might be somewhat palatable when restricted to the Republics of the Union. In this manner it could indicate that the Republics had greater rights, let us say, than the länder in the Federal Republic of Germany or the states of the United States. The conundrum is that the arguments of Soviet federalism were being brought forward to support a more cohesive Socialist bloc. Therefore, sovereignty was being redefined to emphasize the interests of the whole community as essential to the preservation of the interests of its parts. An obligation was thus placed upon each Socialist state to aid any other Socialist nation if its Socialist character were threatened. Therefore, the Soviet-bloc states would have had both their de jure and their de facto positions moved closer to that of the Soviet republics.[43]

Such a view on sovereignty, however, was rejected by the Romanians. In their opinion there could not be a supranational sovereignty, and any derogation of national sovereignty was inadmissible. They also spoke of an organic unity between the individual Socialist state and the Socialist community as a whole, but they emphasized the interests of the parts for the preservation of the entire community. President Ceausescu said at the 10th Romanian Communist Party Congress in August 1969 that:

> By a world Socialist system, we do not mean a bloc in which states have merged with an ensemble, giving up their national sovereignty. . . . Solidarity and mutual assistance among Socialist countries imply relations of equality among all Socialist nations and should not lead to interference into the internal affairs of a people.[44]

This vital difference regarding sovereignty between the Soviet Union and Romania bears a direct relationship to Romania's foreign policy autonomy. The two views on sovereignty can perhaps be best understood by looking at the approach of the two countries to international law. In the case of Romania especially, the maintenance of an autonomous foreign policy and the emphasis on its own concept of sovereignty is especially closely linked to its approach to international law.

JUS COGENS OR JUS DISPOSITIVUM

When the new People's Democracies appeared in the wake of World War II, the Soviet Union was faced with the task of clarifying its legal position vis-a-vis other Socialist states. Pashukanis was censured in the 1930s for stating that the Soviet Union could and did utilize generally accepted norms of international law while imbuing them with a Socialist spirit. While only one other Socialist state was in existence (Mongolia) the Soviet Union could not use a Socialist form in relations with the capitalist states. With the appearance of other Socialist states with similar social structures, the legal relations between them and the Soviet Union could then have both a Socialist content and form. Therefore, the essential ingredient now was whether the Soviet Union had in fact decided to use "Socialist international law" in its relations with other Socialist states, or whether as a signatory to the United Nations Charter it was to use general international law and its core principles of *jus cogens*.

Following the October revolution, the highest principle of relations between workers of different countries was to be that element cardinal for the victory of the proletariat: the principle of Socialist (or proletarian) internationalism. The core of the principle as applied among Socialist states was defined as the construction of Socialism and Communism, and the defense of this achievement in the course of the struggle with the capitalist systems. This part in turn entailed specific rights and duties for each Socialist state in its relation with other states, among them the duty to pursue close cooperation and mutual assistance in all spheres of the construction of Socialism and Communism—particularly the economic sphere.[45]

Socialist internationalism also affected a number of subordinate principles, among them the respect for the sovereignty of Socialist states and noninterference in internal affairs. But, according to G. I. Tunkin, all these subordinate principles were subject to the will of the people[46]—the dichotomy of the Socialist state and the "people," to which we referred to earlier. He wrote that "the Socialist principle of respect for sovereignty obliges Socialist states not only to respect the sovereignty of other Socialist states but also to defend Socialist sovereignty in accordance with the demands of proletarian internationalism."[47] Thus, again, the Czechoslovak intervention in 1968 could be in accord with the subordinate principles of proletarian internationalism.

The question arises, however, whether or not a Socialist international law based on the principles of Socialist internationalism was extant before 1972. Two eminent Western jurists, John H. Hazard and William E. Butler, differed on the matter. Hazard believed that, in the Soviet view, Socialist law was in existence,[48] while Butler believed that Moscow felt that Socialist international law was merely emerging in the early 1970s and that there were only Socialist principles of international relations.[49] Ivo Lapenna, writing in 1975, contended that Soviet doctrine on public international law held the existence of a separate "Socialist international law" to be a reality.[50]

Tunkin, possibly the most influential Soviet expert on international law in the postwar era, insisted that there was in existence a body of general international law which should be taught to the new Soviet generation and used in foreign relations, for he felt that by now this law lacked the principles under which it had earlier supported colonialism. This law, in his view, was moving toward a law of peaceful coexistence. Nevertheless, Tunkin also postulated that another system was growing up alongside general international law—that of the "fraternal" relations of proletarian internationalism. It is true that he referred sparingly to the phrase "Socialist international law" and he did describe proletarian internationalism as a moral and political principle. But in his text, *The Theory of International Law*, published in 1962 and revised in 1970,[51] he did emphasize this new law which in his view uses only the terminology of the principles of general international law but in fact establishes a new law among Socialist states.

Some other Soviet jurists have rejected such an approach to international law. V. M. Shurshalov has written that in relations with one another the Socialist states are applying "the principles and rules of international law but are simultaneously filling the old form with a new Socialist content."[52] Thus, in relations between Socialist states, the form of the law does not change. L. A. Aleksidze, writing in the 1967 *Soviet Yearbook of International Law*, similarly did not distinguish between the principles of Socialist international law and the general international legal principles of jus cogens. Moreover, he maintained that generally recognized norms of contemporary international law possessed an imperative character which included "principles strengthening the fundamental sovereign right of states and peoples, respect for state sovereignty and territorial integrity. . . ."[53]

Nevertheless, it seems that since the 1970 meeting of the Soviet Society of International Law, Tunkin's view that a new Socialist international law has emerged that is new both in content and form has prevailed.[54] Further support for Tunkin was also rendered by V. I. Lisovskii, who found that in its relations with other Socialist states the USSR conformed to principles of "Socialist international law" that were anchored in the concept of proletarian internationalism.[55]

There is further substantial evidence to support the Hazard and Lapenna view that the Soviets have accepted a Socialist international law (with its emphasis on the general "Socialist Commonwealth") in their relations with other Socialist states. Soviet intervention into Czechoslovakia, for instance, could be fitted into the framework of this new law and indeed Tunkin did do so. He wrote, "the events of 1968 in Czechoslovakia have shown how dangerous for the cause of Socialism can be the manifestations of nationalism in conditions of the activization of anti-imperialist forces in a country together with the active support of imperialist reaction."[56]

According to this view, the new law is in line with proletarian internationalism but it is quite different from general international law, especially in the salient concept of sovereignty. Tunkin himself wrote that both general and

Socialist international law respected the concept of sovereignty but that the two understood it differently.[57] As we have seen, Socialist international law was shown to include the principle that what were seen to be inroads by capitalist influence in a Socialist society might be prevented legally. At the same time, Socialist states would insist on the principle of sovereignty as developed in general international law when speaking of relations between themselves and capitalist states. This dual approach, even if it represented, as Butler said, merely principles of Socialist international relations, appeared to strike at the general international law concept of jus cogens—the inability of the parties involved to change the law. A double set of laws posed a very dangerous trap for the Socialist states in Eastern Europe, especially for Romania, who attempted to safeguard its sovereignty on all possible occasions. But there were possible defenses.

The possible pivot of the defense here may be turned on the Soviet claim that they respected jus cogens. Even Tunkin admitted to the supremacy of the principles of jus cogens:

> As is well known, the difference between the principles of *jus cogens* and other principles and norms of international law consists of the fact that derogation from them on the basis of bilateral agreements between states is not permitted. The Vienna convention on the law of treaties of 1969 speaks only of the interrelationship between international agreements (it would be more specific to talk of local international agreements) and the principles of *jus cogens*, but also, the provisions of the convention could be equally applicable to the relationship of customary local international norms and the principles of *jus cogens*.[58]

Nevertheless, Tunkin claimed that Socialist international law, being different from general international law, might be applied as it did not contravene jus cogens. He argued, first, that it would have been a specific norm (being locally applied) of a general law, and, second, that the local norm would hold precedence over the general norm.

The first proposition rested on the principle of *lex specialis derogat generalis*. Socialist law would be a specific form of international law. Tunkin wrote:

> In accordance with the well known proposition according to which a special norm squeezes to the corner a general norm, in those situations when we have (pertinent) Socialist principles and norms, they shall operate.[59]

Yet in view of what Tunkin has written, it is rather difficult to see Socialist law as a specific form of the general international law.

Tunkin's second argument was that jus cogens allowed for the "progressive development of international law and the creation . . . of local international norms which go far beyond the norms of the general international . . . and are a reflection of a higher stage of international integration than general international law.[60] It would be difficult to say that this is merely a matter of interpretation, for when the operation of Socialist international law and proletarian internationalism is taken into account it amounts to an alteration of the substance of jus cogens. As William Butler has said, it is also doubtful that many jurists would find the labeling of a particular local norm "higher" than jus cogens a persuasive argument when the local norm seems intended to permit what jus cogens would proscribe. In addition to these flaws in Tunkin's arguments, the bloc states had the benefit of *omission* in the joint declaration of the June 1976 East Berlin conference; it made no mention of proletarian internationalism. Thus, there were gaps in the Soviet argument, which should have allowed for considerable interposition of doctrinal defenses by those faced with "Socialist international law."

The Romanian approach to the question of international law and sovereignty was considerably different from that of the Soviet Union. The Romanian Declaration of Independence in 1964, issued in face of Soviet pressures for integration, called for national independence and sovereignty and equality among states.[61] The later Romanian view also emphasizes national sovereignty and general international law. Ion Voicu claimed that the norms of contemporary law gave juridical expression to the imperatives of peace and security among countries and peoples.[62] And, of the principles which formed the substance of international legality, he considered sovereignty to be of overwhelming importance in the contemporary epoch. Moreover, he felt that the activation of the other principles, of correlative rights and duties that belonged to the members of the international community, was dependent on the respect for sovereignty.

It should be pointed out immediately, however, that respect for general international law and sovereignty did not make the Romanian view *pro tanto* antipodal to those of the Soviet Union, for the latter also professed to respect these principles. It was rather the Romanian interpretation of these principles that showed the difference. President Ceausescu said in 1976 that:

> One must start in all circumstances from the truth that the principle of sovereignty is of universal validity and the same for all states regardless of their size, or their social order, for it cannot be conceived of but in a single sense and in no case can it be interpreted in a different way from one country to another.[63]

He did not refer to the existence of any form of Socialist international law, but merely Socialist relations among states and included a great deal of emphasis on individual state sovereignty instead of commonwealth sovereignty. Thus, the Romanian leader himself attached a significantly different meaning to legal and quasilegal terminology than was done in the Soviet Union.

As such, despite frequent references to Socialist or proletarian internationalism, the international law that Romania subscribed to was general international law. The UN Charter seemed to be the highest point of reference, together with the principles of jus cogens that were associated with it.

For instance, the Romanian delegate to the UN Legal Conference in 1972, Dumitru Ceasu, declared that there should be a clear definition of terms in international law:

> No reasoning, be it of a political, military or economic nature, be it related to the internal policies of a state can serve as justification for the use of arms against another state.[64]

He also said that national territory was inviolable and that no occupation, not even a temporary one, regardless of motives given, could be condoned. Ceasu, in a way, was merely reiterating the view of President Ceausescu, who had declared following the Czechoslovak intervention that no motive could justify intervention by a Socialist state into the affairs of another.[65]

The key writers on international law and relations in Romania such as V. Duculescu, C. Vlad, D. I. Mazilu, Edwin Glaser, and Gheorghe Moca invariably referred to the UN Chatter to justify their concepts of law among nations, as well as to Marxist-Leninist doctrine. Duculescu tried to enhance the importance of sovereignty by stating that significant documents at the UN could only be adopted by taking into account the interests of national sovereign states.[66] Similarly, Moca, in his very important book *Suveranitatea de Stat*,[67] attempted to bolster his arguments on sovereignty by citing the Declaration of the 25th Anniversary Session of the UN General Assembly of 1970, which specified that states cooperated in accordance with the principles of sovereignty, equality and noninterference in internal affairs.[68] This tied in well with what Ceausescu had said in 1969—that not only must there be respect for the UN Charter but that there was to be only one international law for all countries.[69] This of course hardly fit in with Tunkin's arguments of a specific Socialist international law.

Perhaps the most comprehensive exposition of Romanian views on the principles of international law and relations has been put forward by Alexandru C. Aureliu in his book *Principiile Relatiilor Dintre State.*[70] He stated that all countries, irrespective of their area, the size of their population, their political or economic power, were equal in their exercise of their sovereignty and rights.[71] In turn he felt that sovereign equality consisted of the following principles: (a) relations between states have to be based on free expression of the will of these states; (b) the states enjoy equal rights to participate in the examination of the international problems which affect them; (c) each state is individually the one that can decide whether an international problem presents an interest for it, and this decision does not have to depend on another state; (d) in the framework of international relations and treaties, the states have to occupy equal judicial positions; (e) in international conferences and organizations, states are to have equal rights to participate in debate and have equal roles; (f) the decisions of these meetings can bind only those states that have declared themselves ready to adopt these decisions; (g) noninterference in the affairs of another state constitutes one of the basic principles of contemporary international law.[72]

The whole concept of a centrally directed "Socialist commonwealth" was anathema to Romania. There was such a constant reiteration of this rejection of a center in all Romanian literature that it was bound to permeate its relations with the Soviet Union. In July 1976 Ceausescu reiterated that there "does not and cannot exist a guiding center" for Socialist states.[73] The Romanians were also quick to cite the Moscow Declaration of June 1969, which stated in its final document that "each party, guiding itself upon Marxist-Leninist principles, keeping in mind the concrete national conditions, elaborates its policies in a totally independent way."[74] Romania insisted that her own Communist party was the best judge of problems in the country and that there should be no outside interference whatever.

Such an approach to Socialist internationalism and to "Socialist commonwealth" cohesion stemmed, at least partly, from Romania's attitude toward the dialectical conflict between class struggle and national liberation rights. It is interesting to note how much greater emphasis its theoreticians placed on the latter. Gheorghe Moca, in his book *Suveranitatea de Stat*—which was very favorably received in China and Yugoslavia—expressed the Romanian view of the contemporary epoch when he stated that at that moment there were two trends in international relations: imperialistic states were seeking to impose their own hegemonic will by means of their great relative power, while on the other hand small and middle-sized states were increasingly demonstrating their desire to assert their sovereign rights.[75] The Secretary General of the editorial board of *Lupta de Clasa*, C. Lazarescu, similarly asserted that contemporary international life was characterized by the struggle between the "advanced" anti-imperialist forces and the "reactionary" forces of imperialism.[76]

Again this is not to say that Romania ab initio rejected proletarian internationalism. The term was used very frequently but, as was mentioned previously, the meaning was different from that understood by Soviet theorists such as Tunkin. The flow of strength was from the particular to the general. As Constantin Vlad stated in his paper at the 1972 Prague conference, Romania pursued a foreign policy that it believed to serve its own fundamental interests and implicitly the cause of the national and social liberation of all peoples.[77] In this sense and in this sense only, national and international interests in Romania were blurred.

Another key caveat must be made at this stage. Romania did not enter into direct confrontation with the Soviet Union. As divergent as its view may have been from the norm in the Soviet bloc, it presented them obliquely and gradually. To use communications-theory terminology, it sent out an extended signal. The dissimilarities in these views on the separation of the nation-state and the people and on the content and applicability of Socialist international law in the "Socialist commonwealth" were also presented circuitously by Romania. It incorporated as much as possible of the Soviet view into its theories and attacked the rest indirectly—usually by criticizing Western proponents of "limited sovereignty" and of world integration and government. This esoteric form of communication coupled with partial incorporation should have been a most effective element for the defense of foreign policy autonomy by a smaller Soviet-bloc state.

SOCIALIST INTEGRATION OR SOCIALIST COOPERATION?

The integration of the Soviet bloc had been advocated at various times and to various degrees by Soviet leaders in the postwar era. The two main cooperative organs in Eastern Europe, the Warsaw Pact and Comecon, had likewise been altered to an extent to try to aid these aims. Some of the most influential Soviet jurists also provided legal-theoretical bases for integration, besides the initial Marxist-Leninist doctrine of world working-class solidarity. G. I. Tunkin, for instance, felt that certain rights and duties were derived from the principles of proletarian internationalism for Socialist states in relations with each other, among them the duty to pursue close cooperation.[78]

V. I. Lisovskii, a Tunkin ally, elaborated on this argument by referring to Brezhnev's speech at the 23rd Communist Party Congress in 1966 when the latter had said, in effect, that the national economies of the Socialist states must be integrated to provide for specialization and cooperation of production in order to keep abreast with the technological revolution and with capitalism.[79] Moreover, Lisovskii felt that the East European commercial treaties; the Warsaw Pact; and the treaties of friendship, mutual aid, and cooperation showed that the Socialist states could not limit themselves in their mutual relations to the application of generally accepted principles of international law. Yet to the Romanians, who insisted on strict adherence to general international law, such an attitude remained patently unacceptable.

In effect, as has been seen, it was Khrushchev's attempt at rationalization of production in the Soviet bloc that brought the Soviet-Romanian differences out into the open. The Romanians refused to subscribe to supranational planning and in 1964 issued their "Declaration," which rejected any such planning or restructuring of Comecon into a supranational organization as an infringement of their sovereignty and as contrary to what they perceived to be the essence of Marxist-Leninist doctrine.

Of course, the Kremlin has always maintained that neither the Warsaw Pact nor Comecon were supranational organizations. Indeed, Comecon had an ad hoc type of structure and the Romanians, in objecting to the proposal to give it greater planning and integrating functions, were opting for a status quo, which was formally praised by the Kremlin. As a result, even in 1971, when they finally subscribed to Comecon's comprehensive integration program adopted at Bucharest in July of that year, the Romanians stressed that in their understanding Socialist integration was different from capitalist integration, for the former did not mean any infringement upon national independence and sovereignty and did not lead to the setting up of bodies for suprastate planning and organization. The report of the agreement in the official RCP organ, *Scinteia*, stated:

> The program endorsed reasserts the principles of the Comecon charter, which proclaims that this body was founded on the basis of sovereign equality of the member states [and] proceeds accordingly to the principles of fully equal rights, observance of national sovereignty and interests, mutual advantage and assistance.[80]

The chief writers on questions of sovereignty all agreed that, while cooperation was valuable, it could not be used to derogate from national sovereignty or to set up supranational organizations. Vlad, for instance, attacked Western proponents of integration such as Zbigniew Brzezinski.[81] He contended that a state must develop its economy as a national economy. Integration was to come only as a requirement of "determinism," for if it was forced it was liable to undermine the national life of the people.[82] Thus, in Vlad's view, increased cooperation was to come at the pace of the specific Romanian needs and not those of the Soviet Union, or of the "Socialist commonwealth."

Following the Comecon meeting of June 1975 in Budapest, when extensive plans for integration were drawn up, Romanian theoreticians became even more intense in their rejection of any attempts at supranationality. They contended that in the new economic order that was developing throughout the world the role of the nation-state and the growth of its economy and the preservation of its rights of sovereignty were the sine qua non for development.[83] At the same time they attacked all attempts to proceed with joint planning, usually in the esoteric Romanian manner. This entailed particularly harsh attacks on such straw men as the multinational corporation and transnationalism.[84]

The assumption in this preoccupation with national sovereignty was that by strengthening the nation economically the Socialist world as a whole was strengthened. Again, it was a flow from the particular to the general, antithetical to the Soviet view. The manner in which this flow was to take place was explained by Ilie Radulescu,* who completed the blanket coverage that Romanian theoreticians gave to integration. He wrote that:

> Internal revolutionary forces have a decisive role in changing society on a social basis within the dialectical relationship between the national factor and the international; in fact the national factor, the internal development of the countries, and the increase in their

---

*It is interesting to note the consistency of Radulescu's views from 1965 on, regarding the defense of sovereignty.

economic and technical-scientific potential are responsible for the viability of the international factor.[85]

The same reasoning was applied by Romania in its relations with the Warsaw Pact. Not only did it refuse to recognize any supranational qualities in the Pact but it criticized military blocs by attacking NATO, and carried on an autonomous military policy that, according to it, simultaneously strengthened the entire Socialist bloc through the process of strengthening Romanian defense.

In regard to the conundrum of Socialist integration, it should be remembered that despite its differences with the Soviet Union Romania avoided direct confrontation. Any attacks on Soviet concepts were indirect—usually consisting of demolishing a Western straw man. Communication with the Soviets was again esoteric. In formulating their arguments, the Romanians (as seen in the works of Vlad and Radulescu) were also being skillful at "restriction through partial incorporation." As both Romanian and Soviet policies had gone through shifting perspectives of international relations and law, there was considerable room for maneuver.

CONCLUSION

There were clearly real differences between the Soviet Union and Romania on the broad concept of sovereignty. They disagreed on the hypothesis of a dichotomy in the views and aims of the state on one hand, and the people in a Socialist country, on the other. Similarly, they differed on the content and applicability of Socialist international law, with the Soviet Union declaring that such interventions as that into Czechoslovakia fell within the legality of Socialist concepts and Romania declaring that only general international law was applicable and that no derogation of sovereignty was admissible. They also differed on the dilemma posed by the necessity of emphasizing either the international class struggle or national liberation. Whereas the Soviet Union leaned toward the former, Romania was emphatically on the side of national liberation and sovereignty. As far as integration was concerned, the two parties were also far apart. While the Soviet Union favored increased integration in the Socialist world with added specialization of production and more joint international projects, Romania was opposed to anything but minimal supranational cooperation and vehemently opposed the construction of any supranational structure. While both saw an organic unity between the national and international in the Socialist world, the Soviets perceived the flow of strength from the general to the particular, whereas the Romanians clung to the opposite view.

Nevertheless, it should not be believed that the Soviet position pro tanto excluded that of Romania. The Soviet Union did hold similar views to those of Romania on the endurance of the nation-state. It should also be remembered that the Soviets were signatories to the UN Charter and admitted that general international law was no longer bourgeois law. Even Tunkin was reluctant to reject outright the principle of jus cogens and instead tried to alter it by interpretation. And, similarly, it should be recognized that the Soviet leaders, despite their efforts at Socialist integration, still did not formally admit to supranationality. Thus, there were grounds for compromise if Romania was skillful enough.

Despite its independent stance in foreign affairs. Romania avoided direct confrontations with the Soviet Union. Its assertions of independence, its insistence on sovereignty in terms of general international law were not made through overt attacks on conflicting Soviet concepts. Rather, there had been an esoteric-type of communication where Romanian theorists used very abstract forms to attack Western scholars who expounded identical concepts to those put forth by the Soviet Union. Very significantly, the Romanians also used the concept of exclusion through partial incorporation by repeatedly resorting to Soviet pronouncements to defend themselves.

Therefore, Romania made full political use of active legal defenses in conjunction with the passive ones inherent in the Soviet position. It is recognized that these legal defenses would not have been sufficient in themselves to deter Soviet intervention in Romania, but they formed an integral part of the larger network of passive and active defenses that determined the limits of Romanian foreign policy autonomy.

NOTES

1. *Scinteia* November 13, 1968.
2. Leonid Brezhnev, *Scinteia*, September 25, 1971.
3. G. I. Tunkin, *Teoriia Mezhdunarodnogo Prava*, 2nd ed., Moscow, 1970 in J. H. Hazard, "Renewed Emphasis upon a Socialist International Law" in *American Journal of International Law* vol. 65, January 1971, p. 145.
4. Ralph Miliband, "State and Revolution" in Sweezy and Magdoft, eds., *Lenin Today* (New York: Monthly Review Press, 1970), p. 78.
5. H. Chambre, *From Karl Marx to Mao* (New York: P.J. Kennedy and Sons, 1963), p. 185.
6. V. I. Lenin, *Selected Works*, vol. 9 (London: Lawrence and Wishard Publishers, 1937), p. 336.
7. Miliband, op. cit., p. 81.
8. Ibid., p. 84.
9. E. H. Carr, *The Bolshevik Revolution*, vol. 1 (London: Macmillan and Co., 1950), p. 230.
10. R. V. Daniels, "The State and Revolution," *American Slavic and East European Review* vol. 12, no. 1, February 1953, p. 24.
11. Z. Brzezinski, *The Soviet Bloc: Unity and Conflict* (Boston: Harvard University Press, 1967), p. 105.
12. N. Ceausescu, "Report to the Grand National Assembly," *Lupta de Clasa*, September 1965, p. 10.
13. Ilie Radulescu, "About the Role of Our Socialist State," *Lupta de Clasa*, March 1966, p. 3.
14. Ibid., p. 16.
15. Ibid.

16. V. Duculescu, "The Sovereign State in International Relations," *Era Socialista*, no. 13, July 1973, p. 53.

17. C. Vlad, *Essays on Nation* (Bucharest: Meridiane Publishing, 1973).

18. Ibid., p. 8.

19. See J. V. Stalin "Marxism and the National Question" in *Works*, vol. 2, (Bucharest: EPLR, 1953), p. 218, cited in Vlad, op. cit., p. 16.

20. Ioan Ceterchi, "Faurirea se consolidarea statului socialist," *Era Socialista*, July 14, 1974, p. 9.

21. I. Ceterchi, D. Mazilu, C. Vlad, et al., *Statul Socialist Roman in Etapa Actuala* (Bucharest: Editura Politica, 1976), pp. 223-42.

22. *Financial Times*, (London) May 18, 1976.

23. G. I. Tunkin, "V. I. Lenin i printsipy otnoshenii mezhdu sotsialisti cheskimi gosudarstvami," *Sovetskii Ezhegodnik Mezhdunarodnogo Prava* (SEMP) 1969 (1970), pp. 16-29.

24. W. E. Butler, "Socialist International Law" or "Socialist Principles of International Relations?" in *American Journal of International Law* vol. 65, 1971, p. 797.

25. Ilie Radulescu, op. cit., p. 3.

26. Vlad, op. cit., p. 37.

27. Ibid., p. 45.

28. Ibid., p. 113.

29. Ibid.

30. *Romania Libera*, September 28, 1974.

31. Brzezinski, op. cit., p. 33.

32. G. Ginsburgs, "Socialist Internationalism and State Sovereignty," in *The Year-book of World Affairs* (London: Institute of World Affairs, 1971), p. 43.

33. Jane Degras, ed., *The Communist International 1919: Documents*, vol. 1 (London: Oxford University Press, 1956), p. 5.

34. V. Vorovskii, *Sochineniia*, vol. 3 (Moscow, 1933), p. 475; in William Korey, "The Comintern and the Geneology of the 'Brezhnev Doctrine,'" *Problems of Communism*, May/June 1969, p. 53.

35. Grigori E. Zinoviev, *Kommunisticheskii International*, vols. 83-88, no. 1, 1919, in Korey, op. cit., p. 55.

36. Korey, op. cit., p. 55.

37. Grigori E. Zinoviev, *Sochineniia*, vol. 7, no. 1, pp. 15-21.

38. *Izvestia* (Moscow), March 23, 1919.

39. See J. H. Hazard, "Cleansing Soviet International Law of Anti-Marxist Theories," *American Journal of International Law*, vol. 32, 1938, p. 244.

40. *Pravda*, March 30, 1966.

41. Milovan Djilas, *Conversations with Stalin* (London: Rupert, Hart, Davis, 1962), p. 160.

42. B. L. Manelis, *Sovetskoe Gosudarstvo i pravo* (Moscow), no. 7, p. 17. English version in Hazard, Shapiro, and Maggs, *The Soviet Legal System*, 2nd ed., (New York: F. Dobbs, 1969), p. 34.

43. J. H. Hazard, "Renewed Emphasis . . . ," op. cit., p. 143.

44. *Scinteia*, August 7, 1969.

45. Tunkin, "V. I. Lenin i printsipy . . . " op. cit., pp. 16-29, also see W. E. Butler, op. cit., p. 796.

46. Ibid., p. 27.

47. Ibid.

48. Hazard, Shapiro, and Maggs, op. cit.

49. Butler, op. cit., p. 797.

50. I. Lapenna, "The Soviet Concept of Socialist International Law" in *Yearbook of World Affairs* (London: Institute of World Affairs, 1975), p. 258.

51. Tunkin, *Teoriia* . . . , op. cit.

52. Hazard, "Renewed Emphasis . . . , " op. cit., p. 143.

53. L. A. Aleksidze, "Problema jus cogens v sovremennom mezhdunarodnom prave" in *SEMP*, 1969 (1970), p. 144; also cited in Butler, op. cit., p. 799.

54. See Hazard, "Renewed Emphasis" op. cit., p. 33.

55. V. I. Lisovskii, *Mezhdunarodnoe Prava*, Moscow, 1970, and Hazard, "Renewed Emphasis . . . , " op. cit., p. 144.

56. Tunkin, "V. I. Lenin i printsipy . . . , " op. cit., p. 25.

57. Tunkin, *Teoriia* . . . , op. cit., pp. 493-5.

58. Tunkin, "V. I. Lenin i printsipy . . .," op. cit., p. 18.

59. Tunkin, *Teoriia* . . . , op. cit., pp. 504-505; also see Chris Osakwe, "Socialist International Law Revisited," *American Journal of International Law* vol. 66, 1972, p. 596-7.

60. Tunkin, "V. I. Lenin i printsipy . . . , " op. cit., p. 28.

61. *Scinteia* April 23, 1964.

62. Ion Voicu, "National Sovereignty and the Doctrine of International Law," *Era Socialista*, September 18, 1973, p. 41.

63. N. Ceausescu, *Romania pedrumul construirii societatii socialiste* (Bucharest: Editura Politica, 1976), pp. 301-2.

64. *Scinteia*, November 4, 1972.

65. *Scinteia*, August 22, 1968.

66. V. Duculescu, op. cit., p. 28.

67. Gheorghe Moca, *Suveranitatea de Stat: Teorii Burgheze Studii Critic* (Bucharest: Editura Politica, 1973).

68. Ibid., p. 108.

69. N. Ceausescu, cited by I. Closca, in "The Necessity for a Negotiated Settlement of International Issues," *Lupta de Clasa*, February 1969, pp. 64-5.

70. A. C. Aureliu, *Principiile Relatiilor Dintre State* (Bucharest: Editura Politica, 1966).

71. Ibid., p. 106.

72. Ibid., pp. 106-23.

73. *Tribuna Romana*, July 15, 1976, p. 7.

74. Quoted by A. Rosetti in *Scinteia*, June 20, 1969.

75. Moca, op. cit., p. 133.

76. C. Lazarescu, "The Evolution of the Contemporary World and the Principles of International Relations," *Lupta de Clasa*, September 1967, p. 14.

77. C. Vlad, *World Marxist Review* (Belgrade), July 1972.

78. Tunkin, "V. I. Lenin i printsipy . . . , " op. cit., p. 25.

79. Lisovskii, op. cit., p. 51.

80. *Scinteia*, August 1, 1971.

81. Vlad, op. cit., p. 180.

82. Ibid., p. 92.

83. Ilie Serbanescu, "Noua ordine Economica internationala, conceptii si realitati," *Era Socialista*, no. 6, 1976, p. 43.

84. I. Serbanescu, "Corporatiile transnational si capitalismul de stat," *Era Socialista*, no. 18, 1976, p. 49.

85. Ilie Radulescu, "The National and the International Aspects of Contemporary Economic Collaboration," in *Problems Economice*, no. 8, August 1973.

3

Soviet Interpretations
of the Strategic Limits of
Romanian Policy Deviations

An old East European joke still making the rounds in Bucharest in 1977 was that of the reply a Romanian gave when asked what security meant for his country. "Security for us," he answered, "means keeping the Russians secure enough so that they will leave us alone." The joke demonstrates a great deal of political perception, for the postwar era has shown that the Soviet Union has been most likely to act to enforce conformity in Eastern Europe when it felt that its own security was threatened.

Now, what constitutes security for the Soviet Union defies any simple definition. It must be expressed in both political and military terms; by the former we are thinking of ideological, structural, and economic factors, and by the latter both of strategic and of tactical ones. It is often difficult to differentiate between the political and the military, for the two are at times very closely interwoven and neither may be examined in complete isolation. This chapter, however, will emphasize the military aspects of the Soviet perception of security— it is hoped without losing sight of the political implications. Military considerations of security had a not-insignificant influence in the determination of Soviet action in East Germany in 1953, in Hungary and Poland in 1956, and in Czechoslovakia in 1968.

Romania, which endeavored to pursue an autonomous foreign policy and which, at least according to some Western opinion,[1] had to perform a balancing act to maintain this policy, needed to have a correct perception of the needs of Soviet military security in order to be able to judge correctly Soviet crisis behavior and risk taking. It was necessary for Romania to recognize the right signals and then interpret them correctly. It is specifically the purpose of the next two chapters to examine the parameters that Soviet needs for military security imposed on the conduct of East European states in general and Romania in particular.

Soviet perception of its military security, however, could not be rigid, for it must have been affected by historical and military developments. What constituted military security for Stalin in 1948 may not have done so for Brezhnev in 1968. The development of nuclear weapons and strategic delivery systems must have influenced Soviet policy, as must have the development of detente. Here, though, we propose to examine the theoretical aspects of security perception, the formal and informal decision-making process for Soviet military policies, and the cognizance given to deviant Romanian foreign policy actions. Only then will we turn to the evolution of Soviet military policy toward Romania and analyze some of the Soviet military actions limiting Romanian foreign policy autonomy.

We shall, moreover, examine the domestic formation of the Soviet perception of its military-security needs, scrutinizing the influence of the Soviet military establishment. Its role as an interest group necessitates an analysis of its organizational function, of the policies it has advocated toward Eastern Europe and Romania, and the divergencies within the group insofar as these things can be discerned. Soviet perception of its military security, in general, could have offered Romania some passive defenses for its policies, as could have a Soviet flexibility in formulating its military policy. In assessing whether Moscow took cognizance of Romanian actions as challenges, we should cover the first step toward the more detailed study of how these actions affected Soviet security needs as reflected through the evolution of Soviet military policy.

THE CONCEPT OF SECURITY

The definition of security presents imponderable problems, for it encompasses values that are by and large subjective. In international affairs one is basically concerned with a state's external security. This, in turn, in the past has denoted traditional military security, which naturally enough was a vital concern to the statesmen of the day. Increasingly, however, there has been a broadening of the concept of external security to include political-ideological, legal, and economic considerations. As we have stated earlier, though, the focus here will be military security as it related to the Soviet Union and Romania.

Even the definition of military security involves many problems. It has been suggested that one should incorporate within the notion of military security the concepts of national interests, "objective" power, and force.[2] All of these concepts are to a great extent subjective, for, despite the possibility of quantification of such things as numbers of troops and quantities of weapons, the ultimate decisions are made by the responsible statesmen who bring their own bias to the job. If a vital national interest is to be defined as one over which a state is willing to go to war,[3] this contains a subjective element in the variance of the will, from nation to nation, according to prevailing conditions and national traditions. Using the concept of the "objective" as a desirable image of a future state of affairs[4] again is subjective, for part of a nation's perception would always be determined by human bias. Therefore, military security may be best left as a flexible concept incorporating subjective and objective elements concerned with the physical safety of the state.

Force has traditionally been one of the tools for enforcing this security. The American intervention in the Dominican Republic in 1965 and the Soviet intervention in Czechoslovakia in 1968 demonstrated that both superpowers were willing and able to take unilateral military action if they perceived threats to vital national interests (political and military), within their clearly delineated spheres of influence.

There are, however, serious inherent limitations in the use of force. When a state, especially a superpower, has to resort to the use of force instead of merely threatening the utilization of force, the purpose of the entire operation has begun to disintegrate. There is also a propensity for force to leave a legacy of bitterness or exhaustion which could provide a threat to the newly established order of things.[5] The risks in a Soviet military action against a small state such as Romania would have been smaller than against a more powerful opponent but this did not exclude some of the more serious negative effects. Furthermore, the growth of relative Soviet military power has not necessarily induced a higher Soviet risk-taking propensity vis-a-vis the West and the bloc states. The Soviet intervention in Hungary in 1956 showed an acceptance of risk despite the military-strategic inferiority it had relative to the West. On the other hand, while the Soviet Union enjoyed a tremendous growth in military-strategic power in the 1960s and 1970s, its actions (despite Czechoslovakia) did not show a correlative increase in potentially dangerous ventures.

Of course it may have been to the advantage of the Soviet Union at times to convince an adversary or a target state that it was dealing with a reckless opponent who was unconcerned with the potentially catastrophic consequences flowing from his actions. This, however, did not negate an awareness of risk but could have been part of deterrence. It may well be true that once the Soviet Union decided to use military force in Eastern Europe, the more force it used the less did it perceive the crisis as being risky.[6] Such an attitude, though, represented the modus operandi of the Soviet Union once it decided on an action in Eastern Europe, and not her intentions in intervening.

As we have seen earlier, if Soviet state interests, which by Moscow's definition meant those of world Socialism, could only be safeguarded through the use of military force, then and only then did the Soviet leadership accept the risks entailed in the action (which in turn became a priori just in their minds). In this sense, the use of military intervention would have been a weapon of last resort.

Thus, it appears at the theoretical level that a strong desire for military security did not necessarily make a great power interventionist. The Soviet desire for military security did not have to exclude flexibility in their policy toward Romania. Moreover, if the Soviet Union used military intervention only in extremis, then that could have been a passive defense for Romania.

THE FORMULATION OF MILITARY POLICY

Military policies reflect and in a dynamic manner affect the security per-
ceptions of any state. As the Soviet perception of its security needs affected the
limits it imposed on Romanian foreign policy, the method of formulating Soviet
military policy was of crucial importance to the latter. The influence of the
military establishment and their interaction with the political elements of Soviet
society in the determination of policy would have been the first level of observa-
tion for Romania in discerning the early-warning signals of Soviet action. At the
second level one must contend with the phenomenon that few, if any, organizations are homogenous and that in the Soviet Union as well there may not be a
single "military" mind, but rather within the military itself there may be divergencies of view. If such divergencies are found, then it should be ascertained
what the effects of these divergencies were through an analysis of the formal and
informal structures whereby the various views within the military establishment
could be presented. While it is not possible to discern precisely the thinking of
the Soviet policymakers in military-security matters, it should be useful to locate
some of the signals that conveyed the warning to Eastern European states—and
to the Romanians in particular—that they were about to overstep the bounds
of Soviet tolerance.

Historically, the military in Russia enjoyed considerable influence over
foreign policy. Russia herself behaved much like other big powers in the 19th
and early 20th century and accepted the contemporary European-centered national state system predicated on the theory of the balance of power.[7] The
military leaders in turn emphasized "military necessity" and demonstrated a
predilection for military solutions even when one can see, at least with the
benefit of hindsight, that more important considerations outweighed, or should
have outweighed them. Of the numerous examples of occasions when the Russian
military exercised this type of influence, perhaps the most blatant one would
be that of the insistence of General Sukhomlinov, the Minister of War, and
General Yanushkevich, the Chief of the Russian General Staff, on the military
necessity of general mobilization in July 1914, despite the risk (which was confirmed) of precipitating war.[8] The argument of military necessity that may have
been used in another form for military intervention in Eastern Europe during
the 1950s and 1960s could conceivably have been as persuasive to Brezhnev as
to the Russian leaders of 1914.

In postrevolutionary Soviet history the military has had considerable
influence as well, but on a number of occasions it has alternated between being
a pawn and a player in games played by the party leadership. The role of the
military was not forgotten by any of the leaders emerging from a power struggle
since Stalin's demise. Malenkov was grateful to the army for its role in disposing
of Beria, Khrushchev for its role in supporting him against the "anti-party"
group in 1957, and Brezhnev and Kosygin for its tacit support in dismissing
Khrushchev. Zhukov was temporarily rewarded with the post of Minister of

Defense and a seat on the Politburo, the latter a very uncommon post for a military man in Soviet history. In this period the conservatism of the Soviet military establishment was instrumental in setting the agenda for the next stage in the arms race, with an emphasis on conventional weapons, while the political leadership only belatedly succeeded in putting forth a strategic weapons development that would balance that of the United States.

Since the influence of the military has not been a constant, we are particularly interested in its level and direction since 1965 and how this consequently affected Soviet perception of Romanian actions during this phase. Whatever challenges Romania may have presented to Soviet hegemony, they would have appeared somewhat different if viewed from a military instead of a purely political perspective. Romanian unilateral reduction of the duration of time army draftees were inducted for, or its refusal to participate in Warsaw Pact maneuvers between 1964-67, could have signified a different type of affront to the Soviet military professionals than to the party leaders. Military differences of opinion in turn could have affected considerably the restraints that the Soviet Union placed on Romania.

The influence of the military, though, must be viewed through the decision-making structure in the Soviet Union. Whatever model one may use to analyze this decision-making process one is struck by the preponderance of the power of the Soviet Politburo. An extraordinarily large degree of the business of government in the Soviet Union has been performed at the Politburo level and while (as it will be seen later) the military may have had good access to the top Soviet leadership, it very rarely had direct representation in this body. Similarly, it ought to be kept in mind that because of the traditional emphasis on the primacy of politics in the Soviet Union, the Politburo members had a certain advantage over the military experts in the discussion of military policy. The latter would have been forced to debate their position in political as well as military terms.

Much of the influence of the military was determined by the flux of strength in the Politburo, particularly that of the leader. When the political leadership was weak, the Politburo members vied with each other in demonstrating concern for the defense of the country. They claimed the loyalty of the institutions that derived benefit from such support. Khrushchev sought and received such support against Malenkov, and Brezhnev and Kosygin enjoyed at least tacit military support against Khrushchev. Nevertheless, because in the coup against the latter the army had played only a small part, it was in no position to place its leader into the Politburo as it effectuated with Zhukov after the 1957 crisis. It was only in 1973 that a thoroughly politicized Andrei Grechko was admitted to the Politburo (to 1976). Right after the coup, though, the military did speak up and the new political leadership appeared to view their requests a little more propitiously than Khrushchev had in the 1960s. Thus leadership change was one of the occasions when the military was in a particularly advantageous position to increase its influence in the Soviet policy-making process.

Any analysis of the relationship between the military and political leadership tends to indicate a type of seesaw effect. This kind of influence could affect both the decision of Soviet intervention in an Eastern European country and the execution of such a decision. When the Soviet political leadership pursued an activist role, either by challenging the Western strategic position or by enforcing conformity in the Soviet bloc, it added to the general Soviet strategic problems and increased the difficulties of policy execution by the Soviet military. In the period since 1965, the military seems to have had to extend assistance to the party in order to rectify some of its foreign policy mistakes. They were the ones who moved into Czechoslovakia to arrest the challenges posed by that state, and it was again the military who brought some order out of the chaos in the Middle East following the 1967 Arab debacle. Such crises would naturally have given the military a greater voice in policy formulation either through special professional advisory status or through direct action. This is not to say that effective military influence has been necessarily a force for less tolerance in Soviet foreign policy. There is, for instance, some evidence that the powerful Soviet Chief of the General Staff, Marshal M. V. Zakharov, acted as a counsel of restraint on Soviet policy regarding the military action against China in the summer of 1969,[9] at a time when the Western press was discussing the possibility of a Soviet preemptive nuclear strike.

On the other hand, the military leaders who were less tolerant of diversity also had the opportunity to exercise their influence. While the military must have argued its position in political terms at crisis points such as Czechoslovak deviation in 1968, they could conjoin the security and ideological issues, thereby making their argument that much more persuasive. This must be coupled with the high military security consciousness of the Brezhnev-Kosygin leadership. Brezhnev had fought in Czechoslovakia in World War II with the 18th Army and it could not have been too difficult for such commanders as Marshal Grechko and General Yepishev, the convinced Europeanists,* to persuade him in 1968 of the importance of the Central European equation. When security considerations were at stake in the period of our discussion, the advice of the generals was bound to be weighty even if not conclusive.

Powerful members of the Soviet military had, however, been disciplined when the political leadership felt that they had overstepped the boundary of their bailiwick. Khrushchev dismissed Marshal Zhukov as Minister of Defense and relieved him of his Politburo membership in 1957 when the former attempted to lessen party influence in professional military affairs. He also dismissed the Chief of the General Staff, Marshal Zakharov, in 1963 because the latter opposed

---

*The Minister of Defense, Grechko, and the Chief of the Political Section of the armed forces, General Yepishev, showed repeatedly in their speeches and writings that they believed that the crucial military confrontation would still be in Europe.

what he considered to be adventurism by the leader in the Cuban missile crisis. In the early 1960s the Soviet political leadership also severely criticized the former Chief of Staff Marshal V. D. Sokolovsky after he edited his now-famous book on strategy, for infringing on the prerogative of the political leadership in formulating Soviet strategy.[10] These precedents must have influenced the Brezhnev-Kosygin leadership in ensuring the primacy of the political leadership and keeping the gains of the military at a relatively modest level. The appointment of a civilian, Dimitri Ustinov, to replace Marshal Grechko as Defense Minister upon the latter's death in April 1976 was widely interpreted as a demonstration of Brezhnev's determination to illustrate the primacy of political (and his own) control in the Soviet Union.

The military in turn made the most of the opportunities presented and between 1965 and 1970 they erased both the image and substance of numerical strategic inferiority vis-a-vis the West (though there remained a qualitative gap), as well as greatly improving their capacity for general war by including their general-purpose forces in the development of what they claimed was a better military balance.[11] By 1977 their general-purpose forces could compete easily in many qualitative areas with those of the West.[12] American acknowledgment of mutual assured destruction by the late 1960s certainly gave the Soviet Union a psychological parity. Again, in 1967, the military succeeded in maintaining their hold on the post of Minister of Defense and in the reestablishment of the position of Commander-in-Chief of the ground forces—a post which had remained rather anomalous following Khrushchev's dismissal of the last incumbent, Marshal Chuikov, in 1964. The fact that Moscow did not go through with the rumored[13] appointment of the civilian Ustinov, the secretary of the party in charge of military affairs, as Minister of Defense following Marshal Malinovsky's death gave the appearance that the political leadership was trying to avoid friction with the military.

Thus, the overview of the Soviet military decision-making body shows a powerful, if not necessarily homogenous, lobby. The political leadership made the key decisions and imposed the boundaries on military influence, but the military establishment maintained and at times even slightly augmented its powers of persuasion. In military security matters the political leadership was susceptible to arguments by the military or certain elements of the military to take measures to ensure such security. When it came to enforcing conformity within the Soviet bloc the advice of the generals for intervention, or for that matter for restraint, must have been significant. Therefore, the influence that the Soviet military exerted on Soviet military policy was of more than academic interest to Romania, who was trying to assert its autonomy.

The difference between the various public statements of the top Soviet military leaders may not represent a debate of policy in the Western sense but it does show that there were various military opinions and influences at work. This was illustrated in 1969 in the articles written by the top marshals for Victory Day (May 9). While in the previous Victory Day articles the top-ranking Soviet military leaders all echoed the *Pravda* editorial line, which was strongly anti-Western but included no direct or indirect tirades against China,[14] in 1969 one could perceive significant differences of emphasis among the marshals. The Soviet Defense Minister, Marshal Grechko, in an article entitled "The Great Victory" published in *Pravda* on May 9, evoked the danger of a new war, but in attacking the West he restricted himself to the West German "neo-Fascists" while, very important, he lambasted at length the Maoists:

> The adventurous policy Mao Tse-tung's group, which had proclaimed chauvinist-hegemonial aspirations and anti-Sovietism as their official policy course, cannot but cause concern.

Marshal Grechko also seemed to have changed his opinion on war, which in the previous Victory Day article he had described as "frightful," "devastating," and a "bloody carnage" and had therefore concluded that the Soviet people or Socialism did not need war.[15] Now he talked instead about Lenin's dictum on how to win a war.[16] This may well have reflected a preoccupation on the marshal's part with the problem of a preemptive war against China.

The Commander-in-Chief of the Warsaw Pact forces, Marshal Yakubovsky, took a similar line to Grechko in toning down his anti-Americanism in his May 9, 1969, article in *Sovetskaya Rossiya*, while sharpening his anti-Chinese remarks in comparison with the previous year.[17] He was the only Soviet military leader on this occasion to threaten the Chinese directly if they should attempt again to encroach on Soviet soil.[18] In the same article he called for Socialist "unity"— which seems quite clearly to have been directed at maintaining the European bloc comformity, particularly in the case of Czechoslovakia and Romania. Yakubovsky's virulent language would tend to indicate that he was ready to execute any military intervention order of the party with relish. From Romania's point of view, Yakubovsky certainly would have appeared as a man who insisted on strong conformity within the bloc.

On the other hand, the Soviet Chief of the General Staff, Marshal Zakharov, adopted a substantially different line from that of the *Pravda* editorial on Victory Day 1969. Writing in *Izvestia* on May 9, 1969, he omitted the anti-Mao paragraphs which seemed mandatory to the other military commanders and listed as the most important "provocations" the armed conflicts and wars that he claimed were begun by NATO states in the postwar era. He talked of resistance to imperialism by "all states of the Socialist community"[19] and "all" included China, as the Soviet Union in 1969 still listed the Socialist system as consisting of 14 countries and this number, of course, had to include China. Very significantly, in the same article Zakharov emphasized the need to prevent war because of its grave consequences to mankind. The combination of the Soviet Chief of Staff's reluctance of villify China in his article together with his plan to prevent war would tend to indicate a reluctance on his part to advocate or support a preventive war against China and possibly even intervention against her European "supporters," Romania and Albania.

Thus, in the realm of Sino-Soviet relations, the military differed with each other on how to deal with a possible Chinese threat, and much of the Soviet military differed with the political leadership on the amount of military aid and cooperation to be offered to China even at the zenith of Sino-Soviet relations.[20] John Erikson, for instance, felt certain that in 1969 Marshal Zakharov did advocate restraint against Soviet military action versus China,[21] and when politicians waver the influence of the military man can be very weighty.

The Soviet military's attitude toward the steps that could be taken against China would tend to show a significant difference in military opinion. The intervention in Czechoslovakia in 1968 also coincided with a profound strategic debate within the Soviet military—thus it represented a transitional stage in Soviet strategic thinking. Even during this stage, it must be pointed out, any objections by parts of the Soviet military to foreign policy were not directed against extending Soviet influence abroad or against defending Soviet national security interests in Europe or Asia, but rather involved the implementation of such policies. In the case of Czechoslovakia, the reservations shown by some of the military concerned the damage that the invasion would cause to Soviet-Czechoslovak military relations. The efforts of the Soviet military to have united, efficient military support from the countries of Eastern Europe should not be underestimated. Before the intervention the Czechs were the Soviet Union's natural allies—both because of Slavic affinity and for reasons of historical development. As a result, the two states had close military relationships. The intervention in 1968 changed all this and Moscow had to consider in her contingency planning the possibility, and perhaps the probability, of the unreliability of Czechoslovak forces. This meant additional operational strain on the Soviet military leadership and army to ensure Czechoslovak loyalty in battle and to maintain internal security.[22] Thus there were sound military reasons for a viewpoint opposing the intervention in Czechoslovakia and in Eastern Europe in general.

There is some evidence that certain of the lesser Soviet military leaders were opposed to military intervention in Czechoslovakia as well. Marshal Konev, the Soviet World War II hero, visited Czechoslovakia in May 1968 and after discussions with Czechoslovak President Svoboda, his wartime comrade, he appeared to have been reassured.[23] While it may be argued that this was merely a ploy to get the Czechs off guard, it is true that the invasion only took place at a considerably later date. Just prior to the intervention of the Warsaw Pact forces in August 1968, Moscow also replaced the WTO Chief of Staff, General M. I. Kazakov, with General Shtemenko in order to plan the military action. The removal of General Kazakov, ostensibly for reasons of health, could well have indicated opposition by him to the intervention. He was the former commander of the Southern Group of Forces in the 1950s and was heavily involved with the 1956 suppression of the Hungarian revolt—a man the Soviet Union could certainly have found useful in 1968.

If the Soviet military influenced the Soviet decision makers, through many voices, they themselves were influenced by various factors—including age and locus of service. Until the appointment of the youthful Army General V. G. Kulikov as Soviet Chief of the General Staff in 1971, the top leadership positions were held by the old-guard officers who had held at least divisional command in World War II. While better educated military leaders were being brought in at the intermediate level, the top leadership was still influenced very strongly by the events of World War II and the European perspective that that implied. A greater emphasis on the European theater could also mean a greater interest by such an old guard in maintaining a buffer zone in Eastern Europe and therefore keeping a tighter military reign on the Warsaw Pact countries, including Romania. Marshal Grechko, who took over as Minister of Defense in 1967, had taken part in the liberation of Kiev in 1943 as the deputy commander of the First Ukrainian Front. He favored a hard-line foreign policy and was a supporter of the WTO intervention in Czechoslovakia.

Marshal M. V. Zakharov, a tremendously energetic Chief of the General Staff from 1965 until his death in 1971, had also been a senior commander in World War II. He had been Chief of Staff in the Soviet Far Eastern campaign in 1945, which in effect was a blitzkrieg type of operation against the Japanese forces in Manchuria.[24] While he also took a firm stand in foreign policy—especially vis-a-vis the West in his 1969 Victory Day statement—he also showed moderation in advocating military action in Eastern Europe or China during his tenure as Chief of the General Staff. His moderation in dealing with China may be partly explained by the fact that he must have had considerable confidence in Soviet military capacity in the Far East, for he had demonstrated this at first hand toward the end of World War II. In the case of Eastern Europe, he must have been influenced by his belief in the quick reaction capability of the Soviet Union, which would have allowed him, through this additional option, to be cautious. Second, having had most of his combat experience in the Far East, Zakharov might not have attached the same strategic importance to Eastern Europe as some of the other generals.

All military commanders are influenced to an extent by their personal military experiences and few such experiences could be more compelling than being a senior commander in World War II. Since the old guard held the top positions in the Soviet military (until 1971) they were bound to be deeply influenced by the war and therein by the strategic importance of Eastern Europe, with Zakharov, who served in the Far East at the peak of his war career and who appeared to have been the advocate of moderation on intervention in Eastern Europe during the latter part of the 1960s, being an exception. If the hypothesis that the locus of service in World War II influenced the Soviet military leaders in the 1960s is correct, then that would imply a high security consciousness on their part regarding any wavering of military support in Eastern Europe. However, since most of them took part in military action along the main axis of the German offensive and later defensive moves in World War II, it would follow

Influence of WWII (handwritten annotation)

not only need of arms cumups (handwritten marginal annotation)

that they would have been more sensitive about this same area as the locale of future operations. This in turn would have involved Poland, East Germany, and Czechoslovakia. If the old-guard commanders (with the exception of Zakharov) were to be classified as intolerant of deviation from Soviet policy in Eastern Europe, then such intolerance would also have to have exhibited a regionalism which would have given Romania a much greater leeway merely through her good geographic fortune.

The new Chief of the Soviet General Staff, General of the Army V. G. Kulikov, appointed on September 23, 1971,[25] however, did not fit the mold of the older commanders. His background was bound to be of importance to Romania. Before his appointment to this post, Kulikov had been the Commander of the Soviet Group of Forces in Germany. He was an expert on the strategic situation in the German, Central, and West European territories[26] and his very appointment may well have reflected the priorities of Soviet strategy. His youth (born in 1921) precluded the possibility of his serving in any senior position during World War II and the highest post he held prior to his appointment in Germany was that of Commander-in-Chief of the Kiev Military District, a post he occupied until November 1969.[27] It must be pointed out that Kiev M.D. does not border on Romania and thus to the extent that Kulikov would have been influenced by his previous military service, his interest in the Southern Tier of the Warsaw Pact in general—and Romania in particular—would have been minimal.

Changes in the Soviet and Warsaw Pact military command in 1977 could very well have favored Romania. In a surprise move, General Kulikov was moved from his position as Chief of the Soviet General Staff to the command of the Warsaw Pact forces following the death of its hard-line commander, Marshal Yakubovsky. Kulikov's own position was taken over by General Nikolai Ogarkov, who had previously been in charge of military aid and had been trained as a military engineer. Since Ogarkov was only 59 at the time of his appointment in January 1977,[28] he could not have taken part in any major command role during the Second World War. His thinking, therefore, would not have been influenced in the same way as that of the more old guard of the Soviet military command. Since both Kulikov and Ogarkov were members of the Central Committee of the Soviet Communist Party they could have been influential in moderating Soviet military policy toward Romania.

As a superpower, it was natural for the Soviet Union to have had numerous worldwide strategic and security problems and it would follow that the military would have to have been drawn into the decision-making process by the necessity of including them in the implementation of foreign policy. In this role the military showed reservations about certain Soviet policies, with some factions pressing for divergent policies, for the military itself was far from a homogenous group. The influence combination included at times political and military elements confronting other political and military elements, such as the instance of Shelest and Grechko versus Suslov and Zakharov in the case of the Czechoslovak intervention. If one is to gauge what influence the various military leaders had on Soviet foreign policy—and in this case particularly toward Romania—and to evaluate, for instance, what an advocacy of restraint vis-a-vis Czechoslovakia or Eastern Europe by Marshal Zakharov would have meant, one must also look at the formal and informal structures of military decision making. While the Soviet military had been reshaped, especially by Zakharov between 1965 and 1971, to reflect a greater degree of professionalism,[29] there remained organizational lapses such as the absence of an effective coordinating body for general strategy during this period. Therefore, before we begin an analysis of Soviet military policy, it should be useful to have a look at the military decision-making structure.

THE MILITARY STRUCTURE

Despite the fact that the Soviet Union had achieved superpower status, by the mid-1960s Western opinion held that it was an adolescent as far as its administrative functioning was concerned.[30] Many of the decisions, as far as can be ascertained, were of an ad hoc type with the whole structure often violating the classical features of efficient bureaucracy. While Brezhnev and Kosygin (after 1971, increasingly Brezhnev) tried to develop more orderly procedures and denounced Khrushchev's "harebrained" schemes, the administrative structure even in 1977 was still rigid and therefore movement was often achieved by informal means. If Romania were to assess correctly what the implication was when a Soviet military commander took a tolerant or intolerant view on the type of challenge that it presented to the Soviet Union, it had to evaluate how such military leaders would achieve their own aims. It is the latter that we will attempt to assess here with the caveat that little is known in the West of certain Soviet decision-making bodies.

The Politburo, a group of the top 15 Soviet party leaders which selected its own members by cooptation, has been the top decision-making body in the Soviet Union. Little is known in the West about this body except that only it could make decisions to go to war, to send troops into another country, to deploy combat troops abroad, or to use nuclear weapons.[31] With the exception of Marshal G. K. Zhukov, who had only a short tenure in 1957, and Marshal Grechko (from May 1973 to April 1976), no military man sat in the Politburo in the postwar period. Thus, if the Soviet military was displeased with Romania's refusal to participate in Warsaw Pact maneuvers between 1964 and 1967, they had to find an indirect channel leading to the Politburo. The Party Secretariat was more concerned with the managerial than the deliberative aspects of party leadership and while Secretary Dimitri Ustinov (later Defense Minister and Politburo member) supervised the country's arms production and defense industries, this organization, because of its limited scope, was not the locus where the military men could best exert their influence.

The body to which the military supplied a great deal of its data has been identified by Western observers as the Defense Committee or the Supreme Military Council.[32] The existence of this committee was first mentioned by David Marks of the U.S. State Department, who described it as "a sort of limited National Security Council."[33] During Khrushchev's time, the Defense Committee was known by such names as the Main, the Higher, or the Supreme Military Council. The purpose was the same after 1965, namely to act as a bridge between the party and the military leadership structure. Khrushchev had used it as a forum for delineating the strategic implications of the advent of nuclear weapons.[34] In the Brezhnev-Kosygin era, the indications are that this trend continued and the Committee discussed broad issues of military policy rather than day-to-day management.[35] There have been no indications that even the promotions of Grechko and then Ustinov (April 1976) to the Politburo changed this. As such it was also a good forum for the very top military leadership—which would have consisted of the Defense Minister, and all the Deputy Ministers (including the Chief of the General Staff)—to exercise their influence.

Marshal Grechko and his predecessor, Marshal Malinovski, had considerable power by virtue of their official positions as ministers. The Council of Ministers was empowered to appoint specialist commissions including ones on military-industrial problems, which in turn had armed forces representation. As well as this power that he had through membership in the Council, the Minister of Defense in the Soviet Union had a considerable role in force deployment.[36] Thus, he performed a professional military function as well as that of political conduit. His opinion on operational matters was bound to carry a significant weight and in this manner Grechko's intolerant line on Eastern Europe—especially Czechoslovakia—made him a dangerous foe to those bloc states which tried to deviate from the Soviet line. When he joined the Politburo in 1975, he further increased the danger to Romania.

Marshal Yakubovsky, as the leader of the Warsaw Pact or Warsaw Treaty Organization (WP or WTO) played a crucial role in the Soviet intervention in Czechoslovakia (although operational command for the actual intervention was under the Commander of the Soviet ground forces, Army General I. G. Pavlovsky) and was generally regarded in the West as intolerant of deviation by bloc states. He took over this command from Grechko when the latter became Minister of Defense in 1967 and his position afforded him a modicum of power. The operational heart of the Warsaw Pact, which was concluded on May 14, 1955, between the Soviet Union and Albania, Bulgaria, Hungary, the G.D.R., Poland, and Romania, was the Joint Armed Forces Command the leadership of which, in the figures of the Commander-in-Chief and his Chief of Staff, was always comprised of Soviet officers. In regard to influencing Soviet military policy, Yakubovsky again benefited from his official position through the manner of integration of the WTO command into the Soviet command structure. The Commander-in-Chief of the Warsaw Pact was ex officio one of the three First Deputy Defense Ministers of the Soviet Union[37] and in this role Yakubovsky had good access to the top decision-making forums in the country.

Marshal Zakharov, in his tenure as Chief of the General Staff, was one of the more outspoken military leaders. His influence derived, however, not only from the forcefulness of his personality (and forceful it was) but also from his official position. The General Staff in the Soviet Union since 1965 has had the command attributes of a central coordinating body and it has been described as akin to a "command in being."[38] It was very much like a braintrust of the armed forces. The Chief of the General Staff also had the ex officio position of a First Deputy Minister, thereby forming an efficient link to the political leadership. Consequently, when Marshal Zakharov obliquely condemned Soviet military adventurism through an attack on the "harebrained" schemes of "self-styled military experts,"[39] he must have had considerable influence on the new Soviet leadership for he stayed on as Chief of the General Staff to the end of his life. While his more tolerant views failed to carry the day on Czechoslovakia in 1968, it nevertheless must have provided some comfort to Romania in 1969 to know that there was no unified Soviet military front calling for her disciplining but rather that Zakharov induced some moderation.

The informal structure also affected the flow of influence within the Soviet military. The military "debate" on aspects of strategic policy in the spring of 1965[40] should not be taken at face value, but it did indicate that there were special "lobbies" within the military itself, for instance the advocates of general-purpose forces or the proponents of more advanced logistics systems. These groups would have viewed rather pluralistically a Romanian refusal to participate in Warsaw Pact maneuvers, their reluctance to participate in a joint anti-aircraft system or their refusal to allow passage to Bulgaria for more than a token number of Soviet troops in the 1970s. There were also some rivalries between the traditionalists or the "old guard" in the Soviet military and the emerging group of new technocrats. While between 1958 and 1960 Khrushchev had trimmed a sizable portion of deadwood from the Soviet military, when Brezhnev and Kosygin took over there was still a tremendous need to infuse new blood into the top military leadership.* The advancement of the younger, better educated officers was naturally resented by the old guard, who represented the Front and Army Commanders of World War II. The generation gap in turn must have produced both friction in the strategic concepts of these leaders and further maneuvering for influence within the military. Again, a challenge or irritation from an East European European state would have been viewed differently by the two groups.

Hence, the scenario of the exercise of influence by the military in the Soviet Union is not that of a solid bloc bent on enforcing military uniformity and loyalty in Eastern Europe. First, the influence of the military in decision making as a whole varied over time with that of the strength of the leadership, the activism or risk taking of Soviet foreign policy, and the evolution of strategic

---

*Gen. Col. P. I. Lukashin, on selection deployment and education of Soviet military cadres in *Krasnaya Zvezda*, August 16, 1966. A general survey (in 1965) of all Soviet officers concluded that one quarter should be recommended for promotion.

concepts. While in the period of 1965 to 1977 the Soviet military may have gained in decision-making influence and were indeed a very powerful force, it is also clear that by far the greater preponderance in foreign policy decision making was constituted by the political elements, particularly the Politburo. Second, there were differences among the various military leaders on strategic concepts, in war experiences, in age, and in education. These differences were compounded by some interservice rivalries. While Romania had to contend with military leaders like Marshals Grechko and Yakubovsky, who insisted on conformity in the Soviet bloc even at the price of having to intervene militarily in a bloc state, it also had the benefit of such men as Marshal Zakharov, who would have rather accepted some military and political diversity than alienate a bloc country through an invasion. His successor as Chief of the General Staff had the redeeming quality, from the Romanian point of view, that in line with his personal military experience and his current military expertise he should have had a relatively modest interest in the Southern Tier of the Warsaw Pact, where Romania is located. It is also of importance that because of the formal and informal structure of the Soviet military, the Chief of the General Staff, especially when he was of the caliber of Marshal Zakharov, wielded considerable influence. Therefore, a more tolerant Soviet Chief of the General Staff must have been of considerable help in retarding and perhaps restraining any drastic Soviet military reaction to a Romanian challenge. While the late Grechko's tenure in the Politburo might have had some negative effects for Romania, his replacement by a nonmilitary technocrat in 1976 and appointments of Kulikov and Ogarkov, both younger "technicians," as Commander-in-Chief of the WTO and Chief of the General Staff of the Soviet Army respectively, in January 1977, must have presented valuable advantages. Since Romania was not faced with a united hardline group of Soviet generals urging the politicians to stop any moves of autonomy through military intervention, there was some balance, and if the Soviet ever contemplated such a move during this period it is unlikely that it would have been caused primarily by pressure from military men.

Again, Romania had to understand and gauge correctly the nuances of power and influence in the Soviet Union before it could take full advantage of them. Bucharest expended large sums of money for monitoring the foreign policies of its neighbors through the use of party and academic institutions. In analyzing Soviet policies it had the advantage of dealing with a decision-making process similar to its own. Nevertheless, a true assessment of Romanian understanding can only be derived from its behavior. Flexibility, in the sense of an ability to foresee certain Soviet actions and to adjust to the shifts in Moscow's policies, would provide proof of Romanian understanding. Furthermore, Romanian actions that would have countered Soviet pressures would also have demonstrated Romanian awareness. Therefore, it was Romanian actions and reactions at points of disagreement that would have indicated the accuracy of the Romanian perception of Soviet policy and its formulation.

SOVIET INTERPRETATION OF ROMANIAN ACTIVITIES IN THE MILITARY SPHERE

As Soviet military policy evolved, each Romanian move that deviated from Soviet wishes would have represented a different type of challenge to the Soviet Union and would have brought a different type of response or restriction. Such Romanian moves, as we have seen, had a wide scope and involved such actions as unilateral Romanian troop and length of military service reductions (which constituted foreign policy as well since Romania was a member of the WTO), call for the abolition of military blocs, refusal to take part in Warsaw Pact maneuvers, the passage of restrictive laws on the movement of foreign troops through Romanian territory, constant public reiteration of the defensive nature of the Warsaw Pact, maintenance of military contacts with China and Yugoslavia, the passage 1972 of an "all-horizons" defense law, Romanian refusal in 1974 to allow the construction of a wide-gauge railway from the Soviet Union to Bulgaria which could have been used to carry Soviet troops, its refusal to allow passage to more than a token number of Soviet troops to maneuvers to Bulgaria in the summer of the same year, and finally Romania's continued pressure in 1976 for the transformation of the Warsaw Pact. These Romanian actions seemed to present a challenge to the Soviet Union in Western opinion; it would be helpful, though, to ascertain whether the Soviets in fact took cognizance at all of these Romanian actions.

As with its economic policies, Romania took a different line in its military affairs from the Soviet prescription before Ceausescu came to power in 1965. After joint Warsaw Pact military maneuvers in Bulgaria during 1963 Romania appeared to develop some sharp differences with the Soviet Union, for it refused to proceed with an expected visit to Moscow of its Defense Minister Leontin Salajan until the Soviet military contingent passing through its territory had been withdrawn.[41] The following year Romania again demonstrated its autonomous stance by unilaterally reducing the term of military service to sixteen months and by further reducing the size of its army.[42] It was also at the end of 1964 that Romania rather surreptitiously reasserted its right to Bessarabia. It did this by "uncovering" and publishing an obscure paper of Marx, in which he castigated Czarist policies toward the Romanian majority in that province.*

While there was no Soviet invasion of Romania, or a toppling of the Gheorghiu-Dej regime, the Soviet Union definitely took the Romanian moves as challenges. Military aid to Romania was curtailed and it was given mostly obsolete heavy armaments. The Soviet Union also replied to Romanian encouragement of irredentism with some veiled statements on the rights of the very substantial

---

*The 20,000 copies were sold out in two days after their release.[43]

Hungarian minority in Transylvania.* The precedent of military challenge to the Soviet Union was thus already set by Romania when Ceausescu came to power.

The pattern of autonomous Romanian military policy continued under Ceausescu and in 1966 he called for the abolition of military blocs.[44] During this time Romania also put forward three proposals for reforming the Warsaw Pact: (1) that the command of the Alliance be rotated instead of leaving it in the hands of Soviet Marshals; (2) that there should be unanimity in decision making, particularly in the use of nuclear arms from the territory of a member state; (3) and finally, that financial support for Soviet forces in the German Democratic Republic, Hungary, and Poland should be borne only by those countries where they were stationed, instead of all the members.[45] The lack of implementation of these suggestions are the least indication of Soviet displeasure at Romania. There were further holdups in the delivery of Soviet equipment and the relationship between the two countries deteriorated to the point where Romania did not participate in joint maneuvers until the end of 1967.

Romania posed what was seen as a particularly blatant military challenge to the Soviet Union during the months prior to the intervention in Czechoslovakia when it indicated that it was unwilling to participate in any action against the Dubcek government. Moreover, in the days following the intervention, Ceausescu denounced the whole move in no uncertain terms and called for the withdrawal of the WP troops.[46] Shortly before the intervention in Czechoslovakia in 1968, the Romanians passed a law which gave the Grand National Assembly the exclusive power to authorize the entry of foreign troops into the country—all this at a time when the Assembly was having its long summer recess.[47] As a further irritation to the Soviet Union, Romania, on September 7, 1968, received the British Foreign Secretary Michael Steward on an official visit after the latter had canceled similar visits to Hungary and Bulgaria as a sign of British displeasure at their role in the intervention.[48]

That the Kremlin at least took cognizance of the Romanian actions in 1968 as an irritant is beyond any doubt. *Pravda* vehemently denounced Romanian and Yugoslavian support for the Dubcek leadership following the intervention into Czechoslovakia:

The imperialist circles which are whipping up political hysteria in their countries and in the U.N. have now rushed to their (the counter-

---

*Soviet use of the Hungarian minority rights as a counter to Romanian questions about the provinces that it had to cede to the Soviet Union in 1940 continued during the 1960s and 1970s. The Hungarian press, especially the party newspaper *Nepszabadag* (December 2 and 3, 1964, at Soviet instigation), severely criticized the Romanian treatment of Hungarians. During August 2–8, 1971, the Soviets held military maneuvers with Hungarian and Czechoslovak troops on the Hungarian-Romanian border.

revolutionaries') assistance. It is noteworthy that the leaders of Yugoslavia and Romania who are giving active assistance to the Czechoslovakian anti-Socialist forces have joined this imperialist chorus. And it is precisely in Belgrade and Bucharest that the political adventurers from Prague who find themselves outside Czechoslovakia during this period are weaving their intrigues.[49]

A Soviet accusation of harboring counterrevolutionaries could not be taken lightly by any Soviet-bloc state and since it came on the heels of the suppression of the Czechoslovak regime, Romania had particular cause to worry. Nor was this Soviet attack an isolated case. On September 4, 1968, Nikolai Gribachev, in a very lengthy article in *Pravda*, proceeded to denounce Romanian policy under the guise of denouncing the Romanian writer D. Cobria, who had written an article supporting the Czechoslovak leadership.[50] Gribachev first reminded Cobria, and thereby Romania, that without the help of the Soviet army the country would still be under the rule of the Iron Guard (fascists), whereas now Romania was a member of the Warsaw Pact and had a Socialist system under which it had made tremendous progress. Therefore, in his opinion, it should have been on alert against counterrevolutionaries and Western imperialists who sought to take it and other Socialist countries into the Western orbit.[51]

More than just warning Romania not to denounce the invasion and not to harbor Czechoslovak dissidents, Gribachev also hinted that the Soviet Union may have been making some military moves to back up its demands and obliquely warned against any Romanian military countermoves. Using the frequent Soviet ploy of citing Western reports to discredit, or at times fuel, certain bloc-state actions or fears, he denounced Western allegations of a Soviet buildup of troops on the Romanian borders as Western attempts at intimidating Romania. But, in view of the fact that Moscow dismissed in a similar manner Western reports of Soviet military buildups prior to the Czechoslovak intervention, new denials would have only added more credence to the rumors, and thereby should have intimidated Romania. Gribachev also ridiculed Western reports (in the *Observer*, for instance) that Romania was displaying "an obstinate militancy, that it is training its militia whose numbers exceed that of the regular army, that workers have been armed and receiving training, and that Romania is purchasing captured Soviet arms from Israel. . . . This is designed to frighten the Soviet people." Therefore, Gribachev was signaling to Romania that its military preparations could be construed as a provocation to the Soviet Union. In repeating (though in a disparaging way) the Western allegations that Romania had found an alternate source of military supplies, and particularly one as inimical from the Soviet point of view as Israel, Gribachev indicated that the Soviet government perceived a serious challenge. Moreover, the Kremlin even took Michael Steward's visit as an affront and mentioned that the West saw the very hospitable reception the Romanians accorded him as a symbolic challenge to the Warsaw Pact and Romania's immediate neighbors.[52]

Romanian contacts with Yugoslavia were also suspect to the Soviet Union because it feared the establishment of a Balkan state's bloc or even a Yugoslav-Romanian alliance. When Tito and Ceausescu met at the joint Iron Gates hydro-electric and navigation project on September 20, 1969 (following a prior meeting in July of that year at Turnu-Severin on the Romanian side and Kladovo on the Yugoslav side), they felt the need to issue a statement designed to reassure the Soviet Union that the meeting was not directed against it.[53]

During the first part of 1970 Romania again demonstrated its autonomous military view when its Minister of Defense, General-Colonel Ion Ionita,* wrote in an article in *Scinteia* that Romania's military obligations were restricted to the Warsaw Pact, whose role in turn was to defend member countries against an imperialist attack on Europe.[54] The following week *Scinteia* reiterated Romania's view of a defensive Warsaw Pact and stated explicitly that not only was its army taking orders solely from the Romanian leaders but that any outside interference in affairs of the country or of the army would not be tolerated.[55] It should be pointed out that these Romanian statements came in the wake of the signing of a new Treaty of Friendship and Mutual Aid between Czechoslovakia and the Soviet Union, wherein the former virtually agreed to pursue a joint foreign policy with the latter. Also, back in January of that year, Army General Shtemenko, the Chief of Staff of the Warsaw Pact, wrote of the organization's powerful combined armed forces, which were now allocated by member governments to the combined command.[56] The combined Warsaw Pact command had existed since 1956 but there had been no major military integration. Nevertheless, Marshal Grechko further reiterated the moves toward military integration in the Warsaw Pact in February.[57] It is noteworthy, then, that as late as September 1970, two and a half months after the Romanians signed a treaty of cooperation with the Soviet Union, Ceausescu emphasized at a Romanian military conference that their forces would continue to take their orders from Romanian authorities while continuing to cooperate with all Socialist states, without exception.[58]

The Soviet Union reacted to these Romanian statements of 1970 and it should be remembered that a great state need not use force in international relations to achieve its aims vis-a-vis a small power, but often the threat of force suffices. During July 1–9, 1970, the Soviet Union held Warsaw Pact staff exercises with other member states (but excluding Romania) close to the Romanian border in Hungary.[59] These exercises could have been easily interpreted by Romania as at least a sign of Soviet displeasure.

---

*Romanian military ranks, as in the Soviet Union, do not correspond in translation to Western rank. General-Major, for instance, is the first rank above Colonel, while General-Lieutenant is the equivalent of Major-General in the U.S. Therefore we felt that giving the rank as it appears in Romania should avoid confusion.

On July 8, 1970, Romania signed a treaty of friendship and mutual aid with the Soviet Union, which, despite the inclusion of certain concessions to the Soviet Union, firmly asserted Romanian military autonomy.[60] The treaty differed significantly from that signed between Moscow and Prague. There was no reference to collective obligations of Socialist countries to come to the defense of Socialist achievements, while on the question of foreign policy coordination both parties agreed only to "consult." Moscow did manage to include a clause in the treaty regarding defense against any state or group who would engage in aggression against a Warsaw Pact state, thereby trying to extend the treaty beyond Europe. Romania, however, emphasized the defensive nature of the Warsaw Pact right at the signing of the treaty. The Romanian signatory of the treaty, Premier Gheorghe Maurer, himself stressed this limited power of the treaty and the Warsaw Pact when he declared following the signing in Moscow, that Romania was determined to "honor meticulously the commitments assumed within the framework of the defensive Warsaw Treaty."[61] Thus, no intervention or interference could be allowed in Romania's internal policies, and in a little veiled statement Maurer also insisted on Romania's right to good relations with the Soviet Union's arch-enemy, China, when he said that his country intended to develop good relations with "all countries of the world Socialist system."[62] The fact that Maurer's full statement was published in *Pravda* indicated that the Soviet leaders were aware of Romania's autonomous position even if they did not consider it an outright challenge.

Romania's relations with China consisted of multiple ties ranging from economic to military and the Soviet Union appeared particularly irked by Ceausescu's visit to China in the spring of 1971. The several exchange visits by Romanian and Chinese military and political delegations seemed to reach their zenith with Ceausescu's tumultuous welcome in Peking. The elaborate Chinese praises for Ceausescu's autonomous position highlighted the potential challenge that Sino-Romanian ties presented to the Soviet Union. The Soviet leaders indicated their displeasure with Romania's refusal to conform with bloc policy through its association with the "renegade of the Socialist camp," China, in an important article published by General-Major Ye Sulimov.[63] First of all, he asserted that the defense of the Socialist system required that "no Socialist state remain neutral."[64] Furthermore, whereas Sulimov directed his argument mainly against imperialism, in view of Soviet allegations that China was imperialistic and anti-Socialist, the article also showed a Soviet annoyance at Romania's attempt to play at neutrality in the Sino-Soviet dispute.

In December 1972 a draft of a new defense law was presented to the Romanian Grand National Assembly. The law bound all Romanian leaders to act against any incursion upon Romanian territory and made illegal any cession of territory during war.[65] This decree, which was modeled on the Yugoslav defense law, seemed to be designed for a Czechoslovak 1968 type situation. While the Soviet Union made no public protest regarding the proposed law, there are indications of severe displeasure with Romania. In December 1972, K. F. Katushev, the Soviet Secretary in charge of relations with ruling Communist parties, called in the Romanian ambassador to Moscow for consultation.[66] Furthermore, the December 23, 1972, meeting between Brezhnev and Ceausescu in Moscow was characterized by considerable coolness and indications of disagreement. Whereas Brezhnev's meetings with all the other bloc leaders were supposed to have taken place in "an atmosphere of cordiality, friendship and *complete unity*,"[67] the meeting with Ceausescu took place "in a friendly and frank atmosphere"—the Soviet code words for disagreement.

After 1972 Romania challenges to the Soviet Union more or less reached a plateau. Something of a high point may have been reached during 1974 when Romania apparently refused to grant the Soviet Union a right to build a new wide-gauge strategic railway from Odessa to Varna, Bulgaria, across the Romanian area of Dobrogea, which would likely have been used to transport troops and equipment from the Soviet Union to Bulgaria. Furthermore the Romanians refused passage to Soviet troops which were to take part in summer maneuvers in Bulgaria. Romanian officials, according to Western sources, even circulated rumors that the Soviet Union was attempting to secure a permanent corridor to Bulgaria through Romanian territory.[68] Romania did allow a limited number of Soviet vehicles passage rights, in fact, but these were escorted by Romanian military vehicles.[69] That the Soviet Union took cognizance of these challenges was illustrated by the rather radical step taken by Moscow in issuing a denial in *Pravda* that there was a rift between Romania and the Soviet Union or that they were pressuring Bucharest to allow transit of Soviet troops across the country.[70]

At the 1974 Political Consultative Session of the Warsaw Pact, Romania had proposed the creation of a committee of foreign ministers. During 1975, and particularly in 1976 it pressed very strongly for this. This action plus Romania's rumored attempts to seek purchases of armaments from Western countries during 1975 and 1976[71] increased the disagreement level between the Soviet Union and Romania by 1976. In June 1976 K. F. Katushev and the Chief of the Main Political Administration of Soviet armed forces, General Yepishev, paid a visit to Bucharest shortly before the replacement of Romanian Minister of Defense. This may have seemed innocuous enough taken by itself, but during the first part of the year several "scholarly" articles appeared in Soviet, Hungarian, and Bulgarian publications that appeared to reopen the question of Romania's right to certain parts of its present territory.[72] There were also rumors that during the visit to Romania by Katushev in June the Soviet Union had moved up troops to the Romanian border.[73] While it is difficult to corroborate these rumors it is noteworthy that the Romanian military's newspaper reporting on Ceausescu's friendly meeting with Brezhnev in August at a Crimean resort had a front-page editorial stressing the great readiness of the Romanian army to fight, and reprinted Ceausescu's dictum that everyone must be ready for the defense of the country.[74]

Thus, it appears that the Soviet Union took cognizance of Romanian moves of autonomy that had military implications, considered them a form of challenge, and voiced its disapproval. What this rather cursory preliminary analysis of Romanian challenges was designed to show was that they were not offered in a vacuum of Soviet disinterest. While this, we submit, has been shown, the initial Soviet signs of disapproval do not really indicate the limits that self-perceived Soviet needs of security set on Romanian foreign policy. During the 1960s Western opinion held on occasions that Romania was about to be invaded for breaking the limits of Soviet tolerance. *U.S. News and World Report* claimed that Soviet troop maneuvers during February 1969, in various parts of Eastern Europe and on the Soviet borders with Romania, could be a prelude to the specific type of maneuver which culminated in the military intervention into Czechoslovakia and which now would be targeted against Romania.[75] There was also a claim in September 1969 by the Albanian Communist Party paper *Zeri i Populit* that Soviet troops were massing on the Soviet-Romanian borders in addition to the four Soviet divisions stationed in Hungary, which were taking up action positions.[76]

Whether cognizance of Romanian military actions as challenges—and again we emphasize that the military factor in the Soviet Union is tied in with political and ideological ones—meant that, as the West and Albania suspected, the Kremlin was ready to enforce its views through military action, is the focus of the next chapter.

In this chapter we have attempted to assess only the limits that the Soviet Union placed on Romanian foreign policy autonomy as far as it was determined by the former's theoretical military perception of its security needs. While the concept of external security encompasses political-ideological, legal, as well as military determinants, the last one still remained a key determinant during the 1960s and 1970s. Military security itself is not an objective concept but rather it incorporates a mass of objective and subjective factors that are not necessarily of an exclusive military nature and among which the subjective factor of ideology played no small part in the Soviet Union.

Soviet military policy reflected its security perception and to be able to analyze the former we tried to examine, with the limitation on information that exists in the West, the inputs that went into the formulation of this policy. Among these inputs, the role of the military was significant but we believe that the formal and informal structure of Soviet policymaking, even in military policy, restricted the military to the position of only a powerful advisor. On closer examination it also turned out that what is called the "Soviet military," as in the case of other states, was far from being a homogenous body which advocated restrictive policies of enforcing strict military conformity within the bloc, regardless of the strategic importance of a challenge or of the cost/benefits of enforcement. Romania was faced with both tolerant and intolerant influential Soviet military leaders. Therefore, the military input into Soviet decision making vis-a-vis Romanian challenges was characterized by some flexibility which could have acted as a form of defense for Romanian policies.

The weight that the Soviets placed on these challenges was closely linked with the evolution of their military policy which was a reflection of their general security perception. The military policy incorporated both global, European, and East European concerns. It is this policy, then, that should place the Romanian challenges in proper perspective.

NOTES

1. *U.S. News and World Report*, February 27, 1969, p. 64.

2. See K. J. Twitchett, *International Security* (London: Oxford University Press, 1971), pp. 1–19, for a broader discussion of these concepts.

3. F. H. Hartmann, *The Relations of Nations* (New York: The Macmillan Co., 1967), p. 14.

4. K. J. Holsti, *International Politics* (Englewood Cliffs: Prentice-Hall, 1967), p. 126.

5. Alan James, *The Role of Force in International and U.N. Peace Keeping* (Enstone, Oxford: Ditchley Foundation, 1969), pp. 7–8.

6. J. F. Triska and D. D. Finley, *Soviet Foreign Policy* (New York: The Macmillan Co., 1968), p. 346.

7. For a concise penetrating discussion of the subject see R. L. Garthoff, *Soviet Military Policy* (London: Faber and Faber, 1966), pp. 3–9.

8. M. Florinsky, "The Russian Mobilization of 1914," *Political Science Quarterly*, June 1927. Also see D. Sazonov, *Fateful Years 1909 1916* (London: Jonathan Cape, 1928), pp. 195–214.

9. J. Erickson, "The Soviet Military Effort," BBC Radio 3, December 20, 1971.

10. J. R. Thomas, "Soviet Foreign Policy and the Military," *Survey* vol. 17, no. 3, 1971, p. 134.

11. See *The Military Balance 1965–1966* (London: International Institute for Strategic Studies [IISS], 1965), p. 2, and *The Military Balance 1970–1971* (London: IISS, 1970), p. 6.

12. *The Military Balance 1977–1978* (London: IISS, 1977), pp. 8–11.

13. M. P. Gallagher and K. F. Spielmann, Jr., *Soviet Decision Making for Defense* (New York: Praeger, 1972), p. 43.

14. *Pravda*, May 9, 1968, and see C. Ducval, "Disarray among the Soviet Marshals," *Radio Liberty Research*, May 22, 1969, p. 1.

15. Ibid., p. 3.

16. *Pravda*, May 9, 1969.

17. Marshal Yakubovsky, *Krasnaya Zvezda* (Moscow), May 9, 1968.

18. Marshal Yakubovsky, *Sovetskaya Rossiya* (Moscow), May 9, 1969.

19. Marshal M. V. Zakharov, *Izvestia*, May 9, 1969.

20. J. R. Thomas, "Limits of an Alliance: The 1958 Quemay Crisis" in R. Garthoff, ed., *Sino-Soviet Military Relations* (New York: Praeger, 1966).

21. J. Erickson, *Soviet Military Power* (Whitehall, London: RUSI, 1971), p. 29.

22. Tass International Service in English, February 5, 1970, "Logical questions involved in further development of friendship between Soviet armed forces and the Czechoslovak army" in Thomas, "Soviet Foreign Policy... ," op. cit., p. 135.

23. Thomas, "Soviet Foreign Policy... ," op. cit., p. 136.

24. Marshal M. V. Zakharov, ed., *Final Istoriko me muvuyi ocherk o-razgrome Imperialistichestka Yaponii v 1945 godn*, 2nd ed. (Moscow: Nauko, 1969) in Erickson, "The Soviet Military... ," op. cit., p. 27.

25. *Radio Moscow Domestic Service* 0830 G.M.T., September 23, 1971 in *Radio Liberty Research CRD 285/71* Radio Liberty, Munich, September 2, 1971, p. 2.

26. Ibid.

27. Ibid.

28. *Guardian*, January 10, 1977.

29. Erickson, *Soviet Military Power*, op. cit., p. 29.

30. Gallagher and Spielmann, op. cit., p. 22.

31. M. Mackintosh, "The Soviet Military Influence on Foreign Policy," *Problems of Communism*, September–October 1973, p. 3.

32. Erickson, *Soviet Military Power*, op. cit., p. 29.

33. D. Mark, in U.S., Congress, *Subcommittee on Economy in Government and National Economic Priorities (Part III)*, 91st Cong., 1st sess., June 1969, p. 956.

34. See T. W. Wolfe, *The Soviet Military Scene: Institutional and Defense Policy Considerations*, Rand Memorandum R.M.–4913 PR, June 1977, pp. 11–12.

35. Gallagher and Spielmann, op. cit., p. 19.

36. See Mackintosh, op. cit., p. 3.

37. A. Braun, "The Evolution of the Warsaw Pact," *Canadian Defence Quarterly* (Toronto), Winter 1973–74, p. 31.

38. Erickson, *Soviet Military Power*, op. cit., p. 27.

39. M. V. Zakharov, *Krasnaya Zvezda*, February 4, 1965.

40. Erickson, *Soviet Military Power*, op. cit., p. 7.

41. Garthoff, op. cit., p. 139.

42. *The Military Balance 1964-1965* (London: IISS, 1964), p. 6 and the *Christian Science Monitor*, June 21, 1965.

43. Andrei Otetea, *Notes on Romanians* (Bucharest: Editura Stiintifica, 1964).

44. *Scinteia*, May 7, 1966.

45. New York *Times*, May 17 and May 29, 1966.

46. *Scinteia*, August 22-23, 1968.

47. J. Guillem-Bralon, *Le Figaro*, July 29, 1971.

48. *Scinteia* September 8, 1968.

49. *Pravda*, August 25, 1968, translated in *Current Digest of the Soviet Press*, Joint Committee on Slavic Studies, vol. 20, no. 36, August 28, 1968.

50. D. Cobria, "Czechoslovakia, Friend I am with you" in *Luceafarul*, (Bucharest) August 31, 1968, *Journal of the Writers' Union of Romania.*

51. N. Gribachev, "Prophets and Lessons," *Pravda*, September 4, 1968, p. 3, translated in *Current Digest of the Soviet Press*, vol. 20, no. 36, 1968.

52. *Pravda*, September 8, 1968.

53. *Scinteia*, September 21, 1969.

54. *Scinteia* May 7, 1970.

55. *Scinteia*, May 13, 1970.

56. *Krasnaya Zvezda*, January 24, 1970.

57. See article on Marshal Grechko's position in the *Economist*, February 21, 1970.

58. Ceausescu's speeches in *Scinteia*, September 27 and 28, 1970.

59. *Pravda*, July 1, 1970, pp. 1, 4.

60. For full text of the treaty see *Scinteia*, July 8, 1970, or *Pravda*, July 8, 1970.

61. *Scinteia*, July 8, 1970, and *Pravda*, July 8, 1970, pp. 3-4.

62. Ibid.

63. "Defense of the Socialist Homeland," *Kommunist Vooruzhennykh sil.*, April 1971, pp. 18-24.

64. Ibid., p. 18.

65. *Scinteia*, December 27, 1972.

66. *Pravda*, December 8, 1972, p. 5.

67. *Pravda*, December 24, 1972, p. 1.

68. New York *Times*, August 22, 1974.

69. Ibid.

70. *Pravda*, July 29, 1974.

71. *Times* (London), August 10, 1975, August 18, 1975.

72. New York *Times*, May 31, 1976 and June 26, 1976.

73. T. Rakowska-Harmstone, "Socialist Internationalism Part II," *Survey* Spring 1976, p. 72.

74. *Apararea Patriei*, August 11, 1976.

75. *U.S. News and World Report*, February 27, 1969, p. 64.

76. As reported by Tad Szulc in the *International Herald Tribune* (Paris), September 6, 1969, p. 5.

4

Soviet Military Limitations
on Romanian Foreign Policy
Challenges

The analysis of Soviet military policies and actions toward Eastern Europe necessitates some clarification of methodology. It is not the purpose of this chapter to establish predictive formulae or equations for Soviet military behavior toward Romania, though some predictions may be extrapolated from the analysis, but rather it is to interpret past Soviet policy. While the focus will be on certain periods of discord between Romania and the Soviet Union, the broader analysis of general Soviet military policy will rely considerably on the works of differing authorities in the field such as John Erickson, Malcolm Mackintosh, Raymond Garthoff, T. W. Wolfe, and Michel Garder. The caveat will be that military capabilities do not equate with intention, though they certainly allow for greater flexibility. Whereas the emergence of systems analysis in the 1960s as the principal tool of defense-policy planning in the United States provided a very valuable instrument for the resolution of many military problems, it was not very useful in the analysis of Soviet or East European military policy, even through a methodological reversal of its logical procession. In other words we believe that the Soviet strategic goals could not be defined by using a reverse process from the identification of a certain Soviet weapon system or military capability. If one analyzes past policy, however, an identification of both goals and capabilities would certainly illuminate with greater clarity the general military policy.

In looking at Soviet policy formation in the previous chapter, we employed a rather loose combination of the Organizational Process and Bureaucratic Process Models[1] by examining the importance of institutional interests and the influence of groups and individuals within the bureaucratic system. In this chapter the methodology will involve a blending of the topical and chronological approach with an attempt to keep a division between what is, and what is not known in the field.

By placing the Romanian challenges into the perspective of Soviet military policy, as the latter evolved through the period of the study, we hope to be able to ascertain some of the limitations for Romanian foreign policies as well as to gauge some of the available defenses.

Once the Soviet Union felt that its security was seriously threatened in Eastern Europe, it acted through various military means to protect itself—a phenomenon not peculiar to Moscow. In these instances, the motto appears to have been *nemo me impune lacessit*. It is of importance, though, to ascertain whether there was a pattern to Soviet military action in Eastern Europe. If there was a discernible pattern, it would have been essential for a country like Romania to recognize the types of actions by an East European state, and the circumstances which prompted, or were likely to prompt, Soviet intervention. A pattern would also indicate what constituted the attempt or "go-position" for Soviet military intervention in the bloc countries. This "go-position" may not be sharply delineated during a crisis but for the present definition it would suffice for it to be represented by a point in the crisis at which the Soviet Union was more likely to act than not, in other words when the preparations were complete and there was a preponderance of evidence pointing to Soviet military intervention.

Soviet and Warsaw Pact joint maneuvers have encompassed purposes other than just enhancing military preparedness. Military interventions by the Soviet Union have usually been preceded by some other military moves. Maneuvers, moreover, have the potential to be utilized as a tool for exerting pressure or intimidation against certain nations or groups of nations. For this reason it should be useful to look at the major Soviet and Warsaw Pact maneuvers to discern whether they ever signaled a readiness for military intervention into Romania, or attempts at intimidations, which in turn would have indicated the limits imposed by the Soviet Union on the degree of foreign policy autonomy it would tolerate from Bucharest. All this should again reveal what passive and active defenses were available for Romania.

When Ceausescu succeeded Gheorghiu-Dej, Romania had, as has been seen, already posed a number of important challenges to Moscow. The Soviet Union took cognizance of all of these Romanian assertions of autonomy of foreign policy, and, therefore, the precedent of challenge was established for Ceausescu. The military challenges, moreover, tied in with the entire evolution of Soviet policy up to the time of Khrushchev's political demise.

The end of World War II left Stalin with a tremendous preponderance of military force in Europe, particularly in the eastern half. Subsequently Soviet military policy never lost sight of this fact, and blended it in with the historical Russian view of Europe and postwar strategic developments. The Soviet Union, despite its massive forces in 1945, was still basically a land power and very much Europe-centered. Within Europe the Soviets felt that they had a special case for the domination of Eastern Europe. As Malcolm Mackintosh has written:

> The Soviet attitude to East and Central Europe is based mainly on a combination of military and political factors; politically it is essential that the Soviet-dominated part of the Communist world should include the countries bordering on European Russia; militarily, the Soviet Union needs the "buffer zone" to the West of its frontiers for defensive, internal security and offensive reasons.[2]

Whether one accepts the view that Eastern Europe was to serve as an offensive base or the revisionist view that it was to serve merely defensive buffer purposes there can be little doubt that it was considered to be of great significance by Stalin. He treated Eastern Europe by and large as conquered territory and Romania, which had switched to the Allied side at the eleventh hour, on August 23, 1944, did not escape such treatment. For Stalin, it was the geographic area of Eastern Europe which was of significance, for, with a few exceptions, the Soviet leaders could not count on the reliability of the East European armies, even if they had taken the risks attendant with rearming them.

In the early 1950s though, the buffer zone was imbued with a new dimension as the Soviets extended their air-defense network into the entire belt of East European states to give them protection against American bombers stationed in Western Europe. This network, which extended into Romania,* provided them with a significant improvement in anti-bomber defenses. By the time Khrushchev ascended to power, the Soviet Union had begun to gravitate away from a foreign and military policy which was essentially continental in scope to one entailing an increasingly global perspective. To a great extent, this was occasioned by the development of nuclear weapons and the strategic evolution of the Soviet military forces under Khrushchev. While the Soviet Union only began to have a long-range nuclear capability after 1958[3] (and even then, for several years it amounted only to a kind of *force de frappe*), the effect of nuclear weapons on Khrushchev's thinking was overwhelming. He declared before the 20th Communist Party Congress in February 1956 that, because of the might of the Socialist camp, war was no longer "fatalistically inevitable."[4] Whereas this was a less morale-destroying statement than Malenkov's contention that nuclear war would mean the destruction of Socialist and capitalist countries alike, it demonstrated official Soviet recognition of the destructiveness of nuclear weapons and a willingness on Khrushchev's part to reorient Soviet military policy accordingly. Within the scope of this new policy the significance of Eastern Europe as well as the demands that the Soviet Union would place on it would have changed. A challenge by Romania to the requirements of military conformity would have evoked a different response from that of Stalin—for the response would have been in line with the new general Soviet military aims.

Guardian (Manchester) on May 1, 1958, reported that Soviet guided-missile bases had been established in Romania along the Black Sea coast and in the Carpathian mountains.

When Romania in 1964 unilaterally reduced its armed forces and the introduction time for military personnel, as well as ceasing to participate in further Warsaw Pact maneuvers, it not only diminished its own defense capacity but also reduced its contribution to the general defense of Socialism. Hungary, which decided to pull out of the Warsaw Pact in 1956, discovered that such a military challenge, when coupled with its ideological challenge to the Soviet Union and Socialism, resulted in a prompt Soviet military intervention. While neither the political nor the military challenge posed by the Romanians was nearly as serious, they were potentially dangerous for Bucharest, since the function of the East European forces in Soviet military calculations increased radically under Khrushchev. Despite the Hungarian Revolt, the Soviet leaders placed greater confidence in the East European forces as they became more confident of their reliability. This, as will be seen later, was demonstrated in the reequipment of the WP forces. Within these reassessments, after 1956, partly to ease friction, the Soviet Union negotiated a series of bilateral "status of forces" agreements with various East European states,* and in 1958, for instance, Moscow withdrew its troops from Romania.

The destructiveness of nuclear weapons also induced Khrushchev to believe that he could provide adquate defenses for the Socialist realm by the use of a minimum strategic deterrence force and through repeated pronouncements threatening massive nuclear retaliation. He believed that he could make such a "minimum deterrence" effective by imbuing the Soviet strategic doctrine and the armed forces with a "single incredible option-nuclear war," as John Erickson has written.[6] This reorientation was in part reflected by the rather massive troop reductions effected by Khrushchev between 1955 and 1958.† He proposed further sizable reductions of forces amounting to 1.2 million men on January 5, 1960, but this did not occur because he professed in 1961 that the international pressures at that time did not warrant it.[7]

There is some controversy as to how strongly the military cuts that Khrushchev did effectuate affected Soviet conventional strength—these opinions ranging from the hypothesis that he allowed them to run down,‡ to the contention that he only wished to increase their capabilities while streamlining them (and this involved increased nuclearization).[9] But even if we accept the proposition that Khrushchev was only streamlining the conventional forces, it is apparent that there was an attempt to save on costs, for it is known that the Soviet economy did require massive infusions of funds for the purpose of industrialization. While economic necessities should not be overrated as a causative factor in the reduc-

---

*With Poland in December 1956; with the G.D.R. in March 1957; with Romania, April 1957; with Hungary, May 1957.[5]

†It was reported in *O.F.N.S.* No. 13513, June 3, 1958, "Soviet Survey" that the cut in Soviet forces between 1955 and 1958 totaled 2.14 million troops.

‡Erickson felt that this was the view of the Soviet military.[8]

tion of Soviet forces,[10] Khrushchev did allocate the minimum funds possible for the conventional forces and, as the Cuban missile crisis demonstrated, for the strategic forces as well.

In view of the previous Soviet emphasis on the military security of mass, it would have been unusual if Khrushchev's minimalist approach had been accepted quiescently. The Marshals who had led vast field armies in World War II were unlikely to be content with a mainly nuclear option—and in fact there is evidence of discord. Marshal Konev resigned (officially, for health reasons) as Commander-in-Chief of the Warsaw Pact in 1960[11] to be replaced by Marshal Grechko, who had served with Khrushchev in the Ukraine, while Marshal Zakharov replaced Marshal Sokolovsky as Chief of the Soviet General Staff[12] in the same year.

A solution that would have satisfied both the desire of the traditionalists in the army for conventional mass, and the need of the economy to secure additional funds for industrialization, lay in an increased utilization of the Soviet-bloc nations' military forces. This was put into effect by Khrushchev after 1960 when he began to stress closer military cooperation with Eastern Europe and took concrete measures to improve the efficiency of the Warsaw Pact forces. Included in this was the extension of the mission of these forces from a primary emphasis on defense to a more active joint role in defensive and offensive theater operations.[13] In turn, this entailed joint maneuvers and reequipment. In the early 1960s, therefore, these bloc forces were furnished with new T54 and T55 tanks, anti-tank missiles, self-propelled artillery, and supersonic Mig 21 and S.U. 7 aircraft.[14] These bloc forces, then, augmented considerably the Soviet forces in Europe, which still remained substantial after the retraction of Khrushchev's plan for new cuts in 1960.

With the additional Soviet emphasis on the Warsaw Pact nations in the 1960s Romanian challenges of autonomous foreign policy also inveighed against this Soviet institutional structure. Thus the limits of Romanian autonomy were also influenced by the evolution of the Pact within the larger evolution of Soviet military policy. The Pact established on May 14, 1955, was to serve, according to the Soviet Union, as a counter to the North Atlantic Treaty Organization and as an indicator of the strong Soviet reaction against the rearmament of West Germany. Others, especially in the West, have advanced the argument that the Pact signified the conclusion of a development—a propagandist's culmination of the military integration of Eastern Europe under supreme Soviet command.[15]

Whichever hypothesis for the formation of the WTO is the most valid one, the most significant factor here is the institutional importance that the Soviet Union attached to it. For Moscow demonstrated domestically and externally that it was loath to tolerate challenges to institutions that it deemed essential. Even the latter hypothesis for the Pact formation, however, is predicated on the assumption that the Soviet Union was merely consolidating a prior development and not initiating a new, institutionally led one. In fact, the early evolution of the WTO toward a cohesion institution was quite modest. Supreme authority was to be vested in the hands of the Political Consultative Committee (PCC), which was composed of the First Secretaries of parties, chiefs of states, foreign ministers, and defense ministers. Two auxiliary committees were also established in 1956; a standing committee to work out recommendations on questions of foreign policy; and a Joint Secretariat which was to be staffed by representatives of all the treaty members. The PCC was to confer at least twice a year, but during the first five years it only convened for a total of three times,[16] with the most important one being that of 1958 when a decision was reached to the effect that Soviet troops would be withdrawn from Romania, and that a Joint Armed Forces Command (stationed again in Moscow), would be established.[17] In 1969 the Council of Defense Ministers was established as the highest military body in the Pact,[18] and in 1976 a Committee of Foreign Ministers and a unified Secretariat was added,[19] but it was the Joint Command headed by a Soviet officer who made the operational decisions.

The lax organizational structure with which the WTO emerged was reflected in its charter, which stipulated that each step taken by the organization was to be subject to approval by the participants.[20] In the preamble, the treaty also speaks of "cooperation and mutual assistance in accordance with the principles of respect for the independence and sovereignty of states." The Kremlin itself denied that the treaty provided for, or even permitted any sort of, supranational organs or organizations that could infringe on the sovereign rights of individual members.[21] Article VII of the treaty did furnish a juridical basis for limiting the exercise of the individual state's sovereignty, though, by forbidding their participation in other alliances—and the Soviet Union did exploit the treaty as justification for military intervention in Hungary and Czechoslovakia. But there was no formal move toward or acknowledgment of supranationality in the inchoate stages of the Pact. This at least afforded Romania a degree of flexibility in asserting its autonomy through the utilization of arguments of theory predicated on the precepts of the charter. And it did do so under Ceausescu, by means of emphasizing the defensive character of the Pact and its lack of supranationality.[22]

Informally, the WTO was very much a Soviet creature, with the military command firmly secured in Soviet hands and with the top headquarters located in Moscow. Nevertheless, despite the fact that the treaty furnished Moscow with a framework binding the various Communist states together, it did not in the main rely on it for control. Rather, it employed an elaborate network of bilateral agreements which encompassed all of the bloc states. These treaties of friendship, cooperation, and mutual assistance were initiated during 1947–48 and were renewed in the late 1960s.[23] Thus, there was an alternate channel for the Soviet Union to influence the bloc states, if the WTO was not functioning adequately as a lever of control. In the 1950s, while the WTO was in its organizational infancy, these bilateral treaties constituted the sole de facto organized links. When Soviet military policy in 1960 began to place greater emphasis on East European bloc forces, Khrushchev perceived the benefit of the Warsaw Pact as an instrument of bloc integration and, in upgrading the WTO meetings and contacts, he endeavored to build such a momentum. Romania's opposition to any form of integration and its direct challenge to the WTO in 1964, evidenced by its refusal to participate in joint maneuvers, militated against this momentum and in this respect Gheorghiu-Dej's successful challenge to the WTO institution signified an important precedent for his successor, Ceausescu.

On the other hand, the existence of the network of bilateral treaties with each bloc state afforded Khrushchev an alternate venue for integration and control under a loose WP organization. Consequently, he could be more flexible in accepting challenges to the WTO. Under this organizational adaptability the Soviet government could de facto exclude dissenting Albania from the Pact following the 22nd CPSU Congress in the fall of 1961, and contain Romanian challenges. Furthermore, through the exploitation of the bilateral treaties and nebulous WP organization, the Kremlin could work with groupings within WTO. This afforded Moscow the opportunity to concentrate on the most valuable members to the exclusion and/or containment of dissenters such as Romania. Therefore, even at the height of Khrushchev's quest for bloc integration, the Warsaw Pact afforded a degree of flexibility in accepting institutional challenges and it allowed for the development of a regionalism among the members that would reflect the military and political value attached to them by Moscow.

This evolution of regionalism in the bloc was, in turn, associated with Soviet risk taking in nuclear war and the necessity for reliability of allies. The three northern Soviet-bloc states comprised of the German Democratic Republic, Poland, and Czechoslovakia formed the Northern Tier of the Soviet strategic concept of a two-tier system.[24] The troops of these three nations secured better armaments and in much greater quantity than Romania and the other members of the Southern Tier, and held more frequent maneuvers in conjunction with the Soviet forces.

Risk taking by Khrushchev goes part of the way toward explaining Soviet military concentration on the Northern Tier. Despite strategic inferiority vis-a-vis the West he was not averse to risking crisis—or even war—with the West, as in the case of Cuba in 1962. Risk taking, however, does not exclude risk awareness and Khrushchev may well have thought that it would be to his advantage to convince his adversaries that they were dealing with a reckless player.[25] He realized, though, that he must have forces that could be used quickly and reliably in a nuclear-conventional war scenario. In the Cuban missile crisis he backed down and demonstrated, in his letter to President Kennedy, a full awareness of the consequences of a war.[26] In Europe, the Soviet leader had to have military security, for this was in his own zone of influence, so he maintained strength there at a high level and tried to keep it flexible. Flexibility meant a quick response capability, with good coordination of all services. This in turn required reliable and well-trained troops. While the effectiveness of Soviet forces cannot be questioned, that of the East European states varied. Yet in the Soviet war scenario the forces stationed in Eastern Europe would have seized the strategic initiative in the event of war and advanced west very rapidly (changing divisional headquarters twice a day), on an axis running through Germany, into NATO territory.[27] Geographically alone, this would place a greater emphasis on the Northern Tier.

Concomitantly, Khrushchev had to consider the reliability of the East European troops. Poland and Czechoslovakia retained bitter memories of Nazi Germany and their forces could be relied on for defenses and possibly even in offense against West Germany. In the G.D.R., the Ulbricht leadership was staunchly loyal to the Soviet Union and would have done everything in its power to aid it. In the case of Romania and Hungary, the best the Kremlin could hope for, however, was help in defense. Both countries had a historical enmity toward the Russians, had small industrial bases, and small armies. The Northern Tier states, by contrast, enjoyed the advantage of substantial industrial bases for supplying their troops as well as a more technically advanced population that could learn with greater facility how to operate sophisticated weapons.

While the Khrushchev era witnessed a great increase in the importance of the East European forces in their entirety, in Soviet military planning—which in turn affected dialectically Soviet perception of its military security—this period then also witnessed the evolution of a tier system which, if anything, greatly attenuated Romania's military significance relative to the northern group. Romania, isolated geographically from capitalist states in a remote part of the Southern Tier, modified preciously little the quality of Soviet security by downgrading its own military capabilities. This is not to say that the Soviet Union would not have resented autonomous military moves by Romania, but rather that the Kremlin could afford some flexibility. While Gheorghiu-Dej's actions in this field did not at all set an irreversible precedent of autonomy that would have endowed his successor, Nicolae Ceausescu, with immunity, they did signify another modest step toward further autonomy.

THE IMPACT OF THE ROMANIAN MILITARY CHALLENGES UNDER CEAUSESCU

The change of leadership in Romania in 1965 did not alter the pursuit of autonomy. Ceausescu continued to take a similarly autonomous line toward the Brezhnev-Kosygin leadership as had his predecessor, Gheorghiu-Dej. He did not permit Romanian troops to maneuver in conjunction with Warsaw Pact forces for the next two years, and he did not augment his forces but rather, in 1967, he reduced them rather sharply.* Ceausescu, moreover, delivered a speech in May 1966 in which he called for the abolition of military blocs and for an end to the stationing abroad of foreign troops.[29] Thus he continued the Romanian

---

*Romanian forces were 198,000 in 1965, 201,000 in 1966, and 173,000 in 1967.[28]

challenge (and the Kremlin, as has been shown, did see these moves as challenges) of minimal participation in, and contribution to, the defense of the Socialist realm and asked for what he perceived to be an abatement of military tension. To place these initial Ceausescu challenges in proper perspective we therefore propose to examine briefly the evolution of Soviet military policy under the Brezhnev-Kosygin leadership to ascertain what limits is imposed on autonomy and what defenses it afforded.

While there was considerable criticism of Khrushchev by the new leadership, further analysis reveals that there was no drastic alteration of military policy. There was added effort for overall improvement of military capabilities, and this entailed a change in emphasis rather than a change in direction. While it was still held that a nuclear war implied disaster, the realization was that the problem had to be confronted. Therefore there was a necessity for flexibility, which meant building up forces capable of coping with nuclear, nonnuclear, and mixed nuclear-nonnuclear situations.[30] Strategically, the Soviet Union was confronted with the option of continued inferiority, some form of parity, or a Soviet superiority of a marginal kind. The new leadership rejected the first option and accelerated the already rapid strategic buildup, initiated by Khruchchev. In 1967, for instance, they augmented the number of Intercontinental Ballistic Missiles (ICBM) by 50 percent over the previous year to between 450 and 475, and commenced the deployment of a limited number of Galosh antiballistic missiles around Moscow.[31] The ground forces were not reinstated wholly, but were reinforced. There was a greater investment in "damage limitation" and civil defense organizations, and, in Europe, provisions were instituted for dealing with the contingency of the failure of deterrence.[32] The appointment of Marshal Grechko as Minister of Defense in 1967 seemed to confirm this Soviet concern for establishing capabilities, at all levels of weapons, in a general war. By 1967 the Soviet Union was moving determinedly toward a policy of flexible response. This involved an all-around capability to respond quickly in all environments, nuclear, nonnuclear, and combined, with all the services cooperating effectively.

The Soviet attitude toward the significance of Europe did not change and the important Soviet political commentator, Yury Zhukov, stated this rather succinctly in 1966 when he pointed out, "Like it or not, the Soviet Union is already in Europe and as they say, there is nothing you can do about it."[33] Thus, the global policy still had a European center. As far as Eastern Europe was concerned the Soviet leadership did not display an overt interest in it, but the contention that between 1964-67 "there was practically no Soviet policy towards Eastern Europe,"[34] is an exaggeration.

First, the general Soviet military policy was bound to reflect East European considerations. A flexible response strategy entailed the shaping of East European forces in a way in which they could be integrated into the Soviet effort. While Marshal Sokolovsky reiterated at the time of the 23rd Party Congress the need for preparation to fight in a nuclear war and the paramouncy of strategic nuclear forces,[35] General-Lieutenant I. G. Zavyalov, an influential Soviet military theorist, emphasized the necessity for flexibility.[36] The latter insisted that for such flexibility there had to be a constant state of high combat readiness. Furthermore, he felt that in order to achieve the goals through the utilization of the combined effort of all of the services (but with the decisive role for nuclear weapons), simultaneous action against all groupings of the enemy was needed, together with surprise and a consolidation of success. Thus, while a war with the United States could be completely nuclear in Soviet theory, provisions were enacted to fight a flexible conventional or part conventional war in Europe. The vigorous demands for flexibility outlined by General Zavyalov, and which apparently reflected Soviet policy, imposed a high military demand on Eastern Europe. If anything, Eastern Europe's importance to Soviet security would have been augmented.

It is, moreover, important to note that the Soviet Union was not an adherent of the "gradual response" theories propounded by the United States' Secretary of Defense, Robert McNamara, and felt that once tactical nuclear weapons were brought into action it would be impossible to distinguish between tactical and strategic targets (despite its own flexible capabilities).[37] Thus, her forces were very heavily nuclear oriented and built for quick response.

During the 1970s, the Soviet Union moved to strengthen its general-purpose forces at an increased pace. These were deployed in such a manner as to be able to provide "shock power" through engaging the enemy with high-speed maneuvering elements which could deliver massive firepower in a very brief time. Soviet military doctrine emphasized offensive operations that were to be based on seizing the initiative and exploiting the surprise factor—that is, surprise and speed. The objective in the military doctrine was to paralyze the enemy's command apparatus and to prevent a concentration and buildup of reserves.[38]

The three types of offensive operations outlined by the late Marshal Grechko in a recent book all included these elements of speed and surprise.[39] This did not mean the Soviet forces had no staying power, but it did indicate that for their purposes they had to have a deployment that facilitated rapid regrouping in order to assemble main-strike forces and second, the capacity for major high-speed reenforcement.[40] As well, the Soviet Union laid great stress on armored fighting vehicles, basically the tank, and increasingly emphasized the strike aircraft. Therefore, by the 1970s the East European forces could only cooperate effectively with the Soviet forces if they received more modern equipment, intensified joint training, and improved rapid-deployment capabilities.

Even in the 1960s, though, Romania's refusal for a period of three years to participate in maneuvers rendered its forces less and less useful. In the 1970s, its refusal to allow military maneuvers on its territory and its limited participation in maneuvers outside of the country very severely restricted the value of its forces to the Soviet Union. In the 1960s, the Soviets showed that they already wished to coordinate and integrate Warsaw Pact forces more effectively. M. Padklyuchnikov, in an article entitled "Indestructible Combat Fraternity" published in *Pravda* in May 1966 for the anniversary of the Warsaw Pact, voiced this desire:

> As long as the threat posed by the imperialist aggressors continues to exist, the fraternal armies of the states participating in the Warsaw Pact will join ranks still more closely, and the cooperation of the Socialist countries in the military sphere will continue to strengthen. If the necessity arises, the family of the Warsaw Pact participants, united into a single family, will rise with terrible strength to the defense of the Socialist system and the free lives of our people.[41]

But the Brezhnev-Kosygin leadership did not view the bloc as a unified whole and there is evidence that militarily they maintained the regionalism that developed under Khrushchev. In 1965 the Soviets began to further upgrade the East European forces but the focus of emphasis was on the Northern Tier. Romania was largely ignored while East Germany received "nuclear-capable" weapons such as Frog 44, Scud and Guideline missiles, and supersonic Mig 21 aircraft, whereas only three years before its forces had been obsolete.[42]

The vast logistical buildup required for a more flexible war-making capacity was also taken into account by Soviet military policy. The Soviet armed forces were furnished with great numbers of new transport while under the Air Force Chief of Staff, General Kutakhov, the airlift capacities were vastly increased. Three of the seven airborne divisions could be dropped simultaneously with air portable artillery and light armored vehicles.* In Eastern Europe the growth of logistics capabilities, though, was again centered in the Northern Tier. Large-scale construction was begun on railways in the Polish-Soviet border area and heavy concentrations of anti-aircraft units were placed in the vicinity of railway yards and military stations in Poland, the G.D.R., and Czechoslovakia.[44] Thus, Soviet commanders could move their troops, including entire armies, very quickly to the frontiers of West Germany. The improved logistics, of course, also meant that whatever the nuclear orientation of the Soviet forces, they had an increased capacity for quick "police actions" in Eastern Europe. Greater capacity also fitted in well with the general Soviet bias toward mass, and, furthermore, greater Soviet military power in Eastern Europe tended to reduce the risk element for any Soviet policing actions within the bloc.[45]

In the case of the East European states of the Northern Tier, the Soviet Union delivered massive supplies of sophisticated weapons. Naturally enough this was aided by the tremendously large conventional production of the Soviet Union comprising more than 3,000 tanks per year and 1,800 military aircraft (enough to replace the entire RAF front-line aircraft every six months).[46] All

---

*These capabilities were well demonstrated during the 1970 *Dvina* exercises.[43]

of the three Northern Tier states received massive supplies of tanks and modern strike aircraft. In 1977, Poland had 3,500 tanks, and 745 combat aircraft; Czechoslovakia had 3,400 tanks and 558 combat aircraft, including the SU-7; while the G.D.R. had 2,400 modern tanks and 416 aircraft, largely made up of Mig 21s.[47] As well, in 1976 for instance, they spent respectively 3.6 percent, 3.5 percent, and 6 percent of the GNP on defense. All this compared, for instance, with Romania's position in 1977, whose army had only 1,500 tanks—some of them obsolete—an air force of 327 aircraft with about a third of them 1950s vintage Soviet jets, and an expenditure of only 1.8 percent of the Gross National Product (GNP) on defense—by far the lowest in the entire Soviet bloc.[48] Furthermore, there is a considerable difference between the "burden-sharing" among the East European states. This comprises of the "offsetting" of the stationary costs of Soviet forces in Eastern Europe, of the terms of trade of Soviet weapons, and of the fair share of each in total Warsaw Pact expenditures. This defense burden has been measured to be at a high of 5.5 percent of national income in the G.D.R. in the Northern Tier, to a low point of 2.5 percent in Romania within the Southern Tier.[49] The demands of nuclear war or of blitzkrieg dictated that forces be deployed before war erupted. It was reasonable that deployment would be directed along the main offensive-defensive axis, in the direction of West Germany and Western Europe. Yakubovsky held pronounced views on the desirability of joint training and felt that the preparation for nuclear warfare was to be along the "main axis," in the central battle area of Europe.[50] This, coupled with the reasons that made the Northern Tier countries more likely to be reliable (which reasons continued), made Soviet emphasis on the area logical.

In the 1970s, Hungary occupied an increasingly important role in Soviet strategic planning.[51] Whereas normally it is considered part of the Southern Tier it is certainly much more advanced than the other countries in the group and much closer to the central front. Its territory affords offensive moves both against the West and against Yugoslavia and Romania. As a result Hungary has functioned as something of an anomaly within the Warsaw Pact structure. Soviet forces in Hungary, four divisions strong, have been kept at full strength. Joint maneuvers in Hungary have grown in importance and they usually involve Soviet and Czechoslovak troops exercizing with Hungarian forces. These changes may have ominous meaning for Romania should the Soviet Union ever decide on a military intervention into Romania.

There has been another significant development in Soviet military policy that could affect Romania. During the 1970s, the Soviet Union had acquired a truly blue-water navy. It built large numbers of powerful surface ships, which it deployed in the oceans of the world but particularly concentrated in the Mediterranean. With the benefit of Arab naval bases, it was quickly able to challenge Western supremacy in that sea. With the Soviet emphasis on the Mediterranean there came the possibility that the Soviet Union may also place greater stress on the Southern Tier states in a general shift of perspectives to that area. However, this did not really materialize because of a number of factors. First of all, the Soviet Union was not ably to overcome the Western global naval superiority despite certain claims to the contrary.[52] In the Mediterranean itself, while the West had suffered certain reverses, the Soviet Union lost the use of facilities in Egypt and had been unable to secure rights to Yugoslav ports which would compensate for this. Therefore, the Soviet fleet in the Mediterranean remained inferior to the Sixth Fleet of the United States and the Soviet Union was far from achieving a breakthrough whereby it would have been of advantage to her to shift its strategic emphasis to this new area of opportunity. As such the importance of the Southern Tier remained secondary to that of the Northern half.

As long as Romania remained isolated in the Southern Tier, the Soviet Union could tolerate autonomous Romanian military policies, for Moscow's military security was not seriously impaired. Paradoxically, while Romania's unilateral debilitation of its own regular forces posed a challenge (as seen in Chapter 2) to the Soviet Union, it also lowered the expectation that Moscow could place on the Romanian contribution to the general defense of the Socialist bloc, therein giving it a limited immunity.

Despite regionalism, the Brezhnev-Kosygin leadership did endeavor to strengthen the WTO organization. For instance, at the March 1969 meeting in Budapest of a plenum of the member states' First Party Secretaries and Ministers of Defense, the Soviet leaders tried to secure an accord to further "perfect" the structure and command of the Warsaw Pact. But indications are that they failed. The meeting disbanded after only two hours, and later a Prague radio broadcast stated that there was "an agreement restructuring the Warsaw Pact whereby more attention is paid to the wishes of the individual member countries, and more weight given to the idea of equal rights,"[53] indicating that far from receiving the greater integration that they had wished for, the Kremlin had to acquiesce to a formal extension of equality. The official document that was issued indicated the lowest common denominator upon which all countries could arrive at a consensus; it omitted all references to issues in which the Soviet Union had displayed recent interest[54] (such as support for its dispute with China). Nevertheless, Brezhnev considered the Pact to be of significance and as late as 1971, in his address to the 24th Congress of the CPSU, he proclaimed that "the Warsaw Pact has been and remains the main center for coordinating the fraternal countries' foreign policies."[55]

Romania, and to a lesser extent some of the other East European states, had sought some structural changes in the Warsaw Pact that would allow for more input from the smaller members. Ceausescu had proposed a change in the structure of the Warsaw Pact during the meeting held in 1974 at Warsaw. At the Political Consultative Meeting in Bucharest during November 1976 major changes in fact were introduced. It was announced that a Committee of Foreign Ministers and a unified Secretariat for the purpose of improving the mechanism of political collaboration would be created.[56] It was the creation of this Committee of Foreign Ministers that Romania had sought. To them the effect was to dilute the military character of the Pact by developing its political function. The gain for the Soviet Union from this change (and Romanian challenge) was that the prestige of the Warsaw Pact would increase vis-a-vis NATO.

Thus, the Soviet aim of fortifying the Warsaw Pact during this period, however, had to be tempered by the growth of multilateralism in the organization alongside the old bilateral links. In turn, the concept of multilaterism introduces into any system of alliances the corollary concept of greater autonomy for individual members. And multilateralism in the WTO was to a great extent the result of the military policies of the Soviet Union—a case of military policy determining political action. As the Soviet leaders placed greater reliance on East European forces in the 1960s and 1970s, they had to allow for greater diversity in the Pact.

With this multilateralism, with the regionalism of the tier system, and with the strong bilateral links in the bloc, Romanian challenges to the WTO, even those calling for institutional reform,[57] could be absorbed and contained. Therefore, they were not an unbearable blow against the Soviet institution. Furthermore, Moscow viewed the WTO, along with its coordinating function, also as an instrument for conflict resolution. The Pact meetings, beginning in the late 1960s (with the exception of 1968), ceased to be utilized as mere rubber stamps for approving Soviet foreign policy, but instead appeared at times to provide for a "free vote." In effect the Soviet Union began to employ the organization more for consultation and conflict containment and resolution, and in certain instances watered-down resolutions to what Romania would find acceptable. The value of this conflict resolution approach was demonstrated clearly to Moscow by Romania's willingness to participate in Warsaw Pact meetings while refusing to participate at the meetings of other organizations. Therefore, while the WTO remained important to the Soviet Union, the nature of its organization and institutional development was such that it could absorb and contain Romanian challenges, and, moreover, give the latter a forum where it could vent some of its frustrations relatively harmlessly. In this respect, by channeling Romanian challenges away from flashpoint areas of Soviet foreign policy, the Warsaw Pact acted as a defense for Romanian foreign policy autonomy. There were limits, however—such as Romanian withdrawal from the Pact—which the Soviet leadership, in line with their policy toward Eastern Europe, would not have tolerated; but in the case of most Romanian challenges, we submit that the WTO, instead of acting as an institutional obstacle, performed more as an element of defense.

THE CZECHOSLOVAK PRECEDENT

Romania deviated very seriously from the Soviet line, as we have seen, in August 1968 when not only did it not participate in the intervention into Czechoslovakia but following the event, vehemently denounced it as a contravention of the Warsaw Treaty and asked for a prompt withdrawal of the intervening forces. Much of Western opinion held that Romania could be the next object of the Soviet Union's wrath. Yet, were the two situations analogous? The intervention in Czechoslovakia was prompted by both political and military reasons. Romania, unlike Czechoslovakia, did not exhibit any tendencies toward a "democratization" of Communism which could deteriorate into "bourgeois social democracy," which in turn could mean neutrality. Romania's Stalinist domestic policies hardly posed the danger of contagious disintegration of Communist authority in the bloc, nor did it exhibit any intention of leaving the Warsaw Pact. Yet, despite the fact that Romanian actions posed only a limited political challenge by refusing to follow Moscow's political lead in foreign policy, in this instance, its actions could have had important military implications for Soviet security. In order to put this in perspective, it should be useful to at least gauge the extent to which its actions were analogous to the Czechoslovak challenge to the Soviet military security.

Following the intervention in Czechoslovakia, the Soviet Union and other participants put forth numerous ex post facto security justifications for the intervention. While not all of these reasons can be taken at their face value, they cannot be dismissed as mere rationalizations. First, it must be recognized that Czechoslovakia, by its geographic location, was a member of the more important Northern Tier of the Warsaw Pact, in addition to sharing a border with West Germany. Second, by virtue of its Slavic affinity, its industrial base, and large armaments industries, it figured strongly in Soviet calculations of Warsaw Pact strength. Any hint of it withdrawing from the Warsaw Pact—or even decreasing its contribution to it—would have affected Soviet perception of its security to a an extent that an industrially and military weak, Latinized, remote Balkan state such as Romania could not.

Soviet military policy at this time also demanded a strict military performance from Czechoslovakia. The "flexible response" that the Soviet Union was pursuing by 1968 required a "forward strategy," especially in view of a West German shift toward a "forward strategy."[58] This in turn entailed moving up troop formations on the East-West border with a multiresponse capability. During the 1965 "October Storm" Warsaw Pact maneuvers, the scenario envisaged an East-West confrontation in which the Czechoslovak army was to fight a holding action on its Western frontier during the conventional fighting stage.[59] The Soviet leadership seemed singularly unimpressed by the Czechoslovak performance, and whether it is true or not that they asked to station a number of their own divisions on the Czech-West Germany border only to be refused,* they appeared worried about the security of that very important frontier. The performance of the Czechoslovak forces generally, though, had been good. Thus,

---

*Erickson claims that Novotny refused Soviet requests for the stationing of Soviet troops in Czechoslovakia, which could have avoided a subsequent Soviet intervention.

Soviet criticism here may have been the result of its supersensitivity about the West German border, which in turn would have greatly magnified any mistakes that the Czechoslovak forces may have made. It may also be possible that the Soviet leaders simply wanted their own troops on the border for psychological reasons and that their rumored dissatisfaction was merely an excuse.

By the summer of 1968 the Soviet leadership did indicate (perhaps in exaggerated tones) what appeared to be a genuine concern over the strategic situation when they denounced Sudeten and West German interests in Czechoslovakia.[60] The *Pravda* editorial for the day subsequent to the intervention also voiced this concern over the security of the Czechoslovak borders:

> The commitments the Socialist states undertook in the treaties among them demand that the parties to these treaties ensure the vigorous protection of their borders. What is the situation here with respect to Czechoslovakia's Western borders? On the Czechoslovakia side these borders are in effect open.[61]

The strategic importance of Czechoslovakia's geography was also described by the Soviets. N. Gribachev wrote in *Pravda*:

> Let he who is interested in this—including men of letters—outline the Czechoslovak borders sharply on the map of Europe and see what the situation of the Socialist countries would be. This is a wedge dividing the Warsaw Treaty countries. The G.D.R. and Poland remain to the north and Hungary, Bulgaria, and Romania to the south, without any direct communications between them and soldiers of the Bundeswehr and American soldiers would appear directly on Soviet frontiers.[62]

Moscow, moreover, expressed its fear of a Czechoslovak withdrawal from the Warsaw Pact in its attacks on General V. Prchlik, who merely asked for changes in the structure of the Pact[63] (as had Romania), and whom they succeeded in getting dismissed before the intervention. As well, Moscow reiterated this in later allegations of internal and external plots to take Czechoslovakia out of the Pact.[64] While Soviet stories of plots were most likely fabrications, for Moscow presented little evidence, its fear of a Czechoslovak withdrawal could have been quite genuine in view of their experience of the "democratization" of Communism in Hungary in 1956.

Therefore, there appears to have been few analogies between Romanian and Czechoslovak challenges in 1968, and the impact they made on Soviet perception of security. In Czechoslovakia, the Soviets saw a contagious revisionism that might have neutralized or even taken Czechoslovakia out of the Socialist camp. This, in turn, would have left Soviet strategic plans with a gaping hole in them. The Soviets repeatedly warned Czechoslovakia; and, in intervening, they demonstrated that they were willing to pay the price of the loss of the loyalty of the Czechoslovak forces, and of world condemnation. In a sense, then, they acted in extremis and not because the limits they placed on autonomy were extraordinarily narrow. Romania, on the other hand, merely supported the right of Czechoslovakia to pursue an autonomous internal and external policy. It had no intention whatsoever, as we have seen, of following Czechoslovak domestic reforms or of withdrawing from the Warsaw Pact; but, on the contrary, in 1968 it did participate in joint Pact maneuvers. In 1968 the Soviet Union recognized the necessity for some polycentrism; it had moved a long way from Stalinist demands for bloc conformity, despite the Czech intervention. In breaking the military unity of the bloc on the question of intervention, Romania did not significantly endanger Soviet security as it was reflected in Moscow's military policy—for the Soviets could well assure their security without the use of Romanian troops or territory. Thus, if "Czechoslovakia 1968" was or approximated the limit placed by the Soviet Union on the challenge to its security that it was willing to tolerate, then Ceausescu had no cause for worry in that year. Moreover, the Kremlin did not exclude the utilization of a more sophisticated policy of integration which could seek cohesion without the ultimate deterrence—intervention.

Lastly, in connection with Bucharest's policies in 1968, Romanian-Yugoslav contacts following the WP intervention in Czechoslovakia were particularly irksome to the Soviet Union. Meetings between Ceausescu and Tito raised the suspicions of the Kremlin,[65] as did Romania's contacts with the various Balkan states, for there were several Soviet outbursts against "Balkan Pacts."* There were even rumors in the West that Romania and Yugoslavia had signed a secret defense pact.[66] In the context of Soviet military policy, though, such Romanian actions in the Balkans did not appear as crucial provocations for a number of reasons. While after the Six-Day War in 1967 the Soviet military presence increased sharply in the Mediterranean, the main military concern remained Central Europe. The secondary role attached to the Balkans would have permitted the Kremlin more flexibility in setting the limits of Romanian policy autonomy, and therefore Bucharest's challenge did not necessitate intervention. It is even conceivable that if close Romanian contacts with Yugoslavia were indeed true, these may have functioned less as provocation to the Soviet Union than as a deterrent.

THE CONSTRAINTS AND OPPORTUNITIES OF EAST-WEST SECURITY TALKS

Romania's attempts to pursue an autonomous foreign policy in the 1970s was affected by three different security negotiations between East and West: the

---

*New York *Times*, August 6, 1971, referred particularly to Soviet-inspired attacks by Hungarians in *Magyar Hirlap*.

Strategic Arms Limitation Talks (SALT), the Conference on Security and Co-operation in Europe (CSCE) and the Mutual Balanced Force Reduction Talks (MBFR or MFR). The timing of concrete moves or proposals toward these talks by the Soviet Union and the West was significant. The first proposals for a European security conference were tabled by the Warsaw Pact Consultative Committee in January 1965 and renewed in Moscow in March 1966; then in Bucharest in July 1966; then at Karlovy Vary in April 1967, with additional concrete proposals included; but even this was still rather obscure in terms of mutual force reductions in Europe.[67] It was only at the June 1970 meeting of the Warsaw Pact foreign ministers, however, that it was revealed that the members were amenable to such force reduction discussions.[68] Brezhnev himself first raised the subject of troop limitations in Central Europe in his report to the 24th Party Congress on March 30, 1971; and on May 17, he made his famous "wine tasting" speech where he advocated further understandings with the West.[69] The MBFR talks did not really start to be given serious consideration until 1968 when at the June meeting of the NATO Council of Foreign Ministers in Iceland a declaration was issued suggesting talks with the Soviet Union and the Warsaw Pact states. Therefore, both the Eastern and the Western states wanted more than merely to enhance the military security through these negotiations but also to improve their political image. As such Romania would have to have been extremely cautious in using these negotiations in order to aid its own security.

The first SALT Interim Agreement was signed in 1972, and an Antiballistic Missile (ABM) treaty was concluded as well. What these agreements entailed was a limitation on the total number of land-based and submarine-based ballistic missiles for the Soviet Union and United States and a limitation of the anti-ballistic missiles. In the case of the land-based ICBMs and the submarine-based SLBMs, the Soviet Union had a clear numerical advantage which the United States was supposed to be able to offset through technological superiority and its bomber forces.[70] In November 1974, the Soviet Union and the United States reached an agreement at Vladivostok which set guidlines for a new accord limiting offensive strategic forces until December 31, 1985. This would have placed ceilings of 2,400 on launchers (including heavy bombers) and a 1,320 cap on multiple-warhead launchers, as well as carrying over certain provisions of the 1972 Interim Agreement.[71] In fact in 1977 the Soviet Union possessed 1,477 ICBMs against 1,054 for the United States, but fewer bombers. What these agreements suggest is that the United States had more or less accepted a parity of strategic forces with the Soviet Union. Now it is possible that the Soviet Union, as William Kintner and Robert Pfaltzgraft have written, views parity merely as a transitional stage between Soviet strategic inferiority and Soviet superiority,[72] but even if this is the case the Soviet Union by the mid-1970s at least had the security of a worldwide conceptual acceptance of strategic parity. For Romania a Soviet Union that did not feel on the defensive strategically would have meant a greater degree of security. Since Moscow would not have felt under as much pressure, it need not have sought unquestioning obedience from the less important allies.

It was felt by many observers in the West that the Soviet Union had gained a notable diplomatic triumph with the signing of the Final Act at the CSCE on August 1, 1975.[73] The West recognized the territorial division of Europe and in exchange it only received a Soviet and East European promise on a freer flow of information and people in the so-called "basket three." The Final Act itself is a declaration of intentions rather than a legally binding document and the signatories included an explicit clause in the concluding part which stated that it was not eligible for registration under Article 102 of the Charter of the United Nations. Nevertheless, the Act comprised the most comprehensive document on East-West relations since the war.

What were the gains or the losses for Romania though? Bucharest had sought increased security for Romania, of course, and it had insisted on individual participation at the conference. It was in fact a feature of the conference that Eastern and Western countries agreed that they should negotiate as individuals instead of blocs. If in some ways this was a Romanian challenge to the Soviet Union, it was certainly a containable challenge and the Romanian gain was rather small. The section, however, that was rather important for Romania was that included in Document no. 2 of the first "basket," which dealt with confidence-building measures. This section stated that there was to be prior notification of military maneuvers involving over 25,000 men taking place within 250 kilometers of national frontiers and that an exchange of military observers was to be arranged. While this was designed mainly for East-West relations it had great importance for Romania as well. The Romanian ambassador to the talks, Valentin Lipatti, was insistent prior to the conference that measures must be taken to make effective a policy forbidding recourse to the use of force or to *threatening with force.* He felt and argued that there was a strong link between the political and the military aspects of security.[74] Romania had worked very hard for the inclusion of these notification measures as well as for defining the parameters for future military negotiations that would exclude the use of or the threat of use of force.[75] "Intervention-through-maneuver" and "intimidation-through-maneuver" were used by Moscow against Czechoslovakia and Romania respectively. Therefore it was no wonder that Romania looked at this particular part of the Final Act as a measure to be used to safeguard its security.

Helsinki also accorded Romania the opportunity to improve relations with Moscow without compromising its foreign policy autonomy. We refer in this case to the "basket three" of the accord which sought a freer flow of people and ideas across national boundaries. In this instance, the Romanian leadership had the same vested interest in preventing Western "contamination" as Moscow. Bucharest stressed in practically identical terms to Moscow's that the Helsinki accord was to be viewed as a unitary whole whereby the prohibitions against interference in domestic affairs excluded any Western interest in the right of dissidents, or other "liberal" freedoms in Romania. Ceausescu declared at the Grand National Assembly meeting in 1977 that any foreign actions designed to induce Romanian citizens to leave the fatherland were to be considered unfriendly acts.[76] In 1976 and 1977, there was a major campaign in the Romanian press to discourage immigration through horror stories of the "capitalist crisis." As well, Bucharest did its best to limit contacts between the Romanian population and Western visitors through a published law and through an internal order that was unpublished. Western visitors were forbidden to stay at the residence of a Romanian citizen according to the Romanian law and the internal order decreed that Romanian citizens had to report all contacts with Western visitors. The Romanians summed up their attitude toward most of the Final Act and their compliance on human rights in almost identical terms to Moscow, when they declared before the convening of the Belgrade following-up conference on Helsinki in 1977 that no one was to go to the conference as an "accused or accuser or for reciprocal denunciations."[77]

At the MBFR talks Romania also wanted to participate with equal rights both at the preliminary discussions as well as at the negotiations.[78] The Soviet Union, however, decided to exclude not only Romania but also Hungary from negotiating status. The Northern Tier states were given full status while those of the Southern Tier were only allowed as observers. Thus while all WTO members would be participating nominally, the Soviet Union had already created subgroupings for the negotiations. In that sense the Soviet Union maintained a facade of alliance to alliance negotiations and was able to demonstrate a greater flexibility in the use of the Warsaw Pact. A greater flexibility in the Warsaw Pact would in a limited way aid Romania, but these negotiations also presented dangers. If an accord would have been reached, it would likely have pertained only to the forces in Central Europe to the exclusion of those stationed in Hungary. Therefore it is not inconceivable that Hungary could have been turned into a sort of garage for Soviet equipment and a grouping center for Soviet forces, thereby putting a great deal more Soviet power on Romania's western borders. The talks in Vienna, however, have shown very little progress because of the complexity of the issues involved. Despite years of discussion there had not even been a hint of agreement between the parties.[79] Therefore this kind of danger for Romania should only arise in the rather distant future.

A balance sheet of Romanian gains and losses through these security talks does not show any major change in Romania's position. After Helsinki the Soviet Union may want tighter ideological controls over the bloc states but Romania could reassure it through its very tight control of contact between its people and the Western world. On the other hand, Romania made some limited gains from individual participation. Pierre Hassner had said that the way to increase independence in Europe without a diminution of security was to "make the alignment within the existing groups less automatic and exclusive."[80] Even a militarily secure Soviet Union could not allow that type of independence in the 1970s. Yet the Soviet Union of the 1970s, who apparently achieved strategic parity with the United States, should have felt secure enough in Eastern Europe to continue to permit an isolated, contained Romania some divergence of views, some autonomy (not independence) well within the limits of its tolerance.

THE INFLUENCE OF THE SINO-SOVIET CONFLICT ON SOVIET POLICY

From 1960 onward, Romania often attempted to utilize China as a counterweight to the Soviet Union when it endeavored to posture itself as an honest broker between the two feuding Communist titans. For refusing to adhere to the line of the other Soviet-bloc states in condemning China, Romania was often vilified by the Soviet Union—and at times rewarded by China. The Soviet Union was extremely critical of Chinese support for the Romanian stance subsequent to the Czechoslovak intervention in 1968. And Soviet-Romanian relations became particularly strained following Ceausescu's visit to China in early June 1971, and the disclosure that Bucharest had acted as a channel of communication between the United States and China.

The Sino-Soviet dispute originated in both ideological and military rivalry. The ideological conflict relates perhaps more to the Third World than Eastern Europe, but here we are particularly concerned with the military rivalry and the influence that it had on Soviet military policy as it related to Romania. The Soviet perception of a physical threat from China was at least partly responsible for the limits it imposed on what it viewed as Chinese penetration into the Soviet bloc. The Soviet military image of China was also determined by two factors, one empirical and the other psychological.

On the empirical side, the Soviet Union could point to the sizable clashes between Soviet and Chinese troops that occurred along the Ussuri River in 1969. From as far back as 1964, the territorial integrity of the Soviet Union itself was directly challenged by Mao Tse-tung who, in an interview with Japanese Socialists also criticized Soviet "land-grabbing" in Europe, including the acquisition of Bessarabia from Romania.[81] China did explode a nuclear bomb in 1964, and by the end of the decade it was developing a *force de frappe*. This proliferation of nuclear weapons, coupled with the development of new military technology, could logically add to Soviet insecurity regarding China—particularly since the 1970s Chinese nuclear weapons could inflict considerable damage in the Asian part of the Soviet Union in a first strike. The vast Chinese manpower resources could also have posed new strategic problems for the Soviet Union if it was forced to fight a two-front war in Asia and Europe.

On the other hand, though, the nuclear danger from China only materialized in the late 1960s, while the Soviet Union had been obsessed with a Chinese danger for several years prior to that. Despite its vast military manpower and the possession of a small number of nuclear weapons by the 1970s, China could only contest a superpower like the Soviet Union if the latter refrained from utilizing its massive nuclear weapons capacity; and even then its strength was confined to its own territory.[82] The Chinese lacked the massive logistics support that would have been required for a full-scale invasion of the Soviet Union. The recurring fighting on the frontiers with China, however, must have given the Soviet command an incentive to improve their internal mobility, and, indeed, a large expansion in Soviet logistics did take place.[83] Nevertheless, the necessity to keep more troops in the Far East did not debilitate Soviet defenses in Europe, and during (and for some time after) the intervention in Czechoslovakia in 1968, it had more divisions in Eastern Europe than before, despite the 33 divisions it had deployed along the Chinese border. Furthermore, in the latter part of the 1970s the Soviet high command gave the Sino-Soviet area only second, or at times, third call on resources, after Europe and the Western military districts.[84] Thus, from an empirical point of view, it appears that the Soviet Union could contain China's military and should not have been overly worried by Chinese links with an East European state. Nevertheless, the almost hysterical references to China indicate that the Soviet Union was also heavily influenced by psychological factors.

Despite the conclusion of an agreement with China concerning new technology for national defense on October 15, 1957, two years later, at a time when there was still not the slightest sign of a treaty banning nuclear tests, the Soviet government unilaterally abrogated the pact between the two states and refused to provide China with a sample of an atom bomb or the technical data concerning its manufacture.[85] The Soviet fear of the "Chinese menace" could not be explained away by advancing the argument that the two states conflicted on the concepts of the utility of military power on behalf of world revolution either, for the Soviet decision preceded the break. At the more paranoic level, the Soviets could even envisage a German-Chinese-Japanese anti-Soviet alliance.[86] In the case of Romanian relations with China during 1971, the Soviet Union even spoke of the danger of the formation of a Balkan triangle consisting of Romania, Yugoslavia, and Albania under the tutelage of China.[87] It became apparent shortly afterward, though, to both the Soviet Union and the three accused states, that there simply was a lack of effective Chinese protection for such a hypothetical "triangle."

Thus, there seems to have been at times a potent element of psychological or irritational influence on Soviet policy toward China, which combined with empirical analyses. Sober military advice, such as that coming from Marshal Zakharov in 1969 urging restraints, helped moderate Soviet military policy toward China, but the Soviets were still hypersensitive about any Chinese footholds in Eastern Europe. China's support for Romania following the intervention in Czechoslovakia was undoubtedly morale boosting, but the Chinese had few military options and Chou En-lai admitted as much when he said in 1971 that "distant waters cannot quench local fire."[88] The Chinese could have endeavored to divert Societ action against Romania by "heating up" their own borders with the Soviet Union, but the success of such a move is questionable, for the Soviets demonstrated that they were capable of deploying very large numbers of troops for intervention in an East European state in 1968, while maintaining massive forces in the Far East. Therefore, Chinese efforts would have to have been on a massive scale to divert the Kremlin from a determined move into Romania, and Chou's statement indicated that they were not prepared to risk the potentially disastrous consequences of such a move. A limited Chinese military effort on the Soviet borders would likely have deterred only the most marginal Soviet desire for intervention into Romania, and the latter could ill afford to rely on such protection. While Romania did receive many economic benefits from China, and the Sino-Soviet rift did afford some room for autonomous maneuvering, the psychological or irrational element in the Soviet perception of its military security vis-a-vis China made the limits that the former placed on contacts by Soviet-bloc states with the latter, vague. Ceausescu's flirtation with China in the spring of 1971, instead of providing strong defenses, could well have come close to breaching the limits of autonomy set by Soviet security needs.

THE EFFECTS OF THE DEFENSE LAW

Romania's attempts to build some active defenses may as well have been considered challenges by the Soviet Union and among the most blatant of these, Romania's Defense Law, introduced in December 1972, was likely to irritate the Soviet Union despite its innocuous appearance. It proposed regulations of conduct in case of invasion, which would have permitted the country's leadership to fight on, even in the event of the occupation of large parts of the country by enemy forces, for such occupations were to be denied legal recognition.[89] By proposing decentralization of commands in wartime, the law also provided for more efficient local and guerrilla defenses. These in themselves were hardly an unacceptable challenge to the Soviet Union, but the thrust of the law contained the offensive elements of autonomy. The direction of defense envisioned by the law was toward all horizons, thereby including the Warsaw Pact nations with the capitalist states, as potential invaders. Second, the law was modelled very closely on that of Yugoslavia, thereby suggesting a condominium of the two states. In many ways Romania had no choice but to introduce such a law. The only means a small country had of countering a potential Soviet intervention was through a decentralized defense that would have to be overcome piecemeal even by a large and powerful enemy. Therefore such a defense would deprive that large enemy of speed and by saving the main element of defense from immediate attack, through dispersals, it could also deprive the enemy of surprise. Furthermore if Romania were to take full advantage of possible help from Yugoslavia it had to ensure that its forces were compatible with those of the latter country. Therefore these forces had to be modeled on those of Yugoslavia and had to be geared toward popular or people's war.

Furthermore, the challenge has to be viewed within the Soviet perception of security. Its military policy afforded Romania a certain degree of autonomy by virtue of the latter's geographical position in the strategically less significant Southern Tier, and its lack of common borders with a capitalist state. As a result, the Soviet Union had tolerated a considerable number of autonomous Romanian policies. Soviet response had been to isolate Romania from the other bloc states, and use informal levers or pressure such as embargoing arms or withholding economic aid. The Defense Law merely proceeded to formalize the de facto evolution of Romania's defense policies. While having an informal challenge formalized made it more irritating, this should hardly have induced the Soviet Union to resort to drastic action in view of the fairly substantial limits of autonomy that it permitted Romania previously, and of the defenses inherent in Soviet military policies.

In an attempt to define the limits—in this case the military ones—for Romanian foreign policy autonomy, we found it necessary to examine the threat it posed to Soviet perception of its security needs during this time. For it was Soviet security needs, as reflected through its military policies, that to a great extent set the limits of autonomy in the Soviet bloc. Our analysis, we contend, has indicated that there was a rather favorable prognosis for Romanian foreign policy autonomy, and here we are talking about the lack of danger of the Soviet Union employing that ultimate tool of repression—military intervention. This is not to say that the Soviet leadership could not or did not exploit other subtler means of pressure to contain Romanian challenges, but we contend that there was no necessity for the ultimate deterrent.

Moreover, all this is not meant to imply that the Soviet Union took no notice of Romanian deviation from Soviet policy in its attempts to act autonomously, or that the former did not consider these deviations as challenges to its authority in the bloc. The destructiveness of nuclear weapons, the need for the development of a flexible military posture, and the desire to close the strategic gap with the West induced the Soviet Union to have a more sophisticated approach toward Eastern Europe and move toward regionalism. Beginning with Khrushchev, geographical location on the offensive and defensive axis, reliability, industrial capacity, and technological sophistication helped to enlarge greatly the significance of the Northern Tier members of the Warsaw Pact over the Southern Tier of which Romania was part. This, coupled with the Soviet Union's successful elimination of the strategic gap with the West (and which in turn gave it more confidence), gave it the capacity to contain Romanian challenges by relegating them to a low-level risk to its security. With the exception of the rather anomalous spot of military policy toward and security perception of China, then, Soviet policy allowed fairly wide limits for Romanian autonomy.

Perhaps the above summation indicates a belief that the limits that the Soviet Union places on bloc autonomy can be ascertained through an objective analysis. We do, however, recognize that there are irrational or unpredictable determinants in foreign policy formulation and that, therefore, it should be useful to determine whether the Soviet Union did behave contrary to what our analysis indicated, at least as an extra check. We do know that in the period of

1965 to 1977 there was no Soviet military intervention in Romania, but the question to be answered for the hypothesis of irrational Soviet behavior is whether there was an attempt. For the definition of "attempt" it would be helpful to consider its definition in law, which was very well expressed by Lord Reading. To paraphrase him, acts remotely connected with intervention are not to be considered as attempts to commit it, but acts immediately connected with it are.[90] The preparation for the commission of intervention is not an attempt unless there had been acts that formed parts of a series of acts—in a sense, a trend or tendency—that would have constituted intervention if not interrupted. In practical terms, past Soviet interventions in East European states could define more clearly what constituted the series of acts (or "go-position") that led to intervention. Following this search for such a pattern, or at least a tendency, we propose to look at the major military moves of the Soviet Union and its allies which related to Romania in order to gauge whether they did fit the definition of attempted intervention.

THE WAYS AND MEANS OF INTERVENTION

On four separate occasions since the end of World War II the Soviet Union took military action to try to suppress developments in Eastern Europe that it perceived as political-ideological and/or military threats to its security. While Soviet success in gaining its objectives varied, as had the level of its involvement, it had made an attempt, at least, at military intervention in all four cases. In the G.D.R. in 1953, the Kremlin helped retain the Ulbricht regime in power through resolute military action against the strikers and demonstrators; but in Poland, Soviet troops were returned to the barracks after they ceased their moves on Warsaw, thereby allowing Gomulka and his supporters to consolidate their power over the Natolin (Stalinist) group. In Hungary in 1956, and Czechoslovakia in 1968, the Soviets quickly suppresed regimes which they felt threatened their control of Eastern Europe, through the use of crushing military power. Our purpose here is to see if there was a discernible pattern (or at least a tendency) in these Soviet actions that could show what constituted an attempt or a type of "go-position" for Soviet intervention; and that in turn could classify any military moves that the Soviet Union might have made against Romania in the period after 1965.

Even a cursory search for a pattern in these four instances reveals that, to an even greater extent than in the analysis of general Soviet military policy, it is virtually impossible to separate Soviet political preparations from the military ones. Thus, in probing for the series of moves which made up the attempt at intervention, we will look at political preparation, at military preparation, and then at the corollary ingredients of speed, morale, and surprise in the intervention. Finally, we will look at those elements of deterrence that could mitigate the chances of a Soviet military intervention.

Some Soviet-perceived political misbehavior on the part of the bloc states took place in all the four instances of intervention, but there were some variations in the political charges the Soviet Union drew up in preparation for intervention. The accusation of external links, or catalysts, for a policy unpalatable to the Soviet Union carried particular weight in the series of steps leading to military intervention. In the G.D.R., Soviet troops were told by the high command that the rising was a result of actions by "American Imperialist plots" as well as by "fascist provocateurs,"[91] but these justifications came only on June 17 when the Soviet forces had already come to the aid of the incumbent Ulbricht government. In Poland, however, where Soviet military intervention was stopped before any fighting could take place, there were no Soviet claims that the anti-Natolin group was externally supported or inspired.

The two main test cases, Hungary and Czechoslovakia, though, were characterized by the extensive use of the political device of blaming external (Western) causes for domestic East European upheavals. In Hungary, the Soviet Union appeared to fear that there was a connection with the Anglo-French and Israeli action at the Suez Canal, and that the upheavals in Budapest would set off a whole series of eruptions throughout Eastern Europe.[92] On October 28, 1956, before the final suppression of the Hungarian Revolution, *Pravda* alleged that counterrevolutionary elements supported by the West were threatening the "foundations of Socialist order." In the case of Czechoslovakia, accusations of Western connections came from the Soviet Union shortly before the intervention—almost as a signal. On July 19, 1968, in what retrospectively appears to have been the turning point for Soviet intervention, Moscow disclosed some vague "evidence" which purported to reveal "the perfidious plans of American imperialism and West German revanchism to assist insurgent elements" in Czechoslovakia.[93] And following the interventions in Hungary and in Czechoslovakia, the Soviet Union elaborated at length on charges of Western interference.* Moscow had also indicated that it would not tolerate the withdrawal of a bloc state from the Warsaw Pact.† Therefore, a Soviet warning to Romania of Western plots and interference, with the aim to take it out of the Warsaw Pact, would have been particularly grave.

Hardly less serious than the charge of Western interference has been Soviet warning of domestic disintegration in an East European state. In the G.D.R. the

---

Pravda, August 24, 1968, p. 1, claimed that a conspiracy against Socialist Czechoslovakia had been discovered that aimed to take it out of the Warsaw Pact.

†On August 14, 1968, Brigadier-General Wojceck Baranski, the Deputy Chief of the Polish General Staff, writing in *Krasnaya Zvezda*, p. 3, stated that the West German aim of drawing away from the Socialist states one by one from their alliance could not be tolerated and developments in Czechoslovakia caused particular concern.

Soviet leaders were faced with a situation that developed very quickly from a spontaneous demonstration of some workers in Berlin, rather than something directed or even condoned by the government. As a result, Soviet forces joined the G.D.R. police and government in putting down the revolt, instead of acting against the Ulbricht government, whose loyalty to the cause of Communism and to close ties with the Soviet Union Moscow did not doubt. In Poland, the Soviet leaders were not concerned as much by the domestic policy as they feared a deterioration of Soviet-Polish relations. Brezezinski, for instance, felt that the Soviet Politburo delegation headed by Khrushchev, which came to the Polish capital, a priori conceded the Poles the right to build Socialism in their own way.[94]

On the other hand, in Hungary and in Czechoslovakia, the two countries where Soviet military intervention did replace governments offensive to Moscow, the charge of "counterrevolution" was a significant step toward such intervention. In Hungary, Politburo member G. Marosan called in the Soviet troops on the night of October 23 to suppress a "counterrevolution."[95] In the case of Czechoslovakia, the Soviets alleged in July 1968 that "counterrevolutionary forces similar to those in Hungary in 1956"[96] were at work.

A third step the Soviet Union took in the direction of intervention in Hungary and Czechoslovakia was to try to give the governments of these states a false sense of security. On October 30, 1956, following its first intervention into Hungary, which had left the Nagy government in power, the Soviet leadership issued a declaration that promised to place relations between Socialist states on the five principles of equality, and respect for sovereignty, and moreover they hinted that they might even consider withdrawing from Hungary.[97] In fact, the declaration turned out to be largely a ploy to provide the necessary breathing space for the deployment of Soviet troops for the second intervention, which suppressed the Nagy government. In the case of Czechoslovakia, as late as August 11, 1968, *Pravda* ridiculed what it termed were Western attempts to interpret the Bratislava Declaration as merely a temporary truce between the Soviet Union and Czechoslovakia; and on August 16, the influential Soviet political commentator Yury Zhukov attacked the *New Statesman* for impuning the validity of the Bratislava documents as a solution to the crisis.[98] These statements in *Pravda* must have been aimed, partially at least, at the West, but the surprised reaction of Czechoslovakia, on August 21, to the intervention tends to indicate that they were also aimed at putting the Czechs off their guard.

Soviet military preparations for intervention, in turn, may also be divided into a series of steps. Among these, the first that comes to the surface, in all the cases involved, is that the Soviets had troops stationed within the territory about to be invaded and/or were conducting military maneuvers on it, which led to the intervention. In the first three instances of intervention we cite, the Soviets had troops within the borders of the G.D.R., Poland, and Hungary. Czechoslovakia seems to be the exception in this case, for the last Soviet and WTO troops involved in maneuvers were withdrawn by August 3, 1968.[99] But the maneuvers were part of the preparation. It is worth pointing out that at no time during the period of 1965 to 1977 were Soviet troops stationed or even allowed to maneuver within Romanian territory.

Maneuvers played a key part in the Soviet intervention in Hungary and Czechoslovakia. For especially in the latter where there was no stationing of Soviet troops, the long series of maneuvers, which continued outside Czechoslovakia after the August 3 withdrawal of WP forces, were the immediate military steps preceding intervention. In the G.D.R., the Soviet troops were on maneuvers in the training areas surrounding Berlin just before they intervened in support of the mobile battalions of the People's Police,[100] but it was a relatively small military operation that needed a simple deployment, to which such maneuvers were merely incidental. In Poland as well, no maneuvers were necessary, for on Soviet command Soviet armored troops commenced a straightforward move from their bases near Wroclaw into the direction of Warsaw on October 19, 1956.[101]

The situation in Hungary, however, was quite different from that in Poland and in the G.D.R., for on October 28, 1956, the Soviet Union had to accept the fact that for all intents and purposes four regular armored divisions had been defeated by the Hungarians in Budapest, and, therefore, these forces had to be withdrawn and redeployed.[102] What appeared to be a withdrawal of Soviet troops in Hungary turned out to be a maneuver to complete military preparations, to set up additional operational bases, and to redeploy armor and artillery around Budapest. Only then did the Soviet troops proceed with the second intervention which toppled the Nagy government.

In the case of Czechoslovakia, again, maneuvers seemed a necessary step preceding intervention. The large-scale command and control as well as logistic exercises that preceded the unopposed entry of the Warsaw Pact forces into Czechoslovakia at 11 p.m., August 20, 1968, allowed for a smooth operation, described as of "textbook perfection."[103] The vast forces that took part in the intervention necessitated, reputedly, six months of planning (estimates of the WTO forces taking part ranged as high as 650,000 men).[104] Also, airlifting of large numbers of Soviet troops into Czechoslovakia, including an entire division of airborne troops landed at Rusyne International Airport in Prague, showed the flexibility of the Soviet power to intervene, once proper preparations had been made. The large number of troops and the extensive preparations involved must have provided extra security for the Moscow leadership in the operation, and thereby lowered their perception of risk taking, in this instance.

Another pre-intervention device to which the Soviets resorted was to attempt to sow confusion among the troops of the target state if it showed a willingness to resist. In Poland, the army was loyal to the Gomulka group and refused to take orders from the Soviet-appointed Defense Minister, Rokossovsky.[105] Since no armed conflict took place between Polish and Soviet forces, that was the end of the matter.

In Hungary, however, troops played an active role in the uprising. On October 24, 1956, at the outset of the revolt, Soviet advisors reportedly ordered Hungarian units dispersed. The majority refused, but even after October 27, the Soviet officers continued to spy and to obstruct pro-revolt Hungarian officers from effectively rallying the army to the rebels' side.[106] Before their final military moves in Hungary, the Soviet military also made sure that they trapped the Hungarian military command—through the charade of inviting them for talks and then seizing them.[107] In Czechoslovakia, the Soviet government succeeded in securing the dismissal of General V. Prchlik, a defiant member of the Central Committee of the Czechoslovak Communist Party who was in charge of military affairs, as well as the closing of the Political-Military Academy in Prague, which contained the military elements most loyal to Dubcek.[108] The two actions, preceding the intervention, were bound to have seriously harmed any plans that the Czechs may have had to organize for resistance. Where resistance was offered, or could be organized, then, the Soviet Union appeared keen to interfere as effectively as possible with the opponent's organization of such a defense.

Concomitant with the active steps the Soviet Union took toward intervention, and which made up the attempt or "go position," there were a number of considerations inherent in Soviet action. These included the questions of morale, speed, and of surprise. The first, morale, has always been stressed in Soviet military doctrine.[109] Indications are that during the interventions, where only limited or no organized armed resistance took place, the morale of the Soviet troops remained high. The Soviet soldiers acted with disciplined restraint in East Germany in 1953,[110] with cold efficiency in Hungary in 1956,[111] and with "superb discipline and morale" in Czechoslovakia.[112] There have been very few reported cases of desertion or refusal to obey orders during an intervention.

It is true, though, that all the interventions were of short duration, and that none involved organized resistance by the national Communist party, for even in Hungary it was a case of the Soviet troops rescuing the Communists. The morale of the Soviet troops could well have deteriorated drastically had they become involved in a prolonged antiguerrilla fight organized by one of the national Communist parties. The Soviet military leaders themselves constantly stressed speed in the execution of an operation. This was evident in Soviet military maneuvers,* as well as in war plans, as enunciated by important writers on Soviet strategy.† Military surprise, a factor whose paramouncy was disputed at times in the 1950s, was nevertheless another significant element in Soviet

---

*During the "Dvina," WTO maneuvers *Pravda* emphasized the essence of speed.[113]

†Col. V. V. Larionov, one of the contributors to *Military Strategy*, edited by Marshal Sokolovsky, wrote in *Krasnaya Zvezda*, April 1964 (in Kintner and Scott, op. cit., p. 35) that the aim in war was to win the objectives in a short period of time. "This is what moves to the forefront."

strategy, working in conjunction with speed. Soviet attempts at deceiving the Hungarian and Czech leadership about its intentions before the decisive military actions it took served toward achieving the maximum effects of surprise.

The factors that facilitate Soviet intervention also imply the corollaries that would have tended to inhibit, if not completely restrain, such intervention. In Poland, the readiness of armed workers and the army to fight in support of the government acted as one of the key inhibiting factors on the Soviet Union.* In Hungary, armed resistance to the Soviet forces caused some apprehension, but because the Soviet government believed that the avowedly anti-Communist revolt (as it became in the last stage) could not be contained by the Hungarians, it felt that it had no choice but to act. This is not to say that in a situation where it was not in extremis the Soviet Union would not have been deterred by the prospect of becoming engaged in a slugging match with guerrilla forces—with all the damage that implied to troop morale and to its worldwide image.

While the drawing of a fixed pattern is unfeasible, then, in the analysis of Soviet intervention, several factors do emerge to help define the attempt or "go-position." It appears that the Soviet Union either had troops stationed in the target country, or conducted maneuvers in and out of that country, to prepare for the introduction of a sufficiently large force to ensure a low-risk operation, and to be able to overcome quickly any prospective resistance. Almost simultaneously, political preparatory steps were taken through Soviet accusations of Western imperialist and German revanchist (especially Sudenten Germans') plots linking up with domestic counterrevolutionaries. This combined threat was alleged to be taking the target state out of the WTO and the Socialist camp. In Hungary and Czechoslovakia, the pre-intervention campaign also claimed that the Communist parties of these states were losing control.

The next step (in the case of Hungary and Czechoslovakia) was to delude the target state into a false sense of security. Tactical agreements with the state concerned and the ridiculing of Western speculations and rumors of intervention also acted as a deterrent for that state from preparing itself militarily. In view of Soviet protestations of good intentions, Moscow could have claimed that such military preparations were provocations. Furthermore, in taking action, the Soviet Union considered the desideratum of speedy, effective operations particularly in order to maintain high troop morale.

Not all of the above factors were necessary to constitute an attempt at military intervention, for the requirements varied somewhat with the circumstances. Nevertheless, there had to be some combination of military and political signals and moves from those we described to constitute the attempt, for the existence of a single factor could point in many directions without showing a

---

*Garthoff claimed that a Soviet regiment that attempted to enter Poland from the G.D.R. at Szczecin was fired upon by Polish internal forces loyal to Gomulka and withdrew to the G.D.R.[114]

tendency. In Romania under Ceausescu, the Communist party, as we have seen, was firmly in control and the Soviet Union made no allegations of domestic disintegration nor of any Western plots attempting to join or aid Romanian counterrevolutionaries. Romania limited its participation in the Warsaw Pact, but it did not try to withdraw, for it attempted to keep its challenges within close bounds. During this period, no Soviet troops were stationed on Romanian soil; therefore, the only major steps that could have constituted an attempt to intervene into Romania would have been through military maneuvers and this therein also implied moves designed to interfere with the organization of an effective defense.

ATTEMPTED INTERVENTION THROUGH MANEUVER

The Soviet armed forces, as those of other nations, held important military maneuvers to improve the fighting capacity of their troops in the postwar era. Since about 1961, as we have seen, many of the maneuvers were conducted jointly with the forces of East European states under the aegis of the Warsaw Pact. Large-scale joint maneuvers, in the opinion of the Soviet Union, helped to improve the forms and methods of military operations, as well as strengthening the military links among the Socialist states.[115] Some of these joint maneuvers, as far as can be ascertained from both Soviet and Western sources, were on a mammoth scale—even in the early 1960s.*

While information on Soviet and Warsaw Pact maneuvers is limited—and any analysis will have to take cognizance of this—there is sufficient evidence to support the drawing of an outline of the broader purposes of various such maneuvers from Soviet statements, and from some Western observations. And what does seem fairly certain is that major Soviet and joint Warsaw Pact maneuvers had additional aims to those of increasing military efficiency and bloc military coordination. There are suggestions, for instance, that the vast maneuvers of Soviet and of the three Northern Tier states' forces in the G.D.R., at the time of the Berlin crisis, was a "show of force" designed to intimidate the West.[117]

Under Marshal Grechko, maneuvers assumed an even greater function in the Soviet readiness posture, for the exercise pattern received an ever closer connection with operational deployment; and in the case of Czechoslovakia, it became "mobilization by manoeuvre."[118] Therefore, the large-scale exercise pattern carried the risk (for an opponent) of rapid escalation. A large intervening force could be assembled in Eastern Europe under the guise of maneuvers and, thus, there would be no need to send it directly from the Soviet Union. It is these two roles, especially the latter one, that Soviet and large Warsaw Pact

---

*Gen. P. I. Batov of the Soviet Union reported, for instance, that the maneuvers held in September 1963, in which Soviet, Polish, Czechoslovak, and G.D.R. soldiers participated, had 760 tanks, 800 trucks, and 40,000 men as well as several hundred fighter planes.[116]

maneuvers could perform, which would have been of particular concern of Romania, in view of Ceausescu's quest for autonomy.

It should be reiterated at this point that Romania represented a special case in the Soviet bloc as far as maneuvers were concerned. During the period of our study, no joint military maneuvers were conducted on Romanian soil* and Romania repeatedly called for a cessation of military maneuvers on foreign soil. Furthermore, it ceased participating in Warsaw Pact maneuvers outside its territory for a period of three years until August 1967, when Ceausescu, in a conciliatory gesture, praised the Soviets warmly and declared that cooperation with the Communist world, headed by the Soviet Union, was the keystone to Romania's foreign policy.[120] With the above in mind, we will then examine the implications that large Soviet and Warsaw Pact maneuvers may have had for Romania at crisis points during the period of our study.

In 1965, the year Ceausescu ascended to power, there was relatively little activity in the first half of the year, but a very sizable joint exercise, involving the Soviet Union and the Northern Tier countries, was conducted in the G.D.R. in the latter half (from October 16 to 22, 1965).[121] The maneuver did not relate to Romania, for the scenario envisaged an East-West conflict that involved nuclear weapons. The Romanian Minister of Defense, General Leontin Salajan, did participate as an observer.[122]

The year 1966, a period during which Ceausescu had called for the abolition of military blocs, saw no overt Soviet military moves against Romania through maneuvers. The major exercise of the year was a joint force maneuver called "Vltava" involving Soviet, G.D.R., Czechoslovak, and Hungarian troops on Czechoslovakian territory.[123] This large exercise again had a nuclear scenario, and Western observers felt that West Germany was designated as the "enemy."[124] But the participation of Hungary with the Northern Tier countries also raised speculation that the Soviet plan assumed that Yugoslavia, Bulgaria, and Romania, combined with the obstacles of neutral Switzerland and Austria, were sufficient to isolate the southern and southeastern flank of NATO, thereby enabling Hungarian troops to be moved north.[125] If this hypothesis was correct, then it would tend to indicate that the Soviet Union felt confident in the reliability of Romania in the southern group, despite Ceausescu's statements.

Notwithstanding Romanian establishment of diplomatic relations with West Germany and its refusal to join in the Warsaw Pact condemnation of Israel following the Six-Day War, the Soviet Union did not display any great military interest in Romania during 1967. The several joint Warsaw Pact exercises that did occur were on a modest scale compared with "Vltava" or "October Storm" and involved the Northern Tier. The exception to the latter was a small exercise in the Southern Tier which saw Romanian participation in joint maneuvers for

---

*The last joint maneuvers held on Romanian territory took place in the second half of October 1962, with Soviet, Bulgarian, and Romanian units participating.[119]

the first time since September 1964 (the maneuvers involved Soviet, Bulgarian, and Romanian troops, from August 20 to 27).[126] This, in fact, there appears to have been an abatement of military tension between the Soviet Union and Romania.

The Soviet and Warsaw Pact intervention in Czechoslovakia demonstrated the potential of large maneuvers to be translated into military intervention. A series of maneuvers were initiated by the Soviets, in conjunction with various members of the Pact (with the notable exception of Romania) in March 1968, which continued to exert a steady pressure on Czechoslovakia.[127] In March, the maneuvers were conducted in Hungary and the G.D.R., opposite the Czechoslovak border. The May movements of Soviet troops again had an intimidating aspect, through their locale on the Polish-Czech frontier. At the same time, the Soviet Union held maneuvers on the Romanian frontiers—and this was at the time when Romania was defiantly extending her support to the Dubcek government in its quest for autonomy. It should be emphasized, though (in their relation to Romania), that the May maneuvers near Romania were on a small scale.

The June maneuvers, while not very large, contained the important element of introducing Soviet troops into Czechoslovakia. Western sources believe that a considerable number of the Soviet troops remained in Czechoslovakia throughout July helping to prepare the intervention. (Most of the Soviet force of 16,000 stayed on longer despite repeated Czechoslovak announcement of their departure during July.)[128] The extensive exercises by the Soviet and Warsaw Pact troops throughout Czechoslovakia in June, tend to indicate that the Soviets considered internal reconnaissance and preparation an important step toward intervention. If the Soviet troops did remain longer than the Czechoslovak announcements indicated, this would only reinforce the impression of the great weight the Soviet Union attached to internal reconnaissance before intervention.

"Nemen," the Soviet designation for what they proclaimed to be their largest logistical exercise to date,[129] came in the same month (July) as the publication of "letters" from two groups of Czech factory workers in *Pravda*, in which they claimed that the presence of Soviet forces in Czechoslovakia would be reassuring.[130] The exercise was expanded to encompass the troops of the WTO states that bordered Czechoslovakia, and the Kremlin announced the call-up of reservists. When this particular maneuver was completed, further activity continued through exercises involving communication troops in the surrounding WTO states, but in fact these amounted to a dress rehersal and a continuation of "Nemen" in another form, for the next step was the intervention.

The significant fact that emerges from "Nemen" is the size of the maneuver that preceded the move into Czechoslovakia. While other small land maneuvers had taken place in 1968 in the vicinity of Czechoslovakia, their primary role appeared to be intimidation of the Dubcek regime, while preparation for invasion was of secondary importance. With "Nemen," though, a very large step had been taken toward intervention, for the necessary large force was assembled.

Combined with the political offensive against Prague, it therefore constituted the attempt or "go-position" which the maneuvers of March and May did not. The size of the forces employed also may have been related to the fact that, unlike in the case of the G.D.R., Hungary, or Poland, the Soviet Union did not have forces already stationed in the target state. In the latter sense, Czechoslovakia in 1968 would have had much greater relevance to Romania than the other Soviet interventions.

The intervention itself also revealed two important aspects of Soviet military thinking. Czechoslovakia was infiltrated simultaneously from all of the Warsaw Pact frontiers, not merely the Soviet one.[131] Second, Soviet airborne troops played a significant part in seizing certain key objectives, such as airports.[132]

Thus, it appears that the Soviets used small maneuvers in the first part of 1968 as a means of intimidation. The introduction of Soviet troops into Czechoslovakia was an important step toward the *attempt* to intervene, while the assembly and rehearsal of a massive force attained the "go-position." The intervention itself revealed that the Soviet Union considered it important that it be conducted from all possible sides, and with as many participants as possible, even if these had to include G.D.R. troops, with the psychological and legal complication their participation could cause.

In the light of the above, the small-scale May 1968 Soviet maneuvers may have been an attempt to intimidate Romania, but as they lacked any of the major political-military factors of previous interventions they were not an attempt to intervene militarily. Similarly, postintervention Soviet military strategy, despite some Soviet verbal attacks on Romania, appeared more concerned with West Germany and NATO than in moving against Romania.[133] The bulk of the Soviet forces that took part in the intervention also remained in Czechoslovakia for the first three postintervention months. So the available evidence tends to indicate that it is reasonable to infer that there was no Soviet attempt at intervening in Romania in 1968.

The following year, 1969, was a very busy year for Soviet maneuvers. The frequency of exercise throughout Eastern Europe, in the spring especially, gave rise to Western speculation that they may have been a prelude to an intervention in Romania,[134] who was challenging Soviet tolerance with a scheduled visit by President Nixon in August. This, however, is questionable. The maneuvers the Soviets held in late February and March 1969[135] in the G.D.R. coincided with the West German presidential elections being held in West Berlin on March 5. Tension had been growing over the West German decision to use Berlin as the locale for the convention, and the Soviet and G.D.R. harassment of land access routes indicates that it may be safe to assume that the purpose of these maneuvers was intimidation of West Germany, and not a preparation for intervention into Romania.

"Vesna 69," a large Warsaw Pact maneuver, began in the last days of March with Soviet, Polish, Czechoslovak, and G.D.R. participation.[136] While it involved both staff and ground operations, its locale in Poland, Czechoslovakia, and the G.D.R., as well as exclusive Northern Tier participation, indicated that it was aimed at the West rather than Romania. The anti-aircraft exercises held in Czechoslovakia, Poland, Hungary, and the Western part of the Soviet Union in early April[137] again were too limited in scope to constitute a preparation for a move against Romania.

Exercises of more relevance to Romania did take place in the spring of 1969. More important, Romania did participate in maneuvers that tested tactical and operational preparedness of troops, on Soviet territory, during May.[138] The exercises involved Soviet, Romanian, Hungarian, and Bulgarian forces in sub-Carpathian Russia, east of Czechoslovakia. It was Romania's first joint maneuvers with Hungary since 1962, and, therefore, participation may well have been a Romanian concession. As to the dangers to Romania in this maneuver, it should be pointed out first of all that it was on a rather modest scale, no paratroop exercises were reported, and none of the Northern Tier group of states participated in it. Second, the area in which it was held was situated north of the Romanian Carpathian Mountains, a very strong natural barrier, and also at the farthest border point from Bucharest and Romania's industrial heartland. Thus it was hardly along a logical intervention route. Third, there were no Soviet allegations of a Western threat to Romania, assertions of domestic disintegration, attempts at creating a false sense of security, or interference with the organization of Romanian defense.

There were large-scale WTO maneuvers in September 1969, but they took place at a considerable distance from Romania, in Poland.[139] Known as "Oder-Neisse" in the West, the exercise involved a vast force with Soviet and complete Northern Tier participation, and employed both conventional and nuclear scenarios.[140] The maneuvers appeared to have the dual purpose of attempting to influence the elections in West Germany, which were in progress at this time, and to stress to the bloc the need for a Soviet shield against a "revanchist" Germany.[141] Romania did, however, make the concession of sending her Minister of Defense, General Ionita, to attend the maneuvers alongside all the other bloc ministers.[142]

Small Soviet troop movements during the remainder of 1969 in the vicinity of Romanian frontiers, as well as Black Sea naval exercises, appeared more or less routine to Western observers, and without the potential to be upgraded into an intervention.* There were other large Soviet maneuvers, however, but these were far removed geographically from Romania, and were clearly unrelated to it. While 1969 was a year of considerable military activity, some of which may have

---

Zeri i Populit (Tirana) saw danger for Romania but the Albanians have been the perpetual doomsayers on Soviet intervention. Article by T. Szulc, *International Herald Tribune* (Paris), September 6, 1969.

been designed to pressure Romania, the latter was in no great danger. The small and strategically (that is, for intervention purposes) poorly located spring maneuvers in which it did participate did not even move onto its territory.* Also, it seems from a retrospective political look that the Nixon visit in August would have acted more as a deterrent to, than as a catalyst for, intervention.

The cycle of maneuvers was continued at a high pace by the Soviet Union in 1970, but they were little related to Romania. "Dvina," a very large combined forces exercise, was held in Byelorussia on the Polish border during March, with a scenario which envisioned a Western enemy.[143] The Romanians sent some troops to a small Warsaw Pact maneuver held on the Hungarian-Czechoslovak borders,[144] but it did not participate in the very large Soviet-Czechoslovak maneuvers that followed later in July.[145] Finally, Romania sent a very small contingent of troops to participate in the mammoth "Brotherhood-in-Arms" maneuvers in the G.D.R. during the fall, as a concession. A small controversy developed over the official reports of the size of the Romanian contingent led by General-Major Paul Cheler,[146] but it soon died down. Therefore, during 1970, the Romanian situation was fairly stable.

The following year, however, presented Romania with Soviet and Warsaw Pact maneuvers that gave some cause to worry. While Romania made certain concessions, for instance, by sending its Minister of Defense, for the first time in two years, to attend a meeting of Warsaw Pact ministers during March,[147] it also challenged the Soviet Union through Ceausescu's well-publicized spring visits to China and North Korea. Furthermore, it reportedly turned down a Soviet request for passage of troops across its territory to July maneuvers in Bulgaria.[148] As a result, Soviet-Romanian relations were very strained.

Of the several Soviet and Warsaw Pact maneuvers in the year, two—"Yug 71" and "Opal 71"—had special relevance for Romania. "Yug," conducted in the southern part of the Soviet Union, took place in the first half of June,[149] while Ceausescu was visiting China and North Korea. It was a very large, exclusively Soviet exercise held simultaneously in two widely different areas. The first section was believed to have maneuvered in an area on the Black Sea near Odessa (that is, close to Romanian frontiers), while the second one was several hundred miles away in the north of the Caucasus mountains.[150] While the precise locations are not known, the Soviet coverage of the exercises suggested that the bulk of the forces were in the eastern section, where they followed the standard Soviet scenario of night attack en masse, defense, and some river crossings.[151]

The first section, though, appears to have had a much more varied scenario which would impress any small state such as Romania, close to whose frontiers it unfolded. The maneuvers involved an air assault by a Soviet division, as well as

---

*It was reported in the West that Romania had canceled WP maneuvers on Romanian territory for spring of 1969, in *Times* (London), February 7, 1969.

an amphibious assault by a marine brigade.[152] The implications were not lost on Romania, and Ceausescu stopped off in Moscow on June 25 on his return trip from the Orient in order to soothe Soviet feelings.

As menacing as the Western part of "Yug" may seem, it does not mean that it was an attempt at intervention. Several factors were missing; there were no Soviet accusations of Western threats to Romania, no allegations of counter-revolutionary activity within the country, and no attempts at creating a false Romanian sense of security. The Soviets were acting alone without Warsaw Pact support; since the bulk of Soviet troops were in the Eastern section, the maneuvers near Romania must have been on a limited scale; and finally, there had been no ground Soviet reconnaissance and preparation within Romania. Thus, while this section of "Yug" may have been politically motivated, it showed Soviet capabilities, rather than intent. Ceausescu's stopover in Moscow, therefore, was most likely out of caution and not panic.

"Opal 71" continued Soviet pressure on Romania during August. The exercise, which took place in Hungary and in a small border area in Czechoslovakia, involved Soviet, Czechoslovak, and Hungarian troops.[153] While the maneuvers were not held on the Romanian border but in the northwestern and central parts of Hungary,* they must have impressed the Romanian military observers present with the capacity for intervention they demonstrated. Much like the western section of "Yug," "Opal" involved parachute dropping, air strikes, deep armored thrust into "enemy" territory, and river forgings.[155] Again, as in the case of "Yug," key elements making up the attempt or "go-position" for intervention were missing, so the political purpose vis-a-vis Romania was most likely intimidation.

In 1972, the Soviets conducted only one large-scale maneuver, "Shield 72," in Czechoslovakia,[156] as compared to three major exercises during 1971. The Soviet Union, Czechoslovakia, Poland, Hungary, and the G.D.R. took part, while Romania, along with the other Warsaw Pact members, sent observers. The scenario appears to have envisaged a two-pronged attack from the West into Czechoslovakia, which would be met by both nuclear and nonnuclear responses.[157] If there was a political purpose in the maneuvers, it was most likely directed at showing Pact unity through the reintegration of Czechoslovakia, and not some demonstration versus Romania. Therefore, in 1972 the Soviet Union, despite its differences with Romania, chose not to exert overt military pressure against it.

The year 1973 was a rather uneventful year in Romanian-Soviet relations, as well as in Soviet maneuvers affecting Romania. The main source of friction would have been the visit of a Romanian military delegation led by the Chief of Staff to China in June 1973, but there is no indication that the Soviet Union

---

*The main maneuvers were held at Komarm-Komarno, twin border cities of Hungary and Czechoslovakia, and at Dunaujvaros and Dunafolvaros, which are in central Hungary.[154]

took this as a significant challenge. Its relations with Bucharest were relatively cordial and the Soviet military newspaper reported in February the completion of a ten-day joint Soviet-Romanian staff exercise held in Romania[158] (a staff exercise does not involve maneuvers with troops). The maneuvers that would have had the greatest interest to Romania were the combined Soviet-Hungarian exercises code-named "Vertes-73," involving a scenario of Hungarian troops halting a Western attack from the direction of Austria with the aid of Soviet forces and then counterattacking.[159] The counterattack involved coordinated artillery and tactical air movements and helicopter landings. Therefore, there were some elements similar to those involved in major interventions, but the forces were not large enough. Hungary had been a convenient point in the past for movements to other areas, such as Austria. In the Second World War, for instance, it had been used as a jumping-off point for the German invasion of Yugoslavia and it could be used against Romania. But again several elements were missing in the military preparation—in the size of the operation, in the number of participants involved and not least in the lack of political preparation for such an intervention into Romania. Therefore, these maneuvers, which were held at a considerable distance from the Romanian border, posed no real threat to Romania and only with difficulty could be interpreted even as an attempt to intimidation.

During 1974, there were various causes for Soviet-Romanian friction, ranging from Ceausescu's abolishment of the party Presidium, to Romania's refusal to allow construction of a railway line from the Soviet Union to Bulgaria and its refusal to allow major troop movements across Romanian territory to Bulgaria. In the summer of 1974 the Soviet Union held important joint maneuvers together with Bulgarian forces, in Bulgaria.[160] The maneuvers were on a significant scale but again several elements were missing. Geographically, Bulgaria was a very unlikely place to start an intervention from and no other Warsaw Pact troops were participating besides Soviet and Bulgarian forces. As well, Romania had good relations with Bulgaria and the Bulgarians were careful that maneuvers were not held at too great a proximity to the Romanian border. Furthermore, the political preparation for any sort of intervention was also lacking. Therefore, at best, this was an attempt to pressure Romania, and the latter did make some minor concessions by allowing a token number of Soviet troops to cross its territory to Bulgaria under the supervision of Romanian armored-vehicle escorts.

While 1975 was a rather uneventful year, during 1976 a number of Soviet military moves gave some concern to Romania. Romania's autonomous stance at the East Berlin conference undoubtedly irritated the Soviet Union and in the first part of the year, as we mentioned before, there were several "scholarly" articles published in Soviet, Hungarian, and Bulgarian journals that seemed to question Romania's right to its territory. The Soviet Union held major military maneuvers in the Caucasus region.[161] These maneuvers, held late January and early February 1976, were on a large scale and they demonstrated intervention potential, but they were too remote from Romania. Soviet maneuvers held during May-June ("Sever") near Finland involved over 25,000 troops but the Soviet Union had invited foreign military observers from Western states, so it was unlikely that these moves, particularly combined with the great distance, could have had much meaning to Romania.[162] During June the Soviet Union did move up a number of forces to the Romanian border and then withdrew them, therefore in the strictest sense not performing a military maneuver. Nevertheless, this could be interpreted by Romania as a signal, even though the troops did not have an intervention capacity, the pattern did not fit in with previous interventions, and there was inadequate political preparation for it. There had been a visit to Romania in June by the Soviet Secretary in charge of relations with Communist parties, Katushev, together with the Chief of the Soviet Military Political Directorate, and this may have reflected tension between Romania and the Soviet Union. The Romanian Minister of National Defense was removed from his post in June 1976 but this was done together with a rotation of three other ministers and Ionita did not lose his party position. Therefore, this does not appear to be directly related to the meetings. Nevertheless, some observers in the West believed that the Soviet Union was trying to intimidate Romania,[163] but according to any meaningful level of analysis these moves could not have been more than an attempt at intimidation. The new Romanian Minister of National Defense did visit his Soviet counterpart during November, for the first such ministers' meeting in three years and indications were that Romanian-Soviet relations improved considerably.[164] This was part of the general improvement in Romanian-Soviet relations that followed Ceausescu's visit to Crimea during the year when he met Brezhnev. Soviet-Hungarian maneuvers held in October 1976[165] were routine annual exercises that posed no apparent danger for Romania.

As relations between Romania and the Soviet Union eased somewhat during 1976, maneuvers of the Soviet Union or those of its Warsaw Pact allies appeared to pose no danger for Romania. Soviet, Czechoslovak, and Hungarian officers took part in an eight-day maneuver in Czechoslovakia and Hungary, ending on March 29, 1977,[166] but again in this case virtually every military aspect and political aspect of intervention were missing.

This analysis, we contend, shows that the Soviet Union had within its capacity—and did on occasion use—such maneuvers as a form of pressure on Romania in an attempt to induce it to conform. To that extent, some of the Soviet and joint Warsaw Pact exercises did narrow Romanian limits of autonomy. The credibility of Soviet military pressure, however, was to a considerable extent determined by its willingness to use the ultimate weapon of control—military intervention. If pressure was merely a bluff, and Romania could call such a bluff, then the pressure was bearable and the limits were enlarged. The evidence is that despite Soviet military pressure, Romania made only tactical concessions, and its differences with the Soviet Union continued year after year. Therefore, it is significant to know whether the Soviet Union did make an attempt at intervention, or whether it did reach a "go-position."

The answer, we contend, has to be negative. Of the several crises, the most serious ones appear to have been the maneuvers of spring 1969, and "Yug" and "Opal" in 1971. They all demonstrated how strong a military pressure the Soviets could bring on Romania, but they all lacked a number of key elements that would have transformed them into attempts at intervention. Romania clearly sensed this and following tactical concessions continued to pursue an autonomous foreign policy, which reached its fastigium in 1972, with the passage of an "all-horizons" defense law.

These Romanian policies since 1965 certainly enjoyed Soviet cognizance, and were seen as challenges to Moscow's military security. In turn, Romania was subjected to Soviet pressure, as we have seen in this chapter. In placing these challenges in the perspective of the military policy at the time each one occurred, as well as into the perspective of the general evolution of that policy, certain things became evident. It appears that, despite some fluctuations, Soviet military policy relegated Romania to a position of little strategic significance while simultaneously increasing the role of the states of the northern section of the Soviet bloc. The emergence of regionalism in Soviet policy toward Eastern Europe and in the WTO, consequently, reflected the evolution of Soviet thinking on nuclear weapons, on the resurgence of West Germany as a major power, on the Western Alliance, and on arms and troop limitation talks and agreements. For Romania, Soviet policies formed a certain network of defenses, for inherent in Soviet military policy toward Eastern Europe was the containability of Romanian challenges. Its remoteness from the axis of offensive-defensive operations in Europe, its lack of frontiers with any capitalist states, its small technological base and low reliability in any offensive operations, its poor conventional military effectiveness—which was gravely aggravated both by its unwillingness to cooperate with the Warsaw Pact as well as by Soviet withholding of modern heavy weapons as a form of pressure—all conjoined to relegate it into the lower recesses of Soviet threat perception to its own military security in Europe. When one appends to this the fact that, despite the Czechoslovak crisis in 1968, the Soviet Union did not demonstrate an interventionist behavior in Eastern Europe during the period of our study, then it appears that Romania possessed a formidable set of "passive" defenses for its autonomous position.

We conducted a check on the limits that the Soviets imposed on Romanian autonomy by endeavoring to ascertain whether there had been an attempt at military intervention into Romania, for such intervention has been demonstrated to be the ultimate limit on autonomy in the Soviet bloc. To this end, we tried to discern if there was a pattern, or at least a tendency, in past Soviet military interventions in Eastern Europe and, thereby, define the steps that amounted to the attempt or the "go-position." While we could not discern a clearly defined pattern, we did find that certain actions that preceded Soviet military intervention could provide the preponderance of evidence that constituted a tendency amounting to an attempt.

The empirical test consisted of a review of major Soviet and Warsaw Pact maneuvers in East and Central Europe during 1965 to 1977, and their relationship to Romania. We found these military moves to have posed the greatest danger to Romania in the spring of 1969, and the spring and summer of 1971. On these occasions, certain of the important military factors that preceded previous Soviet interventions in Eastern Europe were present, but they were insufficient to constitute a preponderance of evidence pointing toward a tendency at intervention. They were, therefore, only attempts at intimidation. Accordingly, Romania was not, so to speak, walking the tightrope onto which, the West was convinced, its challenges to Soviet authority had placed it.

On the other hand, it is not sufficient to say that Soviet policy itself constituted inherent defenses for Romanian autonomy. This is only part of the answer, for these defenses, which were "passive" from the Romanian point of view (with the exception of Romania's deliberate lowering of its WTO effectiveness), did not wholly determine the limits for foreign policy autonomy. The limits were not stratic but dynamic, and "active" Romanian defenses had to contribute to the shaping, and perhaps widening, of these limits. The Soviet Union had demonstrated in Eastern Europe, through its preparations for past military interventions, that despite the overwhelming preponderance of its military strength it attached considerable importance to the actions of a small opponent. Consequently, Romania's active defenses, that is, the military actions it took itself, are important. In the next chapter, therefore, we will examine Romanian military policies and actions at crisis points, as well as the control that it maintained over its challenges to Soviet military security.

NOTES

1. See Graham Allison, "Conceptual Models and the Cuban Missile Crisis," *American Political Science Review*, September 1969.

2. Malcolm Mackintosh, "Soviet Aims and Capabilities in Europe" in *RUSI Journal* (London), March 1971 (lecture given on December 2, 1970 at RUSI), p. 23.

3. Carl G. Jacobsen, *Soviet-Strategy-Soviet Foreign Policy* (Glasgow: Robert Mackenzie & Co. U.P., 1972), p. 25.

4. L. Goure, F. D. Kohler, and M. L. Harvey, *The Role of Nuclear Forces in Current Soviet Strategy* (Miami: Center of Advanced International Studies, University of Miami 1974), p. 15.

5. See T. W. Wolfe, *Soviet Power and Europe* (Baltimore: Johns Hopkins Press, 1970), p. 149.

6. J. Erickson, *Soviet Military Power* (London: RUSI, 1971), p. 7.

7. *Revue de Defense Nationale* (Paris) April 1964, p. 625.

8. J. Erickson, "The Czechoslovak Invasion," *Sunday Times* (London), September 1, 1968.

9. Jacobsen, op. cit., p. 24.

10. W. E. Griffith, *The Great Globe Transformed* (Cambridge, Mass.: Europe Center for International Studies, M.I.T., 1971), pp. 17-8.

11. *Pravda* (Moscow), July 25, 1960, p. 1.

12. *Pravda*, May 9, 1960, p. 1, also see Michel Tatu, *Power in the Kremlin*, trans. H. Katel (London: Collins St. James' Place, 1969), pp. 69-72 on the conflict between the marshals and Khrushchev.

13. Wolfe, op. cit., p. 150.

14. R. Garthoff, *East Europe*, September 1965, and *The Military Balance 1962-63; 1963-64; 1964-65* (London: IISS, 1962; 1963; 1964).

15. Hans Von Krannhals, "Command Integration Within the Warsaw Pact," *Military Review* vol. 45, October 1965, p. 43.

16. R.A. Remington, *The Warsaw Pact* (Cambridge, Mass.: M.I.T. Press, 1971), pp. 17-8.

17. *Izvestia*, May 27, 1958.

18. *The Military Balance 1975-1976* (London: IISS, 1975), p. 11.

19. *Globe and Mail* (Toronto), November 27, 1976.

20. "The Warsaw Treaty" New York *Times*, May 21, 1955.

21. G. Ginsburgs, "Socialist Internationalism and State Sovereignty" in *The Yearbook of World Affairs 1971* (London: Institute of World Affairs, 1971), p. 40.

22. N. Ceausescu, *Scinteia*, August 15, 1968.

23. A. Braun, "The Evolution of the Warsaw Pact," *Canadian Defence Quarterly*, Winter 1973-74, p. 32, Figure D.

24. E. Hinterhoff, "The Erosion of the Warsaw Pact and Its Implications," *Ons Leger* (translated), September 1968, p. 7.

25. Hannes Adomeit, *Soviet Risk-Taking and Crisis Behaviour: From Confrontation to Co-existence*, Adelphi Paper No. 101 (London: IISS, 1973), pp. 8-10.

26. R. F. Kennedy, *Thirteen Days* (New York: W.W. Norton & Co., 1969), p. 89.

27. Mackintosh, op. cit., p. 23.

28. *The Military Balance, 1965-66*, p. 7; *1966-67*, p. 8; *1967-68*, p. 4 (London: IISS, 1965; 1966).

29. *Scinteia*, May 8, 1966.

30. Erickson, *Soviet Military Power*, op. cit., p. 8.

31. *The Military Balance, 1967-1968*, op. cit., p. 5.

32. Erickson, *Soviet Military Power*, op. cit., p. 26.

33. *Pravda*, May 20, 1966, p. 5, translated in *The Current Digest of Soviet Press* vol. 18, June 8, 1966, p. 14.

34. J. F. Brown, "Detente and Soviet Policy in Eastern Europe," *Survey*, Spring-Summer, 1974, p. 49.

35. Marshal V. D. Sokolovsky, "On Contemporary Military Strategy," *Communist of the Armed Forces*, April 1966, and in W. R. Kintner and H. F. Scott, *The Nuclear Revolution in Soviet Military Affairs* (Norman: University of Oklahoma Press, 1968), p. 262.

36. I. G. Zavyalov, "On Soviet Military Doctrine," *Krasnaya Zvezda*, March 30, 1967, also in Kintner and Scott, op. cit., pp. 380-5.

37. T. W. Wolfe, *Trends in Soviet Thinking on Theater Warfare, Conventional Preparations, and Limited War*, Rand Corporation Memorandum R.M.-4505-P.R., 1965, p. 41.

38. John Erickson, *Soviet-Warsaw Pact Force Levels*, Washington, U.S.S.I. Report 76-2, 1976, pp. 31-2.

39. P. H. Vigor and C. N. Donnelly, "Freefire," *Armies and Weapons*, September 15 to October 15, 1976, p. 5.

40. Erickson, *Soviet-Warsaw Pact Force Levels*, op. cit., p. 31.

41. *Pravda*, May 14, 1966, p. 5.

42. *Guardian* (London), May 17, 1965.

43. Dvina Voiskovye Monevry . . . Marte, 1970, goda *Moscow Voonizdat*, 1970, p. 192, and in Erickson, *Soviet Military Power*, op. cit., p. 28.

44. *Guardian* (London), May 17, 1965.

45. H. S. Dinerstein, *War and the Soviet Union* (New York: The Rand Corp. and F.A. Praeger, 1962), pp. 200-5.

46. *Flight International* (London), June 5, 1976, p. 1507.

47. *The Military Balance 1977-1978* (London: IISS, 1977), pp. 13-15.

48. Ibid., p. 15 and p. 82.

49. A. Ross Johnson, "Has Eastern Europe Become a Liability to the Soviet Union?" in Charles Gati, ed., *The International Politics of Eastern Europe* (New York: Praeger, 1976), p. 55.

50. Wolfe, *Soviet Power and Europe*, op. cit., p. 26.

51. G. H. Turbiville, "Warsaw Pact Forces in Hungary," *RUSI Journal* vol. 121, no. 4, December 1976, pp. 47-51.

52. A. Braun, "Soviet Naval Policy in the Mediterranean, the 'Sonnenfeldt Doctrine' and Yugoslavia," *Orbis*, Spring 1978.

53. M. M. Boll, "The Dilemma of the Warsaw Pact," *Military Review*, July 1969, p. 91.

54. *The Budapest Appeal*, 1969, in Remington, op. cit., p. 255, Document 7.

55. Remington, op. cit., p. 15.

56. *Globe and Mail*, November 27, 1976.

57. *Scinteia*, May 16 and 28, 1966.

58. Erickson, "The Czechoslovak Invasion," op. cit.

59. Ibid.

60. *Izvestia*, July 30, 1968, p. 2.

61. *Pravda*, August 22, 1968, p. 3.

62. N. Gribachev, ibid.

63. *Pravda*, August 22, 1968.

64. "Conspiracy Against Socialist Czechoslovakia," *Pravda*, August 24, 1968, p. 1.

65. New York *Times*, September 20, 1969.

66. Gabriel Fischer (Professor, Acadia University), personal communication, October 10, 1975, at Conference on "Eastern Europe and Detente," McMaster University, Canada.

67. Peter Nailor, "Problems of Security in Europe," in K. J. Twitchett, *International Security* (London: Oxford University Press, 1971), pp. 116-7.

68. T. W. Wolfe, *Soviet Attitudes Toward MBFR and USSR's Military Presence in Europe*, Rand Report P-4819 (Santa Monica: Rand Corp., 1972), p. 10.

69. T. W. Wolfe, *Some Foreign Policy Aspects of the CPSU Congress*, Rand Report P-4644 (Santa Monica: Rand Corp., 1971), p. 3; and Wolfe, ibid., p. 1.

70. *The Military Balance 1975-1976*, op. cit., p. 3.

71. Ibid.

72. W. R. Kintner and R. L. Pfaltzgraft, Jr., *Soviet Military Trends: Implications for U.S. Security* (Philadelphia: Foreign Policy Research Institute, 1971), p. 3.

73. A. Z. Rubinstein, "Soviet Policy in Europe," *Current History*, October 1977, p. 107.

74. V. Lipatti, "Edificara Securitatii Europeene," *Era Socialista*, no. 2, January 1975, pp. 22-3.

75. N. Ecobescu and S. Celac, *Politica Externa a Romaniei Socialiste* (Bucharest: Editura Politica, 1975), p. 92.

76. *Lumea*, April 21, 1977, p. 4.

77. G. Serafin, *Lumea*, June 9, 1977, p. 7.

78. Constantin Florea, "O politica internationala activa de pace si prientenie intre popoare," *Era Socialista*, March 6, 1973, p. 7.

79. Axel Horhager, "The MBFR Talks—Problems and Prospects," *Defence Review* vol. 9, no. 2, April 1976, pp. 180-3.

80. Pierre Hassner, in *Change and Security in Europe* (London: IISS 1968), p. 17.

81. Dennis J. Doolin, *Territorial Claims in the Sino-Soviet Conflict* (Stanford, California: The Hoover Institute, 1965), pp. 70-1.

82. Klaus Knorr, *On the Uses of Military Power in the Nuclear Age* (Princeton N.J.: Princeton University Press, 1966), p. 169.

83. *The Military Balance 1971-1972* (London: IISS, 1971), p. 6.

84. W. Schneider, Jr., "Soviet General-Purpose Forces," *Orbis*, Spring 1977, p. 101.

85. W. E. Griffith, *The Sino-Soviet Rift*, Document No. 7 (Cambridge, Mass.: M.I.T. Press, 1964), p. 351.

86. J. R. Thomas, "Soviet Foreign Policy and the Military," *Survey* vol. 17, no. 3, 1971, p. 147.

87. Brown, op. cit., p. 56.

88. Chou En-lai in interview with Yugoslav daily, *Vjesnik*, August 28, 1971.

89. Legistatie privind organizarea de stat, *7 Legea nr. 14/1972 privind organizarea apararii nationale a Republicii Socialiste Romania*, Sectia redactionala a *Buletinulni Oficial*, 1973, p. 3.

90. Lord C. J. Reading, in King v. Robinson, 2K.B 342 Court of Appeal, England (1915).

91. Stefan Brant, *The East German Rising* (London: Thames and Hudson, 1955), p. 151.

92. "N.C.," "Czechoslovakia," *Saturday Review*, September 7, 1968.

93. "The Defense of Socialism Is Our Common Task," *Krasnaya Zvezda*, July 19, 1968.

94. Z. Brzezinski, *The Soviet Bloc* (Cambridge, Mass.: Harvard University Press, 1967), p. 257.

95. Ibid., p. 228.

96. T. Alexsandrov, *Pravda*, July 11, 1968.

97. *Pravda*, October 31, 1956, and in Brzezinski, op. cit., p. 230.

98. *Pravda*, August 16, 1968.

99. As announced by the Czech Ministry of Defense, noted in *Survival* (London), IISS, November 1968, p. 358.

100. Brant, op. cit., p. 70.

101. Brzezinski, op. cit., p. 256.

102. J. Erickson, "Meanwhile in Hungary," in A. Moncrieff, ed., *Suez Ten Years After* (London: Butler & Tanner, 1967), p. 122.

103. Tad Szulc, "Soviet Army in Action Impresses West," New York *Times*, September 10, 1968.

104. Ibid.

105. Brzezinski, op. cit., p. 255.

106. Gen. Bela Kiraly, "Hungary's Army: Its Part in the Revolt," *East Europe* vol. 7, no. 6, June 1958, p. 10.

107. Erickson, "Meanwhile in Hungary," op. cit., p. 124.

108. Thomas, op. cit., p. 137.

109. Jacobsen, op. cit., p. 22.

110. Brant, op. cit., pp. 150-1.

111. Wolfe, *Soviet Power and Europe*, op. cit., p. 149.

112. Szulc, op. cit.

113. *Pravda*, March 8, 1970, p. 6.

114. R. L. Garthoff, *Soviet Military Policy* (London: Faber and Faber, 1966), p. 158.

115. Editorial in *Voyenn-Istorischeskiy Zhurnal*, no. 2, February 1973, signed to press January 30, 1973, p. 312. Translated in *Joint Press Release Services* (Washington, U.S. Department of Commerce) vol. 58737, April 13, 1973.

116. *Izvestia*, October 22, 1965, p. 1, translated in *The Current Digest* vol. 17, no. 42.

117. *Guardian*, October 11, 1961.

118. Erickson, *Soviet Military Power*, op. cit., p. 26.

119. *Radio Free Europe Research: Romania*, October 7, 1970, and the New York *Times*, August 29, 1971.

120. *Scinteia*, August 29, 1967.

121. *Soviet News* (London), October 26, 1965.

122. *Izvestia*, October 22, 1965, p. 1, translated in *The Current Digest of Soviet Press* vol. 17, no. 42, p. 8.

123. *Izvestia*, September 14, 1966, p. 2, and September 27, 1966, p. 2.

124. New York *Herald Tribune*, October 14, 1966.

125. *Daily Telegraph* (London), September 19, 1966.

126. *RFE Research: Romania*, October 7, 1970.

127. Wolfe, *Soviet Power and Europe*, op. cit., pp. 479-80.

128. Henry Kamm, "Russian Forces Seem To Put Off Leaving Slovakia," New York *Times*, July 22, 1968 and Richard Eder, "Prague Reported Tense: Soviet Troops on Move," *Washington Post*, July 30, 1968.

129. Wolfe, *Soviet Power and Europe*, op. cit., p. 480.

130. "We Look to Our Friends," *Pravda*, July 30, 1968.

131. J. Pergent, "Les Manoeuvres Geantes Des Armees du Pact de Varsovie," (*Revue Militaire Generale*, November 1971, p. 531.

132. Ibid.

133. David Binder, "Kissinger Urges Defense Step-Up," New York *Times*, September 20, 1968.

134. *U.S. News and World Report*, February 27, 1969, pp. 64-5.

135. *Times* (London), February 21, 1969; announcement made by Tass on February 20, 1969.

136. *Radio Free Europe: Situation Report, Poland*, April 2, 1969.

137. *Guardian*, April 14, 1969.

138. Announced by Tass on May 19, 1969. See *RFE Research: Romania*, May 20, 1969.

139. *Pravda*, September 23, 1969.

140. *Izvestia*, September 30, 1969.

141. *Times* (London), September 29, 1969.

142. *Soviet News*, September 30, 1969.

143. Lieutenant A. Letunovsky, *Krasnaya Zvezda*, March 15, 1970, p. 2, in Joint Press Release Service, no. 60, April 1, 1970.

144. *International Herald Tribune* (Paris), July 10, 1970.

145. *Le Monde*, July 29, 1970.

146. *Le Monde*, October 12, 1970.

147. *Scinteia*, March 4, 1971.

148. J. Guillem-Bralon, *Le Figaro*, July 29, 1971.

149. *Izvestia*, June 16, 1971, p. 6.

150. Major J. F. Meeham, "Summer 1971," *Military Review* (Ft. Leavenworth, Kentucky) April 1972, p. 17.

151. *Pravda*, June 17, 1971, p. 6.

152. *Izvestia*, June 17, 1971, p. 8, and *Pravda*, June 18, 1971, p. 6.

153. *Pravda*, August 1971, p. 1, and September 8, 1971, p. 4.

154. *Nepszabadsag*, August 9, 1971.

155. *Radio Liberty*, C.R.D. 280/71, September 12, 1971, p. 7.

156. *Joint Press Release Services*, 58167, February 6, 1973.

157. G. H. Turbiville, "W.P. Exercises, Shield 72," *Military Review*, July 1973, p. 18.

158. *Krasnaya Zvezda*, February 22, 1973.

159. *Allegmeine Schweizerische Militaerzeitung*, no. 2, 1974, p. 77, and Turbiville, "Warsaw Pact Forces. . . , " op. cit., p. 49.

160. New York *Times*, August 22, 1974.

161. *Soviet Analyst* vol. 5, no. 4, February 12, 1976.

162. *Pravda*, May 24, 1976, and *Guardian*, June 8, 1976.

163. T. Rakowska-Harmstone, "Socialist Internationalism Part II," *Survey*, Spring 1976, p. 72.

164. *Guardian*, November 10, 1976.

165. New York *Times*, October 20, 1976.

166. *International Herald Tribune* (Paris), March 30, 1977.

5

Active Romanian
Military Defenses of
Foreign Policy Autonomy

We have concluded, then, in our analysis of the evolution of Soviet military policy toward the bloc states that Moscow's perception of its security needs contained some passive defenses for Romanian foreign policy autonomy. In some ways these constituted an inherent restraining mechanism on Soviet desires to enforce bloc conformity. Nevertheless, in its quest for security the Soviet Union was not deterred by these defenses from exerting certain types of pressures on Romania in order to induce it to adhere more closely to Soviet policy aims. While Soviet constraints on Eastern Europe ranged from outright military intervention to attempts at intimidation, Romania was fortunate enough, as was seen in the previous chapter, to be confronted only with the latter form of threat. Attempts at intimidation, basically a psychological game of nerves, demonstrated, then, that the passive defenses of Romania did not constitute a sufficient deterrent in themselves to all Soviet pressure. If Romania were to continue to pursue an autonomous foreign policy it had to furnish a countervailing balance through active defenses. Resisting intimidation should have been a key pillar of the entire Romanian policy of autonomy.

In view of Czechoslovakia's lack of armed resistance to overwhelming Soviet power in the 1968 intervention, some arguments were advanced to the effect that it was not possible for any Soviet-bloc state to offer sufficient resistance to defeat such intervention because of the great discrepancy in military power between the Soviet Union and a bloc state. Furthermore, in a pre-intervention crisis the Soviet leaders had been able to call up as many reservists as they wanted to, and to deploy their troop concentrations according to carefully-laid-out plans,[1] whereas a bloc state would have been deterred from doing this by a fear of either provoking the Soviet Union or of giving it an excuse for intervention. While Romania did not have to defend itself solely through the use of

144

its own armed power, as the previous chapters indicated, nevertheless the difficulty of armed resistance is obvious, despite the fact that the present chapter will recognize it as only a part of the network of Romanian defenses. On the other hand, the difficulties of armed defense by a bloc state against the Soviet Union should not ab initio exclude the very possibility of such a defense because of a lack of a geopolitical balance. In terms of deterrence, there is a cost/benefit factor with the result that all a state needs is sufficient armed might to inflict such damage on an aggressor that it would outweigh the benefits of his aggression.[2] Taken together with its passive defenses, then, Romania's active defenses did not have to have a very high level of credibility. Even minimal credibility, though, results from a composite of factors. In active military defense the first ingredient consists of the unambiguous willingness of a state to put up armed resistance, and we will examine whether Romania had indicated such a willingness to resist during crises or disagreement points since 1965. Second, there must be an actual capacity to put up armed resistance.

That in turn entails a broad set of factors that together constitute defensive ability. The first among these was the necessity of the Romanian party leadership to maintain control (and therein unity) over the country's armed forces. We will, therefore, examine the methods employed to maintain such unity and check the support that the armed forces gave the leadership at various crisis points. Second, we will look at the actions that Romania could and did undertake to offset such Soviet desiderata for a successful military intervention as surprise, speed of operation, and maintenance of troop morale. Within this context we shall examine Romania's sounding of alarm at crisis points to avoid being lured into a false sense of security and the actions it took to retard the speed of potential Soviet and Warsaw Pact allied interventions. The latter encompassed both conventional and guerrilla military preparations. Another part of Romanian defenses was made up by its quest for flank support. Specifically, we are concerned with the military aspects of its relations with Yugoslavia, and to a lesser extent with its relations with Bulgaria and Hungary. Romanian relations with China again constituted a possible defense within this sphere. Last, the active defenses could include the very manner of the Romanian military challenges, and our interest here will concern itself with the extent to which the Romanians were skilled enough in dulling the sharper edges of their challenges and in judging how far, during the latter period of our study, they succeeded in placing such challenges within the relative safety of the general European security aims of the Soviet Union.

THE WILL TO RESIST

Any Romanian decision to take active steps for its physical defense had to be conveyed to the Soviet Union in order to perform the function of deterrence. Communication of a willingness to resist, though, should not have presented significant difficulties for Romania. The Soviet Union always kept a close watch on the bloc states and took note of statements made by bloc-state leaders, as well as policy statements appearing in the major party and military publications.* In addition the Soviet intelligence network, which was only partially represented abroad by the very large embassy staffs it maintained in the bloc states, must have made the Moscow leadership aware of any significant steps that Romania might have taken to enhance its ability to resist—should such a decision have been reached by the Romanian leadership. It is indeed difficult to perceive how Romania could have embarked upon any major preparation for defense without Soviet knowledge, had it even desired to do so. The credibility of the active Romanian defenses, then, depended on how effective these defenses appeared under close Soviet scrutiny, once the Romanians made the decision to resist.

Public Romanian reaction during some of the crisis points with the Soviet Union could indicate whether Romania did have a policy of active defenses or whether at least it tried to convey such an impression to Moscow. Ceausescu's first major open crisis came in the spring of 1967. Following Romania's establishment of diplomatic relations with the Federal Republic of Germany in January, the Soviet leaders, and under their direction the rest of the bloc, subjected Romania to vituperative polemical attacks. Ceausescu defended his policies and on May 31 he gave an important address, which took into view the increasing polemics against Romania. While he reiterated that Romania would fight alongside other Socialist countries "for the defeat of imperialist aggressors,"[3] he also issued a warning:

> In speaking of the foreign policy of our Party and government, in emphasizing the fact that the army represents the guarantee of the successful implementation of our foreign policy, I wish to spotlight the fact that the Party assesses highly the activity of our army (and) the full support it gives to Romania's policy of peace and security.[4]

Ceausescu went on to state that the army was to be strengthened and that the military preparedness of the troops would be increased. His statement, "Let every soldier, inspired by the lofty feeling of Socialist patriotism, be ready at any time to serve his homeland and people," indicated that there was a limit to the attempts to intimidate Romania.

Unequivocal Romanian support for Czechoslovakia both before and after the intervention,[5] subjected Bucharest anew to increased Soviet pressure and thereby placed it in a position where it had to demonstrate whether it was pre-

---

*There is an important section of the Soviet Secretariat headed by K. F. Katushev that deals with interparty affairs. Also the Soviet attack on various Romanian writers of newspaper articles indicates that Moscow kept a close watch on the major Romanian publications.

pared to continue with an autonomous foreign policy under such pressure. On August 14, 1968, Ceausescu declared in an article published in the army paper *Apararea Patriei* that in view of the fact that "the threat from imperialism is great," Romania had taken direct steps to strengthen its armed forces. Then he proceeded to list some of the specific measures. Thereafter, at the very time the Soviet and Warsaw Pact forces were commencing their entry into Czechoslovakia, *Apararea Patriei* carried an order of the day to the armed forces by the Minister of the Armed Forces, General-Colonel Ion Ionita, which declared that the Romanian army was to be ready "on a moment's notice" to defend the independence and sovereignty of Romania.[6] The same issue of the paper carried articles on the "excellent fighting ability" of the Romanian armed forces, which the writers felt was well demonstrated in the August 23, 1944, switch to the allied side. These articles further emphasized the vast improvement in the strength of the forces in 1968. Thus the signal to the Soviet Union was clear, namely that in case of intervention Romania was willing to put up armed resistance.

In the first half of 1969, as we have seen, the Soviet Union exerted some of the heaviest military pressures against Romania. Ceausescu's speeches during this period tend to indicate that he continued his policy of reemphasizing to the Soviet Union the willingness of Romania to resort to arms if the defense of its sovereignty required it. As pressure was beginning to mount against Romania in February, Ceausescu declared in a speech before the Great Electoral Meeting held in Bucharest that while at that moment there was no danger from outside reactionary forces, the Romanians nevertheless were on their guard:

> I want to declare that should anybody try to touch our Socialist gains he would come up against the resistance of a 20 million strong, closely united people, determined to fight with all its energies and with abnegation, with every means available in defense of its new life, of the sacred right to liberty and independence.[7]

While at first the speech might appear to be directed against the West, Ceausescu's rejection of the outside "reactionary danger," which was one of the justifications utilized by the Soviet Union in the Czechoslovak intervention, combined with the strained relations with the Soviet Union at that time, would lend credence to the hypothesis that Ceausescu's speech was an esoteric message directed at the Communist superpower.

By May 1969, with Soviet military moves increasing on its borders, Romania called for a new type of interstate relations that would respect the right of each people to decide their own fate. Ceausescu claimed that "Public opinion pronounces itself ever more determinedly against any manifestation of a military character designed to intimidate people and against any demonstration of force which poisons the international political atmosphere."[8] In the following month, he used the well-frequented venue of the reconciliation speech aimed at settling the Sino-Soviet dispute in order to reiterate that disputes between the

Socialist states could be resolved only through negotiations. All other means, he stated (and it must be remembered that there was severe Soviet military pressure against Romania at this time), would only harm the Communist movement and the influence of Socialism in the world. Therefore, not only did Ceausescu indicate that Romania was willing to offer armed resistance, but he also warned that Soviet pressure in itself was damaging the cause of world Socialism as a whole.

While 1970 witnessed a relaxation of military tension between the Soviet Union and Romania, Ceausescu saw fit to continue his liturgy on Romanian willingness to resist military intervention. In a speech before high-ranking military cadres he declared:

> History shows that our people who always worked for the progress of the country also prepared itself for its defenses; it was not infrequent in the past that beside their plows or work-tools, people kept arms, and were ready at any time to defend the land of their forefathers.[9]

Spring and summer maneuvers by the Soviet Union during 1971, however, held close to the Romanian borders did call for a response from Bucharest. As far back as January of that year, when Ceausescu's visit to the Soviet Union's arch-enemy, China, was in the preparatory stage, the Romanian military thought it prudent to issue some advance warning of Romanian sensitivity about its sovereignty. Rear-Admiral Fl. Diaconu, writing in *Apararea Patriei*, claimed that the military archives showed that both the army and the people were hostile to the introduction of German troops in Romania in late 1940 and 1941 (despite an alliance with the Axis powers) and considered it "a grave trespass on national sovereignty."[10] Following the enunciation of this historical rejection of introduction of foreign troops on Romanian soil as a breach of sovereignty, Admiral Diaconu praised extensively the passive resistance of the population to the Germans and the "heroic" general insurrection against Hitlerist Germany during the war, without making any mention of the Soviet role in the "liberation" of August 1944. The latter historical analysis was certainly one way of magnifying the historical capacity of the Romanian people to defend their sovereignty against overwhelming odds.

As Soviet military pressure on Romania heightened in June with Ceausescu's visit to the People's Republic of China, Romanian willingness to resist was reiterated from an oblique, but nevertheless effective, corner. It was strangely enough, the Chinese Prime Minister, Chou En-lai, speaking at a reception for Ceausescu, who outlined the foreign policy of his guest's country. His first statement that "Romania firmly resists subversion by imperialism,"[11] was particularly striking in view of the fact that in Chinese terminology "imperialist" is often the adjectival designation of Soviet foreign policy. But Chou even enlarged on these innuendoes:

> . . . for the defense of the independence and sovereignty of the country, the Romanian people has carried out a difficult struggle

and stood up to pressures. At the moment when the party itself is faced with grave threats of imperialist intervention, the Romanian people under the leadership of the party and the government have strengthened its defensive capacity. At the present moment the Romanian people maintain a high vigilance, and is ready at any time to oppose with a popular war an armed imperialist invasion.[12]

His strong language may not have been compatible with the diplomatic aesthetics of Romanian pronouncement, but its content was in line with previous Romanian pronouncements and policies. It is, therefore, unlikely that his statement did not have Ceausescu's approval and therein it acted very much as a warning to the Soviet Union.

In the latter part of June, when Ceausescu was being accorded tumultuous welcomes in North Korea and Mongolia, *Apararea Patriei* carried a lengthy editorial on its front page celebrating the Day of the Borderguards.[13] It was conspicuous not only in that the newspaper coverage of the event was much more extensive than in previous years, but also in the emphasis on the defensive readiness of these border units which, according to the editors, would be the first to make contact with any intervening military forces. After asserting that the borderguards had a permanent, 24-hour-per-day mission of defense, the editorial went on to state that:

> In the first place, the warm love of the fatherland, and devotion which goes up to sacrifice for the people, for the party, and for the cause of Socialism, are the springs of power and the actions of this soldier. He is irreconciliable with any infraction of our law, [or] trespass across our frontiers. . . . As everywhere in the country, here too in the world of the frontier, the ties among army and people are many and durable.[14]

In the same issue the Minister of the Armed Forces, General Ionita, reiterated this note on the readiness to fight, when he proclaimed that the readiness of the borderguards was a reflection of the battle readiness of the entire people. In the Order of the Day message, he commanded that the borderguards and all the other forces be ready to defend the country. He then declared that the borderguards had the support of the population, the national guard, and youth detachments of the frontier regions.

Throughout the remainder of the month of June, other high-ranking officers such as General-Lieutenant Vasile Milea and General-Major Gh. Gomoiu reemphasized Romania's readiness.[15] The commander of the artillery also wrote that "preparations are intense, so that this branch will be ready to carry out its mission and to be ready at any moment, with the soldiers of the other branches to completely fulfill its missions,"[16] of the defense of Romania. Ceausescu himself perhaps best summed up Romania's attitude to the Soviet military pressures of 1971 when he declared during his visit to North Korea (in the guise of an attack on imperialism in general) that:

> The imperialist policy of dictate and force, of exploitation and en-
> slavement of peoples, represents a permanent danger for liberty and
> quietness of peoples. But, life demonstrates that when the people
> are determined to defend their freedom, independence and national
> sovereignty, there are no forces in the world capable to vanquish
> them.[17]

Thus, at least according to public pronouncements, Romania was not allowing
itself to be intimidated by the Soviet pressures of 1971.

While, as we have shown in the previous chapters, overt Soviet military
pressures against Romania decreased during and after 1972, the latter continued
to declare a readiness to defend itself. But the crowning of this announced willingness by Romania to defend itself came at the end of 1972 with the approval
by the Grand National Assembly of the "Bill on the Organization of the National
Defense of the Socialist Republic of Romania." The speech in the Assembly by
the Minister of National Defense, outlining the main features of the proposed
law, bears note:

> It [the Bill] creates the necessary legislative framework for the
> mobilization of all human and material resources of the country
> for the defense of our fatherland in the event of aggression. . . .
> [and]stipulates that the right to take decision on defense questions
> is a sovereign attribute of the Romanian State, and that the national
> territory is inalienable and indivisible.[18]

In fact, Article I of the law was unequivocal about the obligation to resist intervention:

> It is forbidden to sanction or to recognize any action of a foreign
> state or any situation, regardless of its nature, including general
> capitulation or occupation of the national territory, which in time of
> peace or war might violate the national sovereignty, independence
> and territorial integrity of the Socialist Republic of Romania, or
> which might in any way weaken her defense capability. Any act of
> approval or recognition of this nature is invalid and undesirable, as it
> stands in contradiction to the political system and the highest in-
> terests of our Socialist nation.[19]

The new Defense Law, in an "all-horizons" defense configuration, therefore, gave legal sanctity to a public policy of willingness to resist, which had
apparently become a point for continual recital in post-1967 Romanian public
declarations. After Ceausescu consolidated his own position by late 1966, the
policy down the political and military line was to reject publicly any possibility
of Romania acquiescing to foreign military intimidations. The new law indicated
that Romania intended this policy to become permanently inscribed into its

foreign policy. In view of the several years of reiterating this posture, by 1972 the Romanians must have felt confident enough of having so conditioned the Soviet Union to this that they could safely formalize their stand.

After 1972 the reiteration of the willingness of the Romanians to resist any form of intervention was done in an atmosphere of déjà vu. Nevertheless, in any period of tension or even friction this kind of reiteration served to convey to the Soviet Union an extended signal and to allay the possibilities of misperception by the Soviet Union of Romania's resolve to pursue a certain policy. In 1974, during the process and following the actual changes in the party structure, as well as in the summer and early fall of 1976, the Romanians emphasized their willingness to resist intervention through armed resistance. In 1976, particularly, it is interesting to note that the military paper *Apararea Patriei* printed a front-page editorial that quoted Ceausescu on the need for everyone to be ready for the defense of the country, side by side with the article covering Ceausescu's meeting with Brezhnev in Crimea during early August.[20]

These Romanian declarations again could have acted as an active form of defense and thereby have had a significant deterrent value only if they were believed by the Soviet Union. As Henry Kissinger has written, a bluff believed is more effective than true military capacity not believed.[21] Unfortunately for Romania, Soviet knowledge of the internal affairs of the bloc states had been great enough even in the 1960s and 1970s to detect a pure bluff. Therefore, Romanian declarations would have had little effect if they had not been reinforced by some Romanian military defensive capacity. Again, we are not implying that Romania would have had to possess a military apparatus capable of defeating a superpower aggressor, but rather that the Romanian declarations would have had to have been backed by some concrete military steps. In other words, Romania would have had to maintain some broad (that is, not just purely armed force) military capacity, in order to acquire and maintain some deterrent credibility.

CAPACITY TO PROVIDE ACTIVE DEFENSES

One of the key weaknesses of a target state that any aggressor would search for would be disunity between the political leadership of that state and its military establishment. No effective military defense can be organized by a state unless the military can be relied upon to carry out the orders of the country's leadership. If Romania was to have some credibility, it had to make sure that it satisfied the sine qua non of party-military unity, which in Socialist terminology means party control over the military. Unity in this sense would have increased the efficiency of Romania's defenses by providing good channels of control but, even more important, it would have blocked Soviet attempts to infiltrate or to disrupt the organization of a defense. Therefore, we propose to examine first the methods that the Romanian leadership under Ceausescu employed to control the Romanian military and then look at the actual success that the political leadership enjoyed in this task.

A primary means of control by the Romanian Communist Party was bound to be effected through the use of the military structure and through the closeness of political-military links. Ceausescu was fortunate in that when he came to power in 1965 he was faced with a fairly docile military establishment. The Romanian armed forces were rebuilt very slowly following World War II, partly because of Soviet distrust and partly because of the inability of a weak Romanian economy to support a large force. The old officer corps had been purged and the new ones owed their position to the Communist party. In 1965, then, the Minister of the Armed Forces, General of the Army Leontin Salajan pledged the support and loyalty of the armed forces to the party.[22] Ceausescu sought to maintain this control.

Among the factors that tend to support a hypothesis that he succeeded, is that of the apparently subservient role of the military vis-a-vis the party. In actuality, none of the active military leaders under Ceausescu have had positions in the key decision-making bodies of Romania—the presidium of the party or the Permanent Bureau. Only two active military officers held any sort of senior position in the party in 1972, Minister of National Defense Ionita, as an alternate member of the Executive Committee, and Ion Coman, the head of the army's Political Directorate, as a member of the party's Central Committee.[23] Coman, when he took over as Minister of National Defense in June 1976, was an alternate member of the Political Executive Committee, but his successor as Chief of the General Staff, General-Lieutenant Ion Hortopan did not have even Central Committee membership.[24] This is not to say that the military did not have access to the leadership in order to advise on military matters, but the fact that even the Chief of the General Staff held no senior (that is, Central Committee or above) party position, severely limited the influence of the military in a state where policy decisions were made by the higher party echelons.

Furthermore, Ceausescu and his leadership took concrete measures to increase their control over the country's military forces by certain structural reforms as well as by changing or rotating some of the leadership. The principles of democratic centralism were to determine the entire character of national defense. Accordingly, different defense structures and organizations could be set up while retaining control by the Communist party and in turn by the party leadership headed by Ceausescu. This was reflected in the National Defense Law put before the Grand National Assembly in December 1972. Before, in 1968, the establishment of the National Guards provided a new military branch that could be controlled even more closely than the army, for the Guard units were to cooperate with the local party units, as well as with the central leadership. In 1969, Ceausescu further strengthened his personal control over the military with the creation of the Defense Council.[25] The Minister of the Armed Forces, Ion Ionita, described this organ as having the authority to "make decisions of maximum importance for the defensive capacity of the fatherland and has created an especially propitious framework for affirming the leadership of the party."[26] He further stated that the fact that the President of the Council and, thereby, the Supreme Commander of the armed forces, was also the Secretary General of the party, constituted "an expression and at the same time a guarantee of the unstoppable growth of the leading role of the party."[27] In this manner, Ceausescu, wearing three hats, hoped to achieve direct control over the armed forces.

Even the above arrangement, though, was found unsatisfactory by Ceausescu and his political leadership, for in 1972, as part of the trend of combining party and state functions, they reorganized the Ministry of the Armed Forces under the new title of Ministry of National Defense.[28] This was done under Decree No. 444, the first section of which greatly enhanced the role of the party and Ceausescu in controlling the armed forces. While the last defense Decree, which was passed in 1964, under the leadership of Gheorghiu-Dej, stipulated that the defense ministry was to implement state policy, the new Decree stated specifically in Article I (Section I) that "the Ministry of National Defense implements the *party* and state policy on national defense. . . ."[29] (Emphasis added.) Ceausescu's personal power as Supreme Commander and President of the Defense Council was specifically highlighted by Article 2 of Section I:

> The Ministry of National Defense acts under the direction and guidance of the Party Central Committee, carries out the orders of the Supreme Commander of the Armed Forces of the Romanian Socialist Republic and implements the measures flowing from the decisions of the Defense Council in its field of activity. . . .[30]

As well, it was designated to support and to collaborate with the Central Command of the National Guards and the Union of Communist Youth (Section I, Article 3 and Section II, Article 4, Subsection r).

It bears note that the Ministry with its new and enhanced powers was made subordinate to the Council of Ministers only in its capacity as an "organ of the state administration" (Section I, Article 1), while the day-to-day operation of the ministry was to be in the hands of an administrative council. The latter was to be composed of the minister, the first deputy minister, the deputy ministers, the chiefs of the central commands or directorates, plus experts with high qualifications and long experience, together with other administrative personnel. The last two categories were to be approved by the Defense Council on the recommendation of the Minister of National Defense who had the role of chairman of the administrative council (Section III, Article 8). Thus, the Defense Council, chaired by Ceausescu, was given control as well in the selection of the non-ex officio member of the administrative council.

Furthermore, the new decree gave the role of final arbitrator in disputes between the minister and the majority of the administrative council to the President of the Defense Council, Nicolae Ceausescu (Section III, Article 2).

As well as the Ministry of Defense and the Patriotic Guard, Romania also intended to make full use of the Ministry of the Interior for the defense of the state. It was stipulated that the units of the Ministry of the Interior, which were armed, comprised both of security troops and of the militia, were to fight sabotage, to prevent surprise, to help actively in the resisting of intervention and in case of occupation, to help organize and fight in the resistance movement *according to the general plans approved by the party and state leadership.* [31] The responsibility for the organization and leadership of the entire activity of the various armed youth organizations rested with the Communist Youth Union, [32] thereby further extending the role of the party.

Ceausescu formalized the increase of his personal power over defense through the constitutional amendments in 1974 when he became President of the Republic. [33] According to Article 74 the President automatically becomes the Supreme Commander of the armed forces and chairman of the Defense Council, and had the right to proclaim, if necessary, the state of emergency in some localities or throughout the entire country [Article 75 (13)]. Article 5 gave him the right to confer the ranks of General, Admiral, and Marshal. It is, however, in the manner in which the Defense Law stipulated the declaration of war or the conclusion of peace or armistice that really illustrated the concentration of power in the hands of the leadership of the Romanian Communist Party and Ceausescu in particular. While a state of emergency can be declared by the President according to law, war or partial or general mobilization can only be declared by the Grand National Assembly (GNA) or if it is not in session by the State Council. [34] But the GNA meets rather infrequently and therefore the main responsibility would rest with the State Council, which is made up of the members of the "rubber stamp parliament." The President of the State Council, however, is President Ceausescu. In the case of the signing of a peace treaty following a war or an armistice or any other method of ending armed conflict, the decision must be made by the GNA again, or if it is not in session by the State Council at the recommendation of the Defense Council of the Romanian Socialist Republic. The Defense Council, however, is also headed by Ceausescu in his rule as President of the Republic and Supreme Commander. The Defense Council has the responsibility to examine and coordinate all problems referring to defense of the country, both in peacetime and in wartime. [35] Finally, the Council is responsible not only to the GNA and in the absence of a session to the Council of State, but also to the Central Committee of the Romanian Communist Party.

It appears, though, that Ceausescu was not satisfied with organizational supremacy, but felt the need to rotate and remove certain personnel. There were unconfirmed reports in the West of a possible attempted military coup in the summer of 1971 [36] and a purge and arrest of 40 officers from the Romanian General Staff. [37] However, there had been no confirmation of any of these reports in Romanian military publications and the top armed forces leadership remained the same between 1965 and the end of 1974, so the more likely explanation for any change that may have been detected by Western intelligence may have been due to Ceausescu's predilection (as in the political sphere), to rotate personnel occupying certain positions, in order to prevent the creation of a challenge, rather than as a response to it. There is official evidence of some such changes especially in the removal of Vasile Patilinet, the party secretary in charge of the armed forces from the Secretariat in January 1972[38] and his replacement by a protege of Ceausescu's, Cornel Burtica,[39] a man who had enjoyed a truly meteoric rise. Nevertheless, Patilinet retained a high-ranking position as an alternate member of the party's Executive Committee,[40] a post unlikely to have been given to him if he had been involved in or had even been negligent in detecting an anti-Ceausescu plot. The December 1974 removal of the Chief of the General Staff to an administrative post in Bucharest and his replacement by General Coman, the former head of the Higher Political Committee, was too remote from any possible problems in 1971. What this change may have indicated, however, was a desire on the part of the Ceausescu leadership to emphasize the party's role in the army.[41] In June 1976, Coman became Minister of Defense and his predecessor was shifted to the largely honorific position of Deputy Premier but retained his party position.[42] The replacement of Coman as Chief of the General Staff by a professional officer, General-Lieutenant Hortopan, may well have indicated that a certain phase in Romanian military policies had ended. In 1974, Ceausescu had reorganized the Romanian Communist Party and friction with the Soviet Union had increased until the summer of 1976, when there were moves for a reconciliation, particularly following Ceausescu's visit to Crimea in August. Therefore, the phase where a political officer was put in charge of the General Staff of the Romanian Armed Forces may have represented an attempt by the Romanian Communist Party to have an even tighter control over the armed forces during a period of crisis that abated. The shift of the Minister of Defense to the Deputy Premiership was done together with the change of three other ministers and was likely part of a general rotation. Rotation of personnel, though, in this case as in others, allowed Ceausescu a stringent control over the military.

IDEOLOGICAL INDOCTRINATION

Effective structural or organizational control of the military forces of the nation facilitated another desideratum for achieving unity between the civilian and military leadership of Romania, namely the political indoctrination of the armed forces and the forging of a political alliance (with the military in the subordinate role, of course). The Romanians, after the 1947 Communist takeover, followed the Soviet model of using political officers within the army and conducting intense political indoctrination of the troops. This was continued under Ceausescu and it bore fruit throughout the period of his leadership in the support the party received from the army. For instance, in 1967, when the Soviet Union and the other bloc states were condemning Romanian initiatives with the West, the military leadership attested to the "unshakable" belief in the party.[43]

Just prior to the Czechoslovakian intervention, Ceausescu himself emphasized how essential it was for a Communist party to have political control within its own army. He asserted that:

We start from the consideration that the responsibility and obligation for instruction and education of each national army belongs to the party and the government of the respective country, which are invested by the people with the prerogatives of the overall conduct of the work of fashioning a new order.[44]

Within the same speech he disclosed that as a precaution against the threat from "imperialism" there was intensified work by the political councils and party committees in the army. Consequently, these were contributing greatly to the elevation of the level of political work in all the military units and in cultivating "the militant spirit for implementing the Party's home and foreign policy."[45] Therefore, it appears that at times of political crisis the leadership of Romania made particularly great use of the tool of political indoctrination of the armed forces to ensure unity and support.

This was again evident in the first part of 1971, during the growing Soviet-Romanian crisis over Ceausescu's projected visit to China. At the February plenary meeting of the Central Committee of the Romanian Communist Party, it was decided to further improve the methods of political control within the armed forces.[46] The Plenum was also told that the party organizations within the army were already in the process of being strengthened by "the admission of significant numbers of new members from the ranks of the best officers, non-commissioned officers, and students from military schools."[47]

During later periods of tension between Romania and the Soviet Union, Bucharest emphasized the importance of the party in the armed forces. In 1974 the Chief of the General Staff wrote that command of the armed forces and organization had to follow the party's wishes,[48] and this was only one of the many statements emphasizing the importance of the controlling role of the party within the organization of a Romanian defense. In 1976 again the controlling and guiding role of the party was brought forth. At the Congress on Political Education and Socialist Culture held between June 2 and 4, 1976, Ceausescu himself stressed that patriotism was one and the same with party politics and therefore the party line had to be followed everywhere.[49] During the same month the Minister of National Defense, Ionita, shortly before his dismissal, declared that the willingness of the army to defend the country was mapped out according to the military doctrine enunciated by the Communist party.[50] And in the early fall of 1976 Ceausescu, speaking before the base party activists in the army, declared that the strong unity of the entire Romanian people and of the entire armed forces was reached and was being conducted under the leadership of the Romanian Communist Party.[51] Therefore, the Romanians lost no opportunity, particularly during periods of tension, to strengthen the role of the party in the organization of national defense and, moreover, to enunciate as frequently as possible that this in fact was being accomplished.

MATERIAL INCENTIVES

Structural and indoctrinational control are cogent tools for assuring the obedience of the military in any political system but they do not necessarily suffice in securing total compliance. Often more subtle means of control are necessary and what Western psychologists have termed positive reinforcement, and an aspect of which the Socialist states had designated "material incentives," may help perform this function. Romania, like other states, was bound to find it advantageous to extend to the military, especially the professional section, certain material benefits, which should have helped to retain their loyalty to the party.

As in the Soviet Union, in Romania the officer enjoyed a position of prestige, and when material advantages were added to this, an army career became particularly attractive. Furthermore, the officers of the Patriotic Guard, which was under the direct control of the Romanian Communist Party Central Committee, enjoyed the same privileges as the regular and noncommissioned officers of the army. While some of the benefits available to the professional military man in Romania have been classified information, there have been public statements listing some of the concrete material benefits. In February 1970, for instance, Ceausescu stated that while the economy had grown between 12 and 13 percent in the previous year, the salaries of officers and noncommissioned officers had grown by 16 percent.[52] Since wage increases for the population at large in Romania under Ceausescu had always been considerably lower than the growth rate of the economy as a whole, the 16 percent increase given the military professionals was quite handsome. In fact, an extensive article on the improvements of the military capacity of the Romanian armed forces, which appeared in *Apararea Patriei* on February 17, 1971, revealed that the wages of the officers and noncommissioned officers rose 50 percent between 1965 and 1970—a figure considerably above the national average.

At the end of 1975 new wage increases were announced.[53] As of January 1, 1976, the pay of privates in the army would be doubled, those of noncomissioned officers would increase immediately between 60 to 70 percent, and those of active and reserve officers by 29 percent. Food allowances for servicemen and students were to be increased by 15 percent, while servicemen working on economic projects would be given additional furlough days. The nonremunerative benefits were always considered important for morale. For instance, annual spending on food for the troops was double in 1970 over 1967,[54] and there was also a sharp increase in the amount of money being allocated for the training of military cadres. In the Five-Year Plan ending in 1970 annual expenditure per student increased by Lei 3800 in military high schools, by Lei 4300 in the military schools of the land army, and by Lei 9400 in the Military Academy.[55] The last figure was roughly equivalent to the minimum annual industrial wage in 1970,[56] so all of the increases were substantial. Additionally, there was a sizable improvement in the creature comforts accorded the troops, through a considerable growth in the number of amphitheaters constructed at military bases, and through the procurement of thousands of additional television and radio sets and musical instruments.[57] These increases in expenditure for personnel comforts and wages was reflected in the growth of the military budget from Lei 4.54 bn. in 1965 to Lei 7.0 bn. in 1970 and to Lei 11.3 bn. in 1977.[58] While total Romanian military expenditures may seem small in comparison with those of the Northern Tier states of the Warsaw Pact, they did enjoy a considerable growth, part of which was represented by announced increases in material benefits being extended to the armed forces.

It had long been rumored in Romania that the professional military people had a substantial degree of "unofficial" privileges such as first right to scarce consumer goods, admission to places of entertainment and to holiday resorts. There has, of course, been no official confirmation of these alleged practices, which if true would certainly make military life more attractive, but there has been the release of one official statistic that attested to a most significant privilege. In 1971, it was revealed, again in *Apararea Patriei*, that of the 660,000 flats built during the Five-Year Plan ending in 1970, the families of career soldiers received 17,048.[59] Romania has suffered from a chronic housing shortage since World War II and the situation became extremely acute under Ceausescu's leadership, with the massive shift of the rural population to urban areas in the wake of rapid industrialization. Therefore, housing was the most prized of commodities. While the number of flats allocated to the families of career military men may appear very small in absolute terms, it should be pointed out that these families represented less than 1 percent of the total Romanian population.* The housing allocated to the military professionals represented 2.58 percent of the total built and, as such, these people received at least 2.5 times the new housing per capita compared to the average Romanian. Such a privileged position for the military professionals should certainly have aided in maintaining their loyalty to the party leadership that helped to ensure such benefits.

The Ceausescu regime also endeavored to ensure psychological satisfaction for the career soldier. As in many other societies the wearing of a military uniform in Romania also meant a respected social status, a status that acknowledged military rank. Regular promotion in rank, then, would have become a

---

*The armed forces of Romania under Ceausescu reached a peak of 193,000 in 1969, for a population of 20.5 million. Since the vast majority of the armed forces were conscripts, the career officers with their families were most unlikely to have surpassed 200,000.[60]

psychological necessity for the military professional in maintaining his social status. In Romania this desideratum appears to have been amply satisfied. Promotions were frequent and following yearly announcements of regular army promotions, *Apararea Patriei* issued a particularly long promotion list in May 1971.[61] Minister of the Armed Forces Ion Ionita was promoted from General-Colonel to General of the Army, while General-Lieutenant Ion Coman, Deputy Minister and Secretary of the Higher Political Council of the Armed Forces and General-Lieutenant Ionel Vasile, also Deputy Minister, were both advanced to the rank of general-colonel. Moreover, 17 colonels were promoted to the rank of general-major and three navy captains were made rear-admirals.

On December 28, 1972, as more officers were raised to the rank of general while some generals were advanced a grade,[62] Ceausescu elaborated on the reasons for the promotions:

> This constitutes an expression of the appreciation and belief of the party and government in the activity which you display for the political and military betterment of the troops. At the same time it is in a larger sense an expression of the continuing preoccupation of the party and the state with the strengthening of our armed forces and of the defensive capacity of our Socialist fatherland.

Thus promotions were acknowledged to have the purpose of strengthening defensive capacity and implied in that was the strengthening of the unity between the political leadership and the armed forces. The creation of the office of President of the Republic in 1974, with its exclusive constitutional right of promoting officers to star rank, further strengthened Ceausescu's hand.

THE APPEAL TO PATRIOTISM

When the Soviet Union was rapidly losing territory to the invading Nazi troops in June 1941, and the Soviet military forces appeared on the verge of disintegration, Stalin made a dramatic appeal to the armed forces and the people to fight on. What he asked them to fight on for was not Socialism, or the Soviet state, but Mother Russia. While the Soviet recovery and eventual defeat of Nazi forces came about as a result of a multiplicity of factors, Stalin's appeal to Russian nationalism and patriotism cannot be denied an important role in stiffening armed resistance. It demonstrated that despite the universalist ideology of Socialist states, an appeal to patriotism could be an effective tool in rallying support, particularly military support, to the side of the leadership in a time of crisis. Ceausescu, who endeavored to follow a policy of national autonomy, could hardly have been ignorant of the utility of patriotism.

In the spring of 1967, as the polemical exchanges over Romanian establishment of diplomatic relations with West Germany continued between Bucharest and the other Socialist capitals, the Romanian Communist Party leadership exploited the occasion of the 90th Anniversary of Romanian independence from Turkey to rally army and popular support. *Apararea Patriei* published a long front-page article on the courage and patriotism of Romanian soldiers in past wars against foreign exploitation of the country.[63] Ion Gheorghe Maurer, the Premier of Romania, in a thinly veiled denunciation of Soviet attempts at interference into Romanian affairs, stated that the 1877 liberation meant that henceforth no power would have the right to intervene into the internal matters of the Romanian state or to control its external policies. Furthermore, he asserted that the troops of the Czarist government (which in Maurer's view was only interested in Balkan expansion, and with whom the Romanian principalities had aligned themselves out of necessity), had only traversed Romanian soil on their way to the Balkans after they obtained the right of passage in exchange for the Czar's declaration of his willingness to defend the territorial integrity of Romania, and to respect its right of sovereignty.[64] Not only did such a claim place current Soviet policies vis-a-vis Romania in a rather poor light, but the statement implied that even in a time of national peril, the Romanians had been prepared to restrict an ally, by force of arms, if necessary, in order to preserve their sovereignty.

The Romanian leadership returned time and again to the theme of army patriotism in guarding Romanian sovereignty. Ceausescu, just prior to the Czechoslovak intervention, asserted that there had always been a unity between the army and the people. He noted that, "The Romanian Army has a long tradition of fighting for the liberty of the Romanian people from the old days of Decebal, Mircea the Old . . . to the shoulder to shoulder fight along with the Soviet forces against Nazi Germany.[65]

Throughout the crisis year of 1971, the Romanian leadership stressed anew the past heroism and patriotism of the armed forces. In January 1971, Major C. Cazanisteanu, writing the lead article in *Apararea Patriei*, quoted Ion Cuza, the first Romanian premier, on the readiness of the army and the people in the 19th century to defend the country's territory and independence.[66]

As Soviet military maneuvers commenced to exert pressure against Romania, in June 1971, a special young soldier's edition of *Apararea Patriei* stressed Ceausescu's dictum that "The defense of the fatherland is a sacred duty of all citizens of the Socialist Republic of Romania," and cited the love of country and the sacrifices made in defending independence by such heroes of the past as Nicolae Balcescu, Avram Iancu, Mihai Kogalniceanu, and Gheorghe Marinescu. In the same month the Romanians reiterated time and again their past armed resistance against foreign domination.[67] Following the adoption of the new Defense Law by the Grand National Assembly in December 1972, Ceausescu returned afresh to recount the glorious fighting past of the Romanian army, especially in the battles of Smirdau, Plevna, and Grivita against the Turkish oppressors.[68] The Romanian leadership maintained their faith in the potency of the call to patriotism throughout the 1970s. Repeated references were made to the glorious fighting past of the Romanian people and increasingly to historical studies that "demonstrated" that there had been a natural evolution in the past toward total defense through the involvement of all of the population in resistance.[69] Ceausescu's name was constantly associated with past military and revolutionary heroes, particularly during times of friction with the Soviet Union in 1974 and in 1976. Perhaps the best illustration of this constant recourse to patriotism is the extremely nationalistic new anthem that was introduced in Romania in 1977 that praised the "old fighting renown" of the Romanian people.[70]

In this manner, the Romanian party leadership utilized virtually all of the tools that, according to theoretical models, would ensure armed forces support for the party leadership, or in Romanian terminology, unity. The decision-making structure ensured that political arguments would have the greatest weight and that the military would be in a subordinate position to the party. Regular and intense political indoctrination was designed to ensure that the armed forces would be imbued with the right ideological spirit. Material and status benefits similarly should have ensured that the career soldiers had a vested interest in preserving the status quo. And finally the appeal to patriotism should have drawn on the strain of nationalism that most military men exhibit at a time of crisis. Theoretically, therefore, there should have been a unity of purpose between the Romanian Communist Party and the Romanian armed forces, but one cannot be sure without some empirical checks. Ascertaining the latter is restricted by the very secrecy of military affairs in Romania, as in many other states, that results in numerous conflicts and disagreements being covered up and hidden from public view. The task, however, is not impossible, for public statements of the military leaders and articles in military journals can shed valuable light on military support for the party, especially at times of crisis. As well, retention, promotion, and dismissal of key military leaders again delves importantly on party-army unity. An analysis of the Romanian military's views and security of position should therefore give a reasonably accurate, though by no means perfect, picture of this unity.

ARMY-PARTY SOLIDARITY: THE EMPIRICAL TEST

When Ceausescu succeeded Gheorghiu-Dej in 1965, he had to maintain a low profile while he consolidated his position, for at the time he was at least potentially vulnerable to challenges from the army leadership. Such challenges, however, did not materialize, for in October the then Minister of the Armed Forces, the ailing Leontin Salajan, and his deputy, then Chief of Staff (soon to be promoted to minister) Ion Ionita, both extended their full support to the party leadership.[71] The subsequent replacement of Salajan by Ionita came about as a result of the former's sudden death on August 28, 1966. Ionita, however, owed his promotion to Ceausescu, and this should have helped army-party relations.

It was in a time of external crisis that the armed forces had the best opportunity to demonstrate their attitudes to the party's policies as formulated by the Ceausescu leadership, through the type of support they gave. In May 1967, Ion Ionita, as Minister of the Armed Forces, declared his unequivocal support for the party's position[72] and declared that the troops were ready to fulfill at any time their duty to the party, the people, and the homeland. Ceausescu himself indicated at this time that he was perfectly satisfied with the support that the armed forces were prepared to give to the party's policies.[73]

The Czechoslovak crisis in August 1968 was a period when army-party unity was essential to the Ceausescu leadership in view of increased Soviet pressures. Prior to the intervention, the armed forces leadership came out fully in support of the party line. On August 15, 1968, Ionita declared:

> Our military forces express their full support for the internal and external politics of the party, towards the fulfillment of which we direct our efforts. We support unanimously the actions undertaken by our party for the strengthening of the Socialist system.[74]

Such support served to reassure the Ceausescu leadership, and to warn the Soviet Union that interference would not work.

Following the intervention in Czechoslovakia during the night of August 20-21, though, there appeared a change in army support for the party. Ionita made only one public statement on August 22, when he issued an order that the "Socialist state" was to be defended, and that all military units were to increase their combat readiness.[75] For the next few weeks this was the only statement of support issued by any of the top military leaders. There was, however, general army support for the party, and this was reiterated in each issue of *Apararea Patriei* through to September 25, 1968. All the issues carried front-page articles with an identical title: "Together with the entire people the army expresses its unanimous adherence to the principles of the external politics of the party and the government." On August 28, in an article bearing this title, it was stated that the central organs of the Ministry of the Armed Forces, the general staff, and the army commands had all expressed support for the party and the government and had declared themselves ready to defend the independence and national sovereignty of Romania. There was, however, no mention of any of the top military leaders by name.

In the following issues of the paper the highest ranking officer whose name appeared under the army support article in *Apararea Patriei* was a reserve general, C. Vasiliu Rascanu.[76] Of the active officers signing their names to support articles, none were above the rank of colonel, and moreover a considerable number of them bore Hungarian-sounding names (among the names listed was that of Lieutenant-Colonel Balazs Takacs).[77] It was only on October 16, 1968, that General Ionita, in a speech he delivered at the commencement of a new study year at the General Military Academy, gave details of events in Czechoslovakia and offered his personal support to the party.[78]

The rather strange behavior of the top armed forces leadership in withholding open support from Ceausescu and the party lends itself to three possible hypotheses: first, the army leadership may have opposed Ceausescu's policies and his confrontation with the Soviet Union; second, the top leadership may have fully supported the party's policies, but felt that they had to maintain a low profile in order not to provoke the Soviet Union and to avoid being selected as targets; third, they may have been undecided as to whom to support and were waiting to see what action the Soviet Union was going to take against Ceausescu.

The first hypothesis assumes that Ceausescu had been unable to install an army leadership on which he could rely upon in time of crisis. While this is a possibility, his constant shuffling of the political leadership and the control that he exercised over the armed forces made this unlikely. Nevertheless, if this had been the case would Ceausescu have subsequently tolerated such disobedience and disloyalty? In view of this purging of all political opponents, whether actual or potential, and his egocentric style of leadership, it appears certain that once the crisis was over, he would have purged a disloyal army leadership. It is true that after the Czechoslovak crisis he established the Defense Council and authorized the formation of the Patriotic Guards. The former, though, was designed to improve the chain of command and was in line with certain political changes that Ceausescu had made, while the latter was an attempt to strengthen the country's defensive capacities, rather than an attempt at disciplining the top army leadership. What is crucial regarding the entire first hypothesis is that the top army leadership, including the Minister of the Armed Forces and his deputies (who included the Chief of the General Staff and the Secretary of the Higher Political Council of the Armed Forces), retained their positions until the end of 1974. Some of them even received advancement in military rank. (Ion Ionita, Ion Coman, and Vasile Ionel were all promoted one rank in 1971.)[79] Therefore, the first hypothesis should be considered invalid.

In Czechoslovakia, as we have seen, General Prchlik, the Central Committee chief for military affairs, called for a basic revision of the Warsaw Pact on July 15, 1968.[80] As a result he became the target of Soviet ire, with the consequence that he lost his position and eventually had to be disavowed by the Czechoslovak Minister of Defense and the army leadership,[81] thereby, ending any usefulness he may have had in case the Czechoslovak leadership had decided on a military defense of the country. Romania had declared that it was ready to defend itself against foreign intervention and if it was to organize an effective defense it could not afford to have its top military leaders singled out for Soviet polemical attacks, and pressures intended to inhibit the organization of such a defense. It has been the custom in the Soviet-bloc states (with some exceptions, such as in Czechoslovakia in 1968) that at a time of crisis the top military leadership keeps a low profile while the colonels write the articles. Romania appeared to have been following this pattern and the military was likely organizing quietly, while Ceausescu was stridently denouncing the Soviet intervention in Czechoslovakia. Therefore, the second hypothesis appears to be quite plausible.

In view of our position on the first two hypotheses as being contrapositive, the third one should possess little validity. There was an anomalous development, though, in the intermediate military leadership's retention of their posts after 1968. In 1972, General-Lieutenant Ioan Serb, a ranking member of the Higher Political Council of the Armed Forces of Romania, was fired, and possibly executed, for what were rumored pro-Soviet activities. (The Romanian officially acknowledged that he was no longer a general.)[82] If the allegations were true, then it may have been possible that there was some wavering of support for Ceausescu at the intermediate level in the Romanian armed forces, but it would have had to be very limited to have had escaped his notice. The fact that the top military leadership was untouched by the Serb case would indicate that if there had been any wavering of support within the military, it would have to have been microscopic. Therefore, we contend that the low profile the army leadership presented in the 1968 crisis was due to caution induced by the need to organize a defense and/or to the desire to avoid confrontation. Ceausescu and his party leadership, then, had adequate support for their policies in 1968.

During the spring 1969 crisis with the Soviet Union, the Ceausescu leadership signified that it was confident enough of military and popular support to demand an increased role for small and middle-sized states in the world arena.[83] They insisted on this position, despite the fact that in a conciliatory move earlier Romanian troops took part in Warsaw Pact maneuvers on Soviet soil.[84] Apparently the Romanian leadership did not feel that even such "contamination" could have diminished army support for the party.

As much of 1971 represented a time of grave disagreement between Romania and the Soviet Union, Ceausescu needed the assurance of the unquestioning support of his armed forces in order to resist Soviet military pressures. The military, through the use of *Apararea Patriei*, gave just this type of support during Ceausescu's visit to China in May, when it proclaimed in an editorial that the entire country supported the visit and that everyone viewed the strengthening of the friendship between Romania and China as fortifying world Socialism.[85]

Support for Ceausescu foreign policy intensified in the spring, and banner headlines appeared in *Apararea Patriei* at the end of June proclaiming the army's high appreciation, and total approval of these policies.[86] General Ionita, then Minister of the Armed Forces, expressed his loyalty in the most flowery language:

> The activities of Nicolae Ceausescu are a brilliantly moving example. . . . The armed forces are in a tight unity around the party including its leadership and will give full support to the revolutionary needs, the independence and sovereignty of Romania. All in the army give you their support beloved comrade Nicolae Ceausescu. Thank you comrade for enhancing the prestige of the nation and helping world peace. The soldiers, comrade supreme commander, will always fulfill their duties towards our beloved fatherland—the Socialist Republic of Romania.[87]

There were, moreover, telegrams from various commands voicing their support for Ceausescu's policies and stressing the combat readiness of the soldiers. (Among those pledging support was the commander of artillery and General Vasile Milea and Gh. Gomoiu.)[88] In July 1971, *Apararea Patriei* published telegrams from Ionita, from the Higher Political Council, and from the commanders of every branch of the armed forces giving full backing to Ceausescu regarding his policies toward China, and his foreign policy proposals.[89] As the crescendo of support increased throughout the month, General-Lieutenant Vasile Slicariu and General-Major Gh. Gomoiu voiced their approval and significantly, laid great stress on the soldier's oath to defend the fatherland and the people.[90] And, as Soviet military pressure on Romania was eased by the fall, the Romanian armed forces journal, *Viata Militara*, reiterated the military's "monolithic unity around the party" and its support for the "Romanian Communist Party, and its leadership headed by comrade N. Ceausescu, the most beloved son of the people."[91] Ceausescu thus could hardly have asked for more ardent army support.

During the rest of the 1970s, the pattern of support that developed in the crisis years of 1968, 1969, and 1971, however, appears to have had a momentum of its own. In July 1972, in a speech before the National Party Conference, Ionita praised highly Ceausescu's policies and his concern as supreme commander for the army. He also repeated that the army fully supported the party and its policies.[92] Following the introduction of the Defense Law on December 28, 1972, the top military leadership, on cue, expressed its support for the party. Ionita asserted that since Socialist society consisted of a unitary total, there could logically be only one leadership and as such, the conduct of the defense of the nation could only belong to the party and the constitutional organs of the country.[93]

During 1974 and 1976 the armed forces leadership in Romania constantly reiterated its support for the party leadership, particularly regarding the willingness of the Romanian army to fight for the defense of the country's sovereignty.[94] The changes in the top military leadership at the end of 1974 and in June 1976 can not be explained as instances of disloyalty. The shift of General Gheorghe from the post of Chief of the General Staff to a high-ranking position in the Bucharest municipal government likely resulted out of a combination of factors. There may have been some friction between a professional army officer such as Gheorghe and the irregular forces in Romania, thereby lessening the efficiency of defense. Gheorghe had frequently indicated that he preferred the regular forces. Furthermore, his replacement by General Coman, a political officer, may have indicated a desire by Ceausescu to gain greater political control in the army. Had Gheorghe displayed any disloyalty to Ceausescu it is highly doubtful that he would have been given a high-ranking position in the civilian governmental structure. The replacement of Ionita in June 1976 by Coman again resulted from a likely combination of factors. Ionita had submitted himself to certain sharp criticism in 1975 regarding the efficiency of the military organization, so his replacement may well have indicated an attempt by Ceausescu to increase the efficiency of the Ministry of National Defense by appointing an organization man. Second, the movement of Coman to the Ministry of Defense and his replacement as Chief of the General Staff by a professional officer could also have indicated that Ceausescu was satisfied with the newly increased influence of the party within the armed forces rank and felt confident enough to hand back the operation of command to professional army officers. Ionita's retention of party posts and his designation as Deputy Premier again excluded the possibility that he had displayed any disloyalty toward the top party leadership.

Therefore, we contend that Ceausescu had the benefit of one of the basic ingredients needed for the organization of successful active defense, namely the full support of the armed forces for the political leadership. Through organization, political indoctrination, material benefits, and the appeal to patriotism he achieved a solid army-party unity. The support of the armed forces may have contained some anomalies, as in August 1968, but these were due to tactical considerations rather than flagging support. Ceausescu was in complete command and thus could devote his time to improving the fighting capacity of his armed forces with the full backing of the military leadership. In this sense, then, Romania stood united before any external enemies.

NATIONAL UNITY

Along with maintaining the unity between army and party, Romania had to ensure that the entire population supported the maintenance of the territorial integrity of the country. The population of Romania is far from homogeneous, for it contains a substantial Hungarian minority of about two million, largely concentrated in Transylvania. The latter territory itself had been under Hungarian rule for several centuries until 1918, and a large portion of it had been returned to Hungarian rule under the Vienna Diktat, for the period of 1940 to 1944. It is difficult to gauge how great the irredentist feeling among the Hungarian population of Transylvania has been since 1965, but Romanian rule certainly meant the loss of privileges they enjoyed under Budapest's rule, while the program of Romanianization of Transylvania began under Gheorghiu-Dej certainly was bound to present a threat to their national identity.

Nevertheless, the Hungarians retained certain language and education rights and one of the 16 Romanian provinces was designated as the Autonomous Maghiar Region during the leadership of Gheorghiu-Dej. Ceausescu, an even more chauvinistic leader, maintained an extremely close check on the minorities situation. Formally, the Hungarians had full rights of citizenship.[95] In February 1968, though, he proposed the administrative reorganization of the country (which was shortly enacted into law), into 39 counties instead of the 16 larger regions.[96] The Autonomous Maghiar Region simply disappeared, as it was divided into the counties of Mures and Harghita, and parts were joined to the neighboring Romanian counties. This region had in fact never been substantively autonomous and its importance was rather symbolic. There may have been sound administrative reasons for the country's reorganization, but the abolition of all visible signs of Hungarian autonomy meant that Ceausescu was rejecting even the possibility of irredentism.

During external crises, Ceausescu indicated that he expected the full support of all minorities. In a speech delivered in the largely Hungarian town of Sfintu Gheorghe following the Czechoslovak intervention, in which Hungary had participated, he told his audience that regardless of nationality, "all citizens of Romania—Romanians, Magyars, Germans, and other nationalities—are determined to act with all of their force in support of the policy of the Romanian Communist Party."[97] In another speech before the Plenum of the Council of Working People of the Maghiar Nationality, held in March 1971, Ceausescu returned to the theme of unity when he declared that the construction of Socialism was the responsibility and duty of all the people, regardless of nationality.[98]

In external politics, Ceausescu stressed the lack of any outstanding territorial claims between Hungary and Romania. In emphasizing Romanian-Hungarian friendship, as he did during the visits to Romania of Janos Kadar, the Hungarian Communist Party leader, in 1972,[99] and in stressing that the protection of minority rights were the exclusive responsibility of each country, during Kadar's visit in June 1977,[100] he attempted to deprive potential Maghiar irredentism of external support.

There are indications that the Hungarian minority was not satisfied either with their educational or cultural status. The intense Romanianization in culture through the glorification of the Romanian language and literature and the restrictions in technical education to the exclusive use of the Romanian language all worked to the disadvantage for the Hungarian minority. There is evidence of limited dissent through the emergence of *samizdat* documents in Transylvania.[101] They called for the free use of the mother tongue in all official contexts and for the creation of a special United Nations commission for Transylvania to guarantee their rights of the national minorities, including the German one. These writings, however, appear spontaneous and sporadic. There is no evidence of the existence of any sort of organized dissident movement in Transylvania. They do, however, show that there is considerable frustration among the Hungarian (and German) minorities in Transylvania.

Ceausescu's and the Romanian Communist Party leadership's frequent reiteration of the duty of the Hungarian minority to support the party's policies, and to act in unity with all the other nationalities, coupled with the organizational changes made in the country, indicates that there was a deliberate and persistent policy to stifle any possibility of an irredentist movement gaining ground in Transylvania. If the Hungarian minority had any desire to join territorially their economically and culturally better off conationals across the border, they were certainly denied any opportunity of organizing. And, to the extent to which he succeeded in doing this, Ceausescu countered any potential fifth columns.

THE FIGHTING CAPACITY OF THE ROMANIAN FORCES

Romania's declared willingness to resist an external attack and domestic army-party solidarity constituted significant elements of deterrence to Soviet intervention, and thereby helped enlarge the limits of Romanian foreign policy autonomy. These two elements of deterrence, though, had to be enlarged by some significant additions that would have countervened, at least partially, the apparent Soviet desiderata in interventions in Eastern Europe, namely those of surprise, speed, and maintenance of morale. The denial of surprise is really a case of alerting the Romanian forces and people, and thus not allowing the country to lapse into a false sense of security. Retarding the speed of a Soviet military intervention involved the ability of Romanian armed forces to fight against much greater forces, through the use of regular and guerrilla units. If the Romanians had the potential to put up a prolonged resistance to military intervention by the Soviet Union and its Warsaw Pact allies, this would have been bound to have affected the morale of the intervening forces, and in turn acted as an additional deterrent—that is, if the potential of such a prolonged resistance was perceived by the Soviet Union.

Sounding the Alarm

In declaring its willingness to resist intervention at times of external pressures, Romania was sounding the alarm. These declarations, however, were largely intended for a foreign audience and thus there was a necessity to make the general population aware that there was disagreement with the Soviet Union— that there was a potential danger. This was an essential part of creating an effective defense—effective in the sense that the preparations would have enjoyed a certain level of credibility before the Soviet Union. In view of the efforts of the Soviet Union to lull Czechoslovakia, in 1968 and 1956, into a false sense of security, it was particularly important for the Ceausescu leadership to demonstrate, at points of crisis, that such attempts at surprise did not succeed in the case of Romania.

In mid-August 1968, Ceausescu warned the country on two counts.[102] First, he asserted that since it was no secret there had been mistakes and unjust practices in relations among Socialist states, special care had to be taken that these were not repeated, and moreover that respect for sovereignty was maintained. Second, he announced that since there was a great threat to Romania from imperialism, the party had ordered the strengthening of the army. As at this time the Soviet Union was exerting severe pressure on Czechoslovakia and on Romania, it would have been unlikely that the Romanian population would have construed the term "imperialism" in its standard Socialist usage of depicting Western foreign policy. Following the intervention in Czechoslovakia, Ceausescu again sounded the alarm when he declared that the excuse of "counterrevolution" in Czechoslovakia may be used in the future to justify a move against Romania—a move that Romanians should be ready for at any moment.[103]

During May 1969, the Romanian leadership again made it clear to the population that there was a severe dispute with the Soviet Union. On May 17, 1969, *Scinteia* reported in a front-page article on a one-day visit by the Romanian leaders to Moscow, under the headline, "On the basis of common accord between the leaders of the party and the state of the Soviet Union and the Socialist Republic of Romania." In the commonly understood code for reporting disagreement, the article indicated that the talks had been conducted in a "comradely atmosphere" with a "multilateral, sincere" exchange of opinions on problems of mutual interest. The following day the important political commentator Constantin Milea elaborated on the visit, also in a front-page article in *Scinteia.*[104] While praising the benefit of exchanging opinions between Socialist states, he warned that differences of views could not be solved through the "harmful, anachronistic practices of name-calling and mutual recriminations." Such discussions could only yield positive results, he asserted, if the interests of each state was held as important as the general interest of Socialism. This in turn tied in with Ceausescu's oft-repeated warnings against the use of force in relations among Socialist states.

New external crises or disputes brought further warning to the Romanian population to be on alert. During June 1971, as new Soviet military pressures were applied to Romania, there was additional emphasis on vigilance along "the entire 3152.9 km. frontier."[105] In the fall of 1972, as Romania was formulating its new controversial "all-horizons" Defense Law, Ceausescu warned in *Scinteia* that collaboration among states could only continue if there was "a definite exclusion of force of the threat of force."[106] During the spring and summer of 1974 and the summer of 1976, the Romanians sounded similar alarms.[107]

To the Romanian population, long used to code words in Socialist communications, these statements, made by the Romanian leadership and published in mass-circulation party newspapers and journals, were bound to sound as warnings of danger. Their timing at crisis points appears to have been a deliberate attempt by the Ceausescu leadership to alert the population to all contingencies. And in view of traditional Romanian distrust of the Russians, coupled with Soviet actions in 1956 and 1968, the alert could be brought on through subtle warnings. It also follows that if the general population was alerted to the external danger, the armed forces would have had at least the same benefit. Thus, if it had been the Soviet Union's intention to lull Romania into a false sense of security in order to have the benefit of surprise, it appears that it failed badly.

Romanian Conventional Defenses

When Gheorghiu-Dej lowered the induction period for new conscripts into the army and cut the size of the armed forces during 1964, he decreased the military value of his country as an ally to the Soviet Union. While this action antagonized the Soviet Union, it also provided a passive defense, for it became less worthwhile for the Soviet Union to bother with Romania. In building an active defense, however, the Ceausescu leadership had to create some military capacity to resist an armed intervention, in order to give some credibility to Romania's defenses. This, as we have stated earlier, does not mean that the Romanians had to have the capacity to repulse a full-scale Soviet military attack, but rather that it could put up a fairly prolonged military resistance. The longer such a resistance could last, or had the potential to last in Soviet eyes, the more effective it would have been. Soviet behavior in Eastern Europe in the postwar era indicated that they would have been reluctant to get involved in a large military action requiring several weeks to conclude successfully, and particularly they had no desire to get involved in a Vietnam-type situation.

Romanian armed resistance would have involved its "regular" and "people's" forces. The effectiveness of each, and the manner in which the two were to be coordinated, reflected importantly on the deterrent potential of Romanian military resistance. For the purposes of analysis, we shall examine the "regular" capacity first, because it provides certain key ingredients for all forms of military resistance.

By regular capabilities we include the effectiveness of regular armed forces (army, navy, air forces) and the production and procurement of armaments. During the period of 1965 to 1977 there was no dramatic change in the size of the regular armed forces of Romania,* though there were some fluctuations. One of the most significant changes occurred in 1969 when the forces were increased 20,000 men to 193,000, but the budget was only increased from Lei 5.187 billion to Lei 5.395 billion.[109] The other one occurred in 1971, when the forces were reduced from 181,000 to 160,000, but the budget was increased from a 1970 high of Lei 7.0 billion to Lei 7.50 billion.[110] The discrepancy between troop levels and budgetary allocation could have been the result of qualitative changes, salary increases, and allocation of funds to paramilitary forces. The overall picture, though, indicates that the Romanian regular military forces and military spending were quite small by the standards of the East European states in the Northern Tier of the Warsaw Pact. In a sense, then, Romanian conventional forces themselves did not appear as a powerful deterrent force.

Similarly, it is important to note that in the 1960s the Soviet Union starved Romania of modern armaments. As late as 1977 the Romanian forces did not receive the Sukhoi fighter bomber that equipped other bloc-state air forces or the T-62 tanks.[111] Thus it was essential for Romania to find other means of providing armaments both for the regular or conventional forces, and for the paramilitary ones. The most important sources for armaments, if the forces were to retain any credibility, had to be domestic.

---

*The regular forces numbered 198,000 men in 1965 and 180,000 in 1977.[108]

Unlike Czechoslovakia, Romania had never possessed large armaments industries. However, Ceausescu made serious attempts to build up a domestic source of certain types of armament. At the Ninth Romanian Communist Party Congress in 1967 he announced the decision to speed up the growth of armaments production.[112] Because of the lead time required for the production of even rather unsophisticated weaponry, perceptible growth would only have been noticed in 1968. And, in that year, at the plenary meeting of the Central Committee of the Romanian Communist Party, held in April, measures were taken for further intensifying the domestic production of armaments and training equipment, among them the increased allocation of funds for such production.[113] The Soviet intervention in Czechoslovakia, then, set the stage for a major Romanian quest for as great a self-sufficiency of armaments as the potential of Romanian industry and economy would allow.

Romanian manufacture of certain armaments, in the period following the Ninth Congress, bears note. These included automatic rifles, other small arms, artillery and various types of ammunition, mine-laying and mine-sweeping equipment, mobile points for the direction of artillery fire, equipment for anti-chemical and anti-atomic protection, as well as equipment for the sanitary preservation of food.[114] Within the important field of military logistics, the Romanians produced various types of river and sea craft, pontoon bridges, all types of wheeled military transport, and various tractors, including heavy tracked ones, as well as communications equipment. In addition to small arms and transport, the Romanians also strove to acquire a good maintenance capacity for the heavy equipment that they had acquired. Within this sphere, they produced machines and machine tools for the maintenance of all types of aircraft, as well as other aviation equipment and radar. In addition, they built large repair stations for the maintenance of tanks and heavy military equipment.

While Romania only had a limited capacity for the production of heavy military equipment, in the 1970s it steadily increased its capacity in this sphere. It began the production under license of a light transport British aircraft and began to manufacture the Alouette III helicopters under French license, partly to equip its air force.[115] As well it entered into a long-term agreement with the Fokker firm of West Germany covering the manufacture of twin-jet transport aircraft under license. Much more important, the Romanians are also cooperating with the Yugoslav aircraft industry in the development of the Orao twin-jet (Rolls-Royce engines) fighter and ground attack aircraft to meet the requirements of both air forces.[116] Whereas this may not represent a very large portion of the total heavy and sophisticated equipment requirement for a modern army, by 1975 the Romanians claimed that they were able to supply 66 percent of the total equipment (of all types) of the armed forces.[117] Both in 1975 and in 1976 Ceausescu called for the increased production of sophisticated equipment.[118] The emphasis on building aircraft reflected Romania's concern with defense. For, while the overall military strength of the regular Romanian armed forces did not increase at the same pace as those of the other Warsaw Pact countries, the air force did increase its strength fairly substantially. Between 1975 and 1977 manpower increased from 21,000 to 30,000 and combat aircraft increased from 254 to 327.[119]

Despite the ability of Romania to supply a high percentage of the armed forces' total equipment, the portion of heavy sophisticated equipment was still small and therefore Romania had to seek external sources for such equipment. Since the Soviet Union was reluctant to supply Romania with the armaments it wanted, Bucharest had to turn to the West. It appeared that in 1968 Romania had been able to secure some heavy equipment from Israel[120] and there were persistent but unconfirmed reports that Romania sought to purchase armaments from NATO countries in Europe and from the United States during the summer of 1975.[121] It is a confirmed fact, however, that Romania introduced French helicopters in its air force in 1976 and American jet aircraft in its military transport fleet in 1977.[122] Thus, while Romania's armed forces would have been of very limited use to the Soviet Union in offensive operations where the need for high technology and extensive heavy equipment partially excluded the participation of Romania, a country that spent by far the lowest sum of money per capita on its forces in the entire Warsaw Pact,[123] the defensive capacity of the Romanian Armed Forces was not insignificant. Self-sufficiency in small arms in many types of ammunition, in road transport coupled with the possession of elaborate repair facilities and some manufacturing facilities, enhanced this defensive capacity. The purchase of foreign arms and particularly the collaboration in the production of aircraft with Yugoslavia, which was again geared toward Romanian defense and not offensive operations, acted in a manner that could help Romania's active defenses. The Soviet Union may have been irritated at Romanian collaboration with Yugoslavia, and its purchases of Western equipment, but if Romania succeeded in overcoming these objections it would be creating a unique armed force within the Warsaw Pact. In concrete terms, this went against the extremely high level of standardization of the Warsaw Pact forces, a standardization which the Soviet Union viewed as absolutely essential in the creation of compatible forces capable of rapid offensive operations. In going against this trend Romania was effectively removing itself from the Warsaw Pact military structure, slowly, but through a definite, perceptible trend and thereby decreasing its potential use to Moscow and the Warsaw Pact further.

In addition to providing the regular armed forces with a secure domestic supply of certain armaments, the Ceausescu leadership also undertook certain organizational reforms to increase its efficiency. Local commanders were given greater decision-making powers and initiative was stressed.[124] This limited decentralization was also emphasized by General-Major Ion Suta of the infantry and tank command, who claimed that such army decentralization was tied in with that of the paramilitary forces, such as the Patriotic Guards.[125] In addition, a great accent was placed on improving instruction within the armed forces, and *Apararea Patriei* noted on November 1972 a high degree of satisfaction by the military commanders on the progress that had been made. Therefore, Romania, especially after 1968, had taken steps that should have enhanced considerably the ability of its regular armed forces to offer resistance to a military intervention.

Defense by People's War

Romania, however, does not appear to have had to limit armed resistance to the regular army forces. Domestic production of light armaments would have facilitated the creation of paramilitary units and these in fact had been in existence since World War II. Such forces, though, were small and their role was geared more toward domestic security than national defense. In 1968, however, in the aftermath of the Soviet intervention in Czechoslovakia, there appeared signs of a change in Romanian thinking. Ceausescu announced before a mass rally in Bucharest on August 21, 1968, that a decision had been made to form an armed Patriotic Guard, consisting of "workers, peasants, intellectuals and defenders of our Socialist native land."[126]

The decision could be viewed on three planes. First, the organization of the Patriotic Guards helped rally popular support around Ceausescu and the party leadership. The organization of defense against an external threat proved to be a unifying force in other states. Second, it is likely that Ceausescu realized that if in the future the passive defenses that Romania possessed, failed and the Soviet Union decided on military intervention, Romania's small regular forces would have had a limited credibility as a force capable of providing prolonged resistance. Third, if Romania were to take advantage of Yugoslav support it had to create forces that were compatible with the Yugoslav concept of people's war. In a developing state of only 20 million people, the best way to overcome a deficiency was by promoting total or people's warfare, which would have involved guerrilla activities alongside those of the regular forces. Since guerrillas could be trained in a short time and equipped inexpensively from domestic production, Romania could call upon a large reservoir of manpower. (General-Major Constantin Oprita estimated that in 1972 Romania could call up between 4.68 million to 6.245 million citizens for military duty or 23 percent to 32 percent of the population.)[127] The Romanians also estimated that if they structured their forces for people's war it would take an army of between 700,000 and one million men to maintain an occupation in case of defeat and that this would be difficult to sustain for a long period, even for the largest power.[128] As a result, Romania not only formed the Patriotic Guard but also began the military training of factory workers and university students.

The first intimation of an official shift in the entire defensive strategy of the country (and not just the formation of the Patriotic Guards) came through a rather esoteric type of communication, frequently used by Romania to publicize sensitive matters. The September 25, 1968, issue of *Apararea Patriei* carried an extensive front-page interview with Professor Radu Vulfe on scenes from Traian's column that depicted the Daco-Roman wars. What was emphasized in the interview was Decebal's (the leader of the Romanians' predecessors, the Dacians) fight in the mountains, through guerrilla warfare, against the overwhelming forces of the Romans, and the very serious losses the latter suffered. Since *Apararea Patriei* had not been previously a forum for abstract theoretical discussion or of analysis of obscure historical details, the article appeared somewhat anomalous. As it coincided with Ceausescu's insistence on building up the "people's" military forces, it was likely signifying a shift toward the total war concept, which involved guerrilla warfare.*

The Romanian Chief of the General Staff, General-Colonel Ion Gheorghe, also emphasized that a future war could only be a people's war (that is, involving the entire population). Consequently, preparations for such a war had to involve, in his opinion, the readying of the army, the reservists, the Patriotic Guards, and the armed youth, in a manner that took cognizance of the involvement of the entire people.[130] In February 1971, the Plenum of the Central Committee of the Romanian Communist Party gave its wholehearted approval to an integrated approach to armed resistance. It especially stressed the need for effective cooperation between the regular army and the Patriotic Guards.[131] Furthermore, the Minister of the Armed Forces, Ion Ionita, in an article also published in 1971, declared as quite axiomatic that an anti-imperialist war would have to be a people's war with the result that "all people must be ready for the defense of the fatherland, not merely some."[132]

If the change in the direction of planned Romanian resistance to that of people's war was significant, so was the role that each armed force element was to play within the total defense. The function of the Patriotic Guards was bound to be particularly important, for they represented the spearhead of the irregular forces, as the armed youth forces were to be formed around them.[133] However, it is in the determination of the importance of the main elements of armed resistance, that there appeared to have been some differences among the top military leaders of Romania.

Ionita himself emphasized the role of the Patriotic Guards, seemingly to the disadvantage of the regular army.[134] The considerable extent to which he downgraded the role of the army is, however, questionable, for after 1968 he spoke mainly in political terms and his emphasis on the irregular forces was always expressed within the context of preaching the total readiness of the nation. General-Colonel Ion Coman, then the Secretary of the Higher Political Council of the Armed Forces and a Deputy Minister of Defense, similarly, stressed the importance of the irregular forces. But he was thinking in even broader terms than Ionita, for he viewed the defense of the country as involving not only the entire people but also as being a confrontation on multiple planes, encompassing the military, the political, the ideological, the psychological, and

---

*Ceausescu declared again at the 10th Party Congress in 1969 that an anti-imperialist war could only be a people's war involving the entire population.[129]

so on.[135] Since the party in his opinion had to control all of these factors through a unified post at the top (Ceausescu), the regular army's role would appear diminished in face of the magnitude of the total factors involved. It did not mean the total devaluation of the army in favor of the people's or irregular forces, but Coman's omission of defining the role of the army could be interpreted as a slap in its direction.

The Commander of the Patriotic Guards, General-Lieutenant Vasile Milea, contemplated a very large role for people's forces in any defensive war. He felt that they were meant to fulfill the "sacred duty" of each citizen toward the country and that in fact these forces, which included the Patriotic Guards, the local civil and anti-aircraft defenses, and the youth training detachments, would strengthen dramatically the nation's military defense system.[136] The Patriotic Guards themselves, in his opinion, represented one of the principal forms through which the party's concept of national defense was materialized. Moreover, these formations, he asserted, had the additional benefit of local bases whereby the people could integrate defense and economic production.

On the other hand, General-Colonel Ion Gheorghe, the Chief of the General Staff, accented the role of the army despite his acceptance of the concept of people's war.[137] He noted that the partisan war concepts, for instance, appeared in countries where social liberation was the object and once it was attained the partisan or guerrilla formations were transformed into a regular army.[138] Furthermore he alleged that Marx and Engels themselves had insisted that the need to arm the people did not negate the role of the army. General Gheorghe confidently asserted that the party considered the army as the principal component of the entire system of national defense. He reminded the reader that the army had certain unique characteristics that made it indispensable as the major defensive tool. These were (1) The army had a tighter structure than any other organization, and a flexibility not linked to local conditions; (2) The army was fully equipped in all the weapons categories and, could repulse aggression on land, on the seas, and in the air; (3) The army's professionalism enabled it to train other resistance units. It could also school the citizenry in patriotism, and it was capable of aiding in social and economic activities; and (4) While other units of the military system had a territorial dependency, and could occasionally come under the powers of the local administration, the army was exclusively subordinated to the supreme leadership organs of the state, and the supreme national command led by the Supreme Commander of the Armed Forces, Nicolae Ceausescu.[139]

Thus, it would appear that both the commander of the Patriotic Guards and the Chief of the General Staff were each jockeying for a more powerful position while the Minister of the Armed Forces and the top political officer were leaning toward the guerrilla war concept of using irregulars. The "debate" among the military leaders, however, must be placed in the proper context. An irrevocable change had taken place in Romanian military policy after August 1968. Paramilitary or irregular forces had been increased from 50,000 men to more than 700,000 by 1977—the largest such force among the bloc states.[140] Romania was to fight a "total" war according to the Yugoslav model in case of intervention, for this was the policy laid out by Ceausescu and all the military leaders accepted it. The "debate" among the generals was of a "democratic-centralism" type with each trying to enhance his own bailiwick. It was natural that there would have been some rivalry between the regular army and the Patriotic Guard, with its supporting units. But it was not a rivalry that sought an exclusive role for either since it was made clear to them, and they accepted it, that there had to be close cooperation for an effective defense. The Patriotic Guard and the other irregular forces were made up of a very large number of men and indications are that the Guard in particular was given fairly extensive training. Nevertheless, the regular army had to be given the primary coordinating role in the defense of the country, for they were the best organized, trained, and equipped element. They were, however, only one element in the defense and the superior position accorded them should not diminish the great importance attached to the irregular forces, or the significance of the change in Romanian military thinking after 1968.

The views of Constantin Milea and Ion Gheorghe thus were not irreconcilable. Milea did acknowledge in a position paper that the Patriotic Guards would fight together with the army as a *subordinate* element.[141] For his part, Gheorghe rejected an exclusive role for the army, as restricted to states where the ruling class did not trust the people. In Romania, he felt the army would fight in conjunction with the Patriotic Guards and the subordinate units of the Ministry of the Interior.[142]

Romanian war scenarios reflected this conciliation between regular and popular forces. The initial contact with an invading enemy was to be made by the popular forces, such as the Patriotic Guards. According to General Milea they would not fight in the manner of regular troops but instead, would avoid head-on action in favor of flank, rear, and hit-and-run blows. Within the interior of the country, according to him, the popular forces would assure the security of the principal economic targets. If there were an enemy breakthrough and the latter occupied Romanian territory, the popular forces were to aid any encircled Romanian regular army troops, and constantly harass the enemy in order to destroy its morale.[143] The latter task, therefore, is very much a step toward classical guerrilla warfare, especially with the emphasis on destroying the enemy's morale.

Other irregular forces were to play an important role in the defense of the state as well. The forces of the Ministry of the Interior in particular were assigned the role of counterespionage and the prevention of strategic surprise.[144] While they of course had the other role of fighting against the enemy and of participating in resistance once a part of the territory was occupied by the enemy, this role of preventing surprise was designed to deprive an opponent of a key desideratum for victory. Ceausescu had stated repeatedly that foreign agents would try to infiltrate Romania and that this must be guarded against by the security troops and the militia of the Ministry of the Interior. And in preventing surprise these forces would ensure that the enemy was not capable of creating the type of confusion that would facilitate his aggression. As surprise has always been a key element of Soviet military strategy its prevention had to be an indispensable element of defense. Along this line, anti-aircraft defenses constituted another important element of the Romanian defense and, therefore, they organized local anti-aircraft units. Tremendous emphasis was placed on these units to resist air strikes by the enemy or any other diversionary moves.[145] They were to cooperate closely with the other defenses as part of the Ministry of National Defense, particularly with the regular territorial anti-aircraft defenses of the main armed forces that appeared to have been the Romanian equivalent of the Soviet PVO-Strany.

General Gheorghe, despite his emphasis on the regular army, merely elaborated on the above scenario without substantially changing it. He agreed that the popular forces were to fight first in a retarding and harassing action, with only occasional help from regular army units. He wrote:

> Being the most efficient element of the military system, it is indicated that the army will be launched into action at the decisive moment, after the invader was harassed physically, psychologically and politically and diminished and traumatized by the initial rebuff of the territorial fighting formations and some elements of the army.[146]

He also allowed that in all fighting there was to be a constant link between the popular and the regular armed forces.

Of course there were organizational difficulties. The command structure was rather complicated, for the President of the Republic, the Central Committee, the Ministry of the Interior, the Ministry of Defense, and the Organization of Communist Youth all had a part to play in the defense. Perhaps there was even some continued friction, for Gheorghe was replaced by Coman at the end of 1974 as Chief of the General Staff and the latter himself replaced Ionita as Minister of National Defense in June 1976, when a professional military officer was brought in as Chief of the General Staff. If the hypothesis for these changes is even partially correct, then the appointment of a professional military officer, Hortopan, as Chief of the General Staff in 1976 would indicate that the problems had been solved and that the Romanians were able to reorganize their forces according to the war scenarios postulated earlier by Generals Gheorghe and Milea.

Romanian policy on armed resistance and their war scenarios suggest a number of strengths. If the bulk of the regular armed forces were to be held back from an initial response in the case of an invasion, the intruder could make greater progress against irregular forces, but he would have been denied the chance to deal a knock-out blow to the most powerful element of the armed forces. The latter, with the benefit of local terrain, shorter supply lines, and popular support, could deliver heavy blows at its own choosing. This type of defense, far from allowing for a speedier invasion, would have deprived a potential invader, such as the Soviet Union, of one of their key desiderata, speed in consolidating an intervention. The prolonged guerrilla-type warfare envisioned in the Romanian scenario, especially when involving the mass of the population and combined with regular army units, would have been particularly demoralizing to an intervening force trained for quick, clear-cut victories. Romanian territory itself has large mountainous regions ideally suited to guerrilla warfare and this was not lost on its military leaders.* The flexibility envisaged by Romanian plans for armed resistance when faced with a much stronger opponent, in fact, involves what in boxing terminology is called "rolling with the blow" and countering with "short jabs." If successful, such a tactic would have resulted in prolonged resistance—a heavy blow to Soviet morale, which had not been faced previously with armed resistance organized by a bloc-state Communist party.

So while the regular Romanian armed forces were weak by the standards of the Northern Tier states of the Warsaw Pact, and would have been of little value to the Soviet Union in offensive and in certain defensive operations along the axis running within that Tier, this did not reflect Romanian capacity to resist armed intervention. After 1968, the regular army became an integral part of a much larger defense system where its shortcomings in heavy and sophisticated equipment were not as significant. The flexible system of total defense, backed by domestic production of small arms, ammunition, and transport equipment, supported by mass mobilization and territorial resistance making maximum use of terrain, all made for prolonged resistance, even against such a disproportionately large opponent as the Soviet Union. The Romanian system of armed defense in its totality, as opposed to merely its regular armed forces, then, we contend, had credibility for the Soviet leaders (who have always been well informed about the bloc states), who were bound to be influenced by these developments.

FLANK DEFENSES

Since the deterrent value of Romanian armed resistance to intervention increased parallel with the time it could prolong such resistance, it would follow that the Soviet Union, had it decided to intervene in Romania, most likely would have attempted to use the method it had employed in Czechoslovakia, namely an all-points-of-compass attack, to overcome resistance quickly. To

---

*Colonel Gheorghe Stanciulescu, a section chef of the Center for the Study and Research of military history and theory, as well as a frequent contributor to military journals, laid special emphasis on the Carpathian redoubt in case parts of Romania were occupied, as well as on other mountainous and wooded areas.[147]

countervene this, Romania in turn would have had to attempt to protect its flanks and to try to neutralize intervention from those quarters. In case of Soviet intervention, Romania would certainly have been attacked from the north and east, directly from the Soviet Union, and from the northwest by Soviet troops stationed in Hungary. It is its southern and southeastern borders that could have been left untouched, if Bulgaria and Yugoslavia did not cooperate in an attack. In such a scenario, the Romanians could have attempted to hold the southern portion of the country along a highly defensible line of Transylvanian Alps and Carpathian Mountains, which cut across virtually the entire country, and along the rivers Siret and Danube. Within the area south of this line, Romania has its capital, the oil fields of Ploesti, and the bulk of its industry and agriculture. Even if Romanian defenses, as the intervention continued, were contracted into the central mountain core, it would have been invaluable for it to hold on to the south for as long as possible.

Relations with Yugoslavia

Romanian-Yugoslav relations were blessed by the absence of any territorial dispute between the two states, or of historical animosity between the two peoples. Furthermore, as Yugoslavia was not a member of the Warsaw Pact and Tito had been one of the most ardent supporters of polycentrism, there was no question of Yugoslav participation in a military intervention in Romania. Rather, what was of importance to Romania was the help Yugoslavia would have given it in case of a Soviet and Warsaw Pact intervention. Since much of the border between the two states consists of the same mountain chain, separated only by a river, the Yugoslavs had the potential to provide key external help if the Romanians resorted to guerrilla warfare against the aggressors. Yugoslav popular resistance against the Nazis in World War II also provided the Romanians with an example of guerrilla war, and the Romanian Defense Law of 1972 was modeled on that of Yugoslavia.

Relations between Romania and Yugoslavia were close and contacts at crises points are particularly significant. Ceausescu visited Belgrade in June 1968, and in their speeches both he and Tito not only praised the close relations of cooperation between the two nations, but also emphasized the benefit of such cooperation to the entire Socialist camp.[148] On August 24, 1968, Ceausescu again met Tito at Vrsat, Yugoslavia, just across the border, where they exchanged views "on problems of bilateral and international relations" of interest to both countries.[149]

Contacts continued between the two leaders, especially at crisis points and their speeches gave the impression of ever closer links. Following Soviet pressure on Romania in 1969, the two leaders met in the autumn, at the twin border cities of Turnu-Severin (Romania) and Klardovo (Yugoslavia) and Tito stressed the development of multilateral relations between the two states. It is interesting to note that he mentioned these relations as "political, economic, and of *other nature.*"[150] (Emphasis added.)

Tito and Ceausescu met again in November 1971, this time in Romania. There were allusions to military cooperation both in Tito's speech, when he mentioned that there was now a tradition to meet at least once a year and that both countries must guard their independence and sovereignty,[151] as well as in Ceausescu's address, when he mentioned that "It was not only once that our peoples fought jointly for their national and social liberation."[152] This meeting was particularly salient in view of the fact that Romania had just resisted spring and summer Soviet military pressures.

As tensions between the Soviet Union and Romania increased in the wake of Soviet maneuvers in Bulgaria, Tito and Ceausescu met for the twelfth time during June 1974. At this meeting they held up Romanian-Yugoslav relations as an example of international collaboration and in the joint communique they stressed the necessity that "countries and people of the Balkans arrange for themselves their reciprocal relations" and of turning of the Balkans into a zone of peace.[153] In 1976 as tensions increased again between Romania and the Soviet Union, two high-ranking Yugoslav military delegations paid visits to Romania in June and July while in September of that year Ceausescu made a visit to Yugoslavia where he was given a tumultuous welcome.[154] He and Tito reconfirmed the five principles of international relations and stated that it was the duty of all nations to refrain from intervening "*under any pretext or any circumstance*" (emphasis added) in the internal or external affairs of another state.[155]

Romanian-Yugoslav cooperation extended to a great many fields. Joint hydroelectric projects on the Danube were part of an ever-increasing economic cooperation that saw trade between the two countries increase 2.8 times between 1971 and 1975.[156] The two countries had seen eye to eye on autonomy in foreign policy, they used pretty well the same language in asserting rights of sovereignty at the East Berlin conference in 1976, they shared similar views of Eurocommunism in external affairs, and they both denounced the so-called "Sonnenfeldt Doctrine" in 1976. The Yugoslavs have even claimed in discussions with Western officials that they often participate at various negotiations and meetings of Communist parties merely to support the Romanians.[157] All this would indicate a mutual recognition of the interdependence of the two states. There has even been a rumor in the West that Bucharest has a contingency plan in case of Soviet intervention whereby Ceausescu and his entire leadership group would fly to Belgrade and if necessary on to Peking where they would form a government in exile, thereby further prolonging resistance to the Soviet Union.[158]

It has been suggested by some Western observers that after 1968 the Romanians and the Yugoslavs had entered into a secret defense alliance.[159] While it was in Yugoslavia's interest to see an autonomous Romania, even the leadership of the former never admitted to such a treaty. The numerous contacts between the two countries, especially at times of crisis, and the frequent consultation of the military leaders does, however, suggest some sort of understanding. This could range from a full military alliance to supplying the Romanian defenders, in case of attack, with arms and ammunition, or to an agreement to give the Romanian leadership refuge in case of defeat. All of these could have helped buttress Romanian defense credibility and thereby helped enlarge the limits of its autonomy. Even if the Soviet leaders were not aware of the precise nature of Romanian-Yugoslav relations, the very possibility of an alliance could have acted as an element of deterrence. So at the minimum Romania had one secure border, and possibly a valuable ally.

The Hungarian and Bulgarian Flanks

In the case of the Hungarian border, Romania did not have much hope of immunity in the event of a Soviet intervention against the Ceausescu leadership. Besides the fact that the Soviet troops in Hungary would have participated in an intervention, the Soviet Union had the power to order Hungarian participation. Hungary won the right for domestic reform at the price of following rather unquestioningly Soviet foreign policy dictates. Moreover, Moscow could have bargained with Hungary over the large Maghiar minority in Transylvania, and over possible territorial adjustments. Romania tried to maintain good relations with Hungary[160] (though these were affected by Budapest's concerns for the Magyars of Transylvania)[161] but in a Czechoslovak-type of crisis, its Transylvanian frontier was vulnerable.

On the other hand, the situation with Bulgaria was quite different. With the cession of southern Dobrogea to Bulgaria in 1940, there remained no outstanding territorial claims between Bucharest and Sofia. Relations between the two states had been very cordial under Gheorghiu-Dej, and Ceausescu deliberately cultivated this friendship.

In its approach to relations with Bulgaria, Romania stressed regional stability. Having lived in one of the world's most volatile regions, the Balkan people, including the Bulgarians, would have placed a high price on stability and security. Ceausescu relied on the argument for security in all of his references to the Balkan region. He and the Bulgarian leader, Todor Jivkov, exchanged very friendly visits virtually every year.[162] During the signing of a new Treaty of Friendship and Mutual Cooperation with Bulgaria on November 19, 1970, Ceausescu emphasized the great contribution he felt Romanian-Bulgarian friendship made to the stability of the entire Balkan region.

Warm relations between the two countries continued in the latter part of the 1970s. In 1976, for instance, the leaders of the two countries paid mutual visits to each other and praised with the greatest warmth their relationship in the joint communique they issued.[163] Cooperation between the two states increased through joint hydrotechnical complexes, rapidly developing trade, and contacts at all levels of government. Romania had to be very careful in its handling of

Bulgaria both because of Yugoslav-Bulgarian animosity and because of the extreme closeness of Bulgarian-Soviet relations. The latter resulted at times in Bulgaria's acting as a proxy for Moscow in Balkan relations.

Therefore, Romania tried to place its relationship with Sofia within the context of easing tensions in the entire Balkan region. This entailed improving relations with all of the states and Bucharest did make very strenuous efforts at enhancing its relations, particularly with Turkey and Greece. It was instrumental in the convening of the conference of Balkan states at the end of January 1976 (the first such conference since World War II) in order to try to stabilize Balkan relations. Romania had previously proposed a denuclearization of the Balkans in 1957 and 1969. Now it had the support of the Greek government, but unfortunately this conference did not gather much of a momentum largely because of Bulgarian opposition, the latter apparently acting on orders from Moscow. Nevertheless, the continuing good relations between Romania and Bulgaria demonstrated that the Sofia leadership did consider security important. Romania thus attempted to show that both countries could reap benefits from mutual collaboration and good relations and that both had a vested interest in stability. Translated into military terms an attack on Romania would have had a destabilizing effect on the entire Balkan region and therefore would have been contrary to Bulgarian interests.

Romania undoubtedly hoped that, in case there was a Soviet intervention, Bulgaria would have remained neutral. It is true that the latter, in the period under study, did not have Soviet troops stationed on its soil, and those that participated in joint maneuvers did not constitute a large force. Nevertheless, in view of the staunch loyalty of Bulgaria to the Soviet Union, neutrality may have been too optimistic a quest. Still, in view of the good Romanian-Bulgarian relations, which were meticulously maintained by Ceausescu, and in view of Bulgarian interest in stability and security, the Romanians could reasonably have expected that the Bulgarians would not have made more than a token contribution to any military intervention in Romania. It is unlikely that the Soviet leaders would have been unaware of this restraint on their Bulgarian allies. Such Bulgarian restraint, in turn, would again have lent additional credibility to the Romanian willingness to put up armed resistance. For it was unlikely that the Soviet leadership in the 1970s had Stalin's power to make the Bulgarian participation effective by mere threats against them.

THE POLITICS OF DEFENSE REORGANIZATION

As with the political challenges that it posed to the Soviet Union, Romania had to be careful that the military challenges were not abrasive but rather were offered in a palatable form. This involved both diplomacy and small concessions. In preparating its active defenses, Romania had to be particularly careful that these did not become in themselves provocations to the Soviet Union—provocations justifying intervention. Romanian manner or style would best be illustrated by its conciliatory actions (if any), especially during the crisis periods of 1968, 1969, and 1971.

On August 14, 1968, Ceausescu justified the strengthening of the Romanian army by claiming that the Romanian Communist Party was fulfilling its duty not only to its own people but also to the cause of Socialism.[164] He went on to re- assure the Soviet Union that in the future Romania would always be ready to fight against imperialism allied with Socialist states, and he emphasized in par- ticular, that nothing could budge or weaken his nation's friendship for the Soviet Union. Following the Czechoslovak intervention, Ceausescu received Marshal Yakubovsky in Bucharest,[165] thereby demonstrating that despite rather strong polemics between the two states, Romania was willing to keep the lines of com- munication open.

In the spring of 1969, under intense Soviet pressure, Romania decided to compromise and allowed its troops to take part in Warsaw Pact maneuvers on Soviet soil.[166] The number of troops taking part was small but Romania made it clear that it still considered itself a member of the camp with an obligation to participate in the strengthening of the joint defenses. Furthermore, during the tense period of 1971 the Romanians reiterated their support for military co- operation among the Socialist states.[167] Ceausescu himself told a popular rally held in Bucharest in August 1971 that the party envisioned the cooperation of not only economic and social bodies with those of the other Socialist states, but also that of the army.[168]

Subsequent Romanian actions showed that they were prepared to imple- ment some of the promises of military cooperation with the Soviet Union. While Romania did not allow Warsaw Pact military maneuvers on its soil it did allow joint map and staff exercises as a means of compromise. During the periods of friction in 1974 and 1976 the Bucharest leadership maintained contacts with the Soviet Union and tried to reassure them that Romania was complying with the general concepts of Socialist defense. In 1976, for instance, Ceausescu was very emphatic in stating that Romanian defense was not directed against anyone but was merely designed to assure the "triumph of Communism in Romania."[169]

Therefore, Romania made concerted efforts to ensure that, in strengthen- ing its active military defenses, it did not provoke the Soviet Union. It even blunted its challenges with concessions in order to avoid an open confrontation. Furthermore, it strove to keep the lines of communication open with the Soviet Union, even if this meant welcoming visits from such opponents of bloc-state autonomy as Marshal Yakubovsky. This was all a conscious, deliberate effort and in that sense it constituted an element of active defense.

CONCLUSION

The focus of our analysis in this chapter was the efficiency of the Romanian "active" military defenses that, together with the "passive" defenses, should have helped deter Soviet intervention or intimidation. In effect, we wanted to discern if these active defenses could enlarge or in the very least stop the limits of Romanian foreign policy autonomy from contracting.

Romania declared openly a willingness to resist by armed force any intrusion upon its national territory. This declared willingness would have had little deterrent value unless it was believed by the Soviet Union which, with its excellent intelligence network, was unlikely to accept a simple bluff. Romania passed the first hurdle in organizing a credible military defense, for evidence showed that under Nicolae Ceausescu there was a strong unity between the armed forces and the party leadership, thereby depriving any external enemy of the chance to drive a wedge between various sections of Romanian society in order to weaken the nation's resistance capacity.

Army-party unity was effected skillfully by the Ceausescu leadership through the formal military decision-making structure, through political indoctrination, through material incentives, and through appeals to patriotism at times of crisis. An empirical analysis of military behavior at crisis points indicated that the party's control methods functioned well. At the decisive points, the armed forces lined up solidly behind party policy. As well, Ceausescu took steps to protect the territorial integrity of the country by eliminating any threat of irredentism from the Magyar population of Transylvania, however remote this threat may have been. By eliminating the Maghiar Autonomous Region in 1968, Ceausescu went far in stifling any identification that the large Hungarian minority had or could have developed with a territorial unit.

As far as the effectiveness of the actual Romanian forces was concerned, the criteria for evaluation was the extent to which they could deprive the Soviet armies of three of their key desiderata which they demonstrated in interventions in Eastern Europe, namely surprise, speed, and morale. In the case of the first point, the Romanian political and military leadership appeared to have done a credible job in alerting the country and the armed forces to the external dangers in times of crisis.

Speed and morale are closely linked together, for by involving the Soviet armies in a prolonged war, Romania would also have struck a serious blow at their morale. The extent to which the Romanian forces could have put up a prolonged resistance against extremely powerful Soviet and (likely) Warsaw Pact forces depended on their actual fighting capacity. The regular, or conventional armed forces, had been improved by Ceausescu and the domestic source of weapons had been greatly increased. Nevertheless, by the standards of the Northern Tier states of the Warsaw Pact, the regular Romanian forces were still small and weak. In 1968, however, the institution of the Patriotic Guards and local defense units under the concept of "people's war" radically altered the entire scenario of Romanian armed resistance.

The use of popular forces did not merely add a large mass to a small regular army but instead changed drastically Romania's concepts of armed resistance. After 1968 the regular army became part of an integrated scheme of total defense. Its bulk was to be held back in reserve, safe from a knock-out blow by superior invading forces, while the irregular or local forces delayed and harassed the enemy in classic guerrilla-warfare style. All of the armed forces were to fight with flexibility, using the defensive potential of local terrain and, if necessary, were to continue the fight in the Carpathian redoubt. The Defense Law, introduced in December 1972, warned the potential intruder that even if he succeeded in occupying large tracts of Romanian territory, no surrender would be made.

In addition to building a credible force to resist Soviet intervention, Romania sought to safeguard its territorial flanks by developing close, friendly relations with its neighbors. While not much could be done on the Hungarian frontier, Romania developed very close ties with Yugoslavia, thereby acquiring a potential ally. In the case of Bulgaria, Romania, while failing to establish as close links as with Yugoslavia, nevertheless developed a friendly cooperation that could have resulted in Bulgaria giving the Soviet Union only token support in case of an intervention in Romania. With some of its frontiers safe, Romania's capacity for prolonged resistance to Soviet intervention was enhanced and therein lay its credibility.

Last, Romania used its diplomatic skills and willingness to offer some concessions while pursuing a general policy line, in order to dull the edge of its military challenges to Soviet security. As in the political sphere, Romania sought to present its challenges obliquely and to avoid a direct confrontation with the Soviet Union.

Thus, we submit that Romania had built up important and effective "active" military defenses that fitted in well with its extensive "passive" defenses. Together they helped provide Romania with fairly wide limits for foreign policy autonomy—limits that may well have been unique among the Soviet-bloc states. As significant as these "defenses" were, they were, of course, part of a larger "defense" network that included political "defenses" as well as legal and institutional ones.

NOTES

1. E. Hinterhoff, "The Erosion of the Warsaw Pact and Its Implications," *Ons Leger*, September 1968, p. 8.

2. F. S. Northedge, *The Use of Force in International Relations* (London: Faber and Faber, 1973), p. 18.

3. Nicolae Ceausescu, "Speech Made at the Meeting of the Basic Active of the Armed Forces," May 1967, in *Romania, On the Way of Completing Socialist Construction* (Bucharest: Meridiane Publishing, 1969), p. 307.

4. Ibid., p. 308.

5. Ceausescu gave full support to the Czechoslovak leadership in an August 14, 1968, speech published in *Apararea Patriei*, Central Organ of the Ministry of the Armed Forces of Romania (weekly, Bucharest), August 15, 1968, and denounced the intervention on August 28, 1968, in *Apararea Patriei*.

6. *Apararea Patriei*, August 21, 1968.

7. *Scinteia*, February 29, 1969.

8. *Scinteia*, May 25, 1969.

9. N. Ceausescu, *Cuvintare le Consfatuirea cadrelor de baza din Ministerului Fortelor Armate, February 5* (Bucharest: Editura Politica, 1970), p. 6.

10. F. Diaconu, *Apararea Patriei*, January 13, 1971.

11. *Scinteia*, June 9, 1971.

12. Ibid.

13. *Apararea Patriei*, June 23, 1971.

14. Ibid.

15. *Apararea Patriei*, June 30, 1971.

16. Ibid.

17. "Speech Delivered at the Korean-Romanian Friendship Great Meeting Held in Pyongyang," June 14, 1971, in N. Ceausescu, *Romania, On the Way of Building Up the Multilaterally Developed Socialist Society*, vol. 6 (Bucharest: Editura Politica, 1972), p. 102.

18. General Ion Ionita, *Apararea Patriei*, December 29, 1972.

19. *Legea nr 14/1972, Buletinul Oficial*, 1973, Sectia redactionala, p. 3.

20. *Apararea Patriei*, August 11, 1976.

21. Henry Kissinger, *American Foreign Policy* (London: Weidenfeld and Nicholson, 1969), p. 61.

22. *Scinteia*, October 24, 1965.

23. *Conferinta Nationale a Partidului Comunist Roman 19-21 Julie, 1972* (Bucharest: Editura Politica, 1972), pp. 549-55.

24. *Apararea Patriei*, August 25, 1976.

25. *Scinteia*, March 15, 1969.

26. *Apararea Patriei*, May 5, 1971.

27. Ibid.

28. "Decree on Organization and Operation of the Ministry of National Defense," *Buletinul Oficial al Republicii Socialiste Romana*, part I, no. 130, November 21, 1972, pp. 1048-51.

29. Ibid., p. 1049.

30. Ibid.

31. Mihai Loghiade, "Unitatile Ministerului de Interne" in I. Cernat and S. Stanislav, eds., *Apararea Nationala a Romaniei Socialiste* (Bucharest: Editura Militara, 1974), pp. 171-4.

32. *Legea no. 14/1972*, op. cit., p. 58.

33. *Constitution of the Socialist Republic of Romania* (Bucharest: Meridiane House, 1975).

34. *Legea no. 14/1972*, op. cit., p. 6.

35. *Legea No. 14/1972*, op. cit., pp. 7-8.

36. *Radio Free Europe Research: Romania*, March 6, 1972.

37. *Corriere della Sera* (Milan), February 19, 1972.

38. *Radio Bucharest*, January 24, 1972, in *Radio Free Europe Research, Romania*, January 25, 1972.

39. *Scinteia*, February 17, 1972.

40. *Conferinta Nationale. . . ,* op. cit., p. 554.

41. *Informatia Bucurestiului*, December 3, 1974, and *Radio Bucharest*, December 7, 1974, 21:00 G.M.T.

42. *Agerpress* (Bucharest), June 16, 1976.

43. General-Colonel Ion Ionita, *Apararea Patriei*, May 10, 1967.

44. *Apararea Patriei*, August 15, 1968.

45. Ibid.

46. *Apararea Patriei*, April 7, 1971.

47. Ibid.

48. Ion Gheorghe and Oliver Lustig, *Stiinta Conducerii si Comanda Militara* (Bucharest: Editura Militara, 1975).

49. *Apararea Patriei*, June 9, 1976.

50. *Romania Libera*, June 14, 1976.

51. *Scinteia*, October 2, 1976.

52. Ceausescu, *Cuvintare la Consfatuirea. . .* , op. cit., p. 7.

53. *Scinteia*, December 30, 1975.

54. *Apararea Patriei*, February 1971.

55. Ibid., p. 5.

56. *Anuarul Statistic al R.S.R. 1971* (Bucharest: Directia Centrala de Statistica, 1971), p. 146.

57. *Apararea Patriei*, February 17, 1971.

58. *The Military Balance, 1965-1966* (London: IISS, 1965), p. 7; *The Military Balance, 1970-1971* (1970), p. 17; and *The Military Balance, 1977-1978* (1977), p. 15, respectively.

59. *Apararea Patriei*, February 1, 1971.

60. *The Military Balance, 1969-1970* (London: IISS, 1969), p. 14.

61. *Apararea Patriei*, May 12, 1971.

62. N. Ceausescu, "Cuvint la solemnitatea Inaintarii in grad a unor generali si ofiteri superiori," in N. Ceausescu, *Romania pe Drumul Construirii Societatii Socialiste Multilateral Dezvoltate*, vol. 7 (Bucharest: Editura Politica, 1973), p. 952.

63. *Apararea Patriei*, May 5, 1967.

64. *Apararea Patriei*, May 10, 1967.

65. *Scinteia*, August 15, 1968.

66. *Apararea Patriei*, January 21, 1971.

67. "150th Anniversary of Revolutionary Movement of 1821," *Apararea Patriei*, June 16, 1971.

68. *Scinteia*, December 30, 1972.

69. Ioan G. Stoica, "Apararea Patriei," *Familia* (Bucharest), Seria V-a Anul 10, no. 5, May 1975, p. 5.

70. *Lumea* (Bucharest), November 3, 1977, cover.

71. *Scinteia*, October 24 and 25, 1965.

72. "Speech Made at the Basic Active of the Armed Forces of the Socialist Republic of Romania," May 31, 1967, in Ceausescu, *Romania, On the Way of Completing Socialist Construction*, op. cit., p. 299.

73. Ibid., p. 300.

74. *Apararea Patriei*, August 15, 1968.

75. *Scinteia*, August 23, 1968.

76. *Apararea Patriei*, September 4, 1968.

77. *Apararea Patriei*, September 11, 1968.

78. *Apararea Patriei*, October 16, 1968.

79. *Apararea Patriei*, May 12, 1971.

80. *Survival* (London, IISS), November 1968, p. 357.

81. Ibid.

82. New York *Times*, February 18, 1972.

83. N. Ceausescu, "Romania si Securitates Europeana," *Scinteia*, May 25, 1969.

84. *Scinteia*, May 22, 1969.

85. *Apararea Patriei*, June 9, 1971.

86. *Apararea Patriei*, June 30, 1971.

87. Ibid.

88. Ibid.

89. *Apararea Patriei*, July 14, 1971.

90. *Apararea Patriei*, July 21, 1971.

91. *Viata Militara* (Bucharest: Editura Militara), November 9, 1971, p. 16.

92. Ion Ionita, in *Conferinta Nationala a Partidului Comunist Roman 19-21, July 1972* (Bucharest: Editura Politica, 1972), p. 350.

93. Ion Ionita, "Coordonate ale appararii nationale a Romaniei," in Colonel I. S. Cernat and E. J. Stanislav, eds., *Politic si Social in Doctrina Militara a Romaniei Socialiste* (Bucharest: Editura Politica, 1974), p. 14.

94. *Apararea Patriei*, August 11, 1976.

95. Ionel Nicolae, "Politica Particului Comunist Roman in Problema Nationala," *Era Socialista*, no. 1, January 1975, p. 31.

96. N. Ceausescu, "Exposition on the Improvement of the Administrative Organization of the Territory of the Socialist Republic of Romania," *Scinteia*, February 16, 1968.

97. *Scinteia*, August 27, 1968.

98. *Scinteia*, March 13, 1971.

99. *Scinteia*, February 26, 1972.

100. *Lumea*, June 23, 1977.

101. *Economist*, December 17, 1975, p. 6.

102. *Apararea Patriei*, August 15, 1968.

103. *Scinteia*, August 21, 1968.

104. Constantin Mitea, "Interesul dezvoltarii relatiilor de prietenie se colaborare Romano-Sovietice al cauzei socialismului si pacii," *Scinteia*, May 18, 1969.

105. *Apararea Patriei*, June 23, 1971.

106. *Scinteia*, September 19, 1972.

107. *Apararea Patriei*, August 11, 1976.

108. *The Military Balance 1965-1966*, op. cit., p. 7 and in *The Military Balance 1977-1978*, op. cit., p. 15.

109. *The Military Balance 1969-1970*, op. cit., p. 14.

110. *The Military Balance 1971-1972* (London: IISS, 1971), p. 11.

111. *The Military Balance 1977-1978*, op. cit., pp. 2-5.

112. General Ion Ionita, *Apararea Patriei*, May 5, 1971.

113. N. Ceausescu, *Apararea Patriei*, August 14, 1968.

114. *Apararea Patriei*, February 17, 1971.

115. *Jane's All the World's Aircraft 1976-1977* (London: Jane's Yearbooks, 1977), p. 150.

116. Ibid.

117. Simion Pitea, *Economia si Apararea Nationala* (Bucharest: Editura Militara, 1976), p. 130.

118. Ibid., pp. 46-7.

119. *The Military Balance, 1975-1976* (London: IISS, 1975), p. 4, and *The Military Balance 1977-1978*, op. cit., p. 15.

120. *Pravda*, September 4, 1968, and *Toronto Jewish News*, June 15, 1968.

121. *Times* (London), August 10 and 18, 1975.

122. *The Military Balance, 1976-1977* (London: IISS, 1976), p. 4 and *The Military Balance 1977-1978*, op. cit., p. 15.

123. *The Military Balance, 1977-1978*, op. cit., p. 82.

124. General-Colonel Ion Gheorghe, "Deciziunea comandantului," *Apararea Patriei*, March 31, 1971.

125. I. Suta, "Consideratii asupra fizionomiei actiunilor militare in razboiul intregului popor," in Cernat and Stanislav, eds., *Politic si Social. . . ,* op. cit., pp. 93-5.

126. *Scinteia*, August 21, 1968.

127. "Consideratii privind rolul factorului demografic in apararea armata a Republicci Socialiste Romana" in Cernat and Stanislav, eds., *Politic si Social. . . ,* op. cit., p. 79.

128. Iulian Cernat, "Scopurile Politico-Strategice ale Razboiului Integrului Popor" in Cernat and Stanislav, eds., *Apararea Nationala. . . ,* op. cit., p. 104.

129. N. Ceausescu, in *Congresul al X-lea al Partidului Comunist Roman* (Bucharest: Editura Politica, 1969), p. 55.

130. *Apararea Patriei*, February 3, 1971.

131. *Apararea Patriei*, April 7, 1971.

132. Ion Ionita, "P.C.R.–Fauritorul si conducatorul armatei noastre populare," *Apararea Patriei*, May 5, 1971.

133. General-Major Paul Marinescu, "Debate on the Defence of the Fatherland," *Viata Militara*, October 1971, p. 4.

134. *Apararea Patriei*, December 6, 1972.

135. General Ion Coman, "Trasaturi ale conducerii apararii," in Cernat and Stanislav, eds., *Politic si Social. . .*, op. cit., p. 20.

136. General Vasile Milea, "Garzile patriotice in sistemul national de aparare," in Cernat and Stanislav, eds., *Politic si Social. . .*, op. cit., p. 101.

137. General Ion Gheorghe, "Rolui armatei in sistemul national de aparare," in Cernat and Stanislav, eds., *Politic si Social . . .*, op. cit., pp. 26–33.

138. Ibid., p. 29.

139. Ibid., pp. 29–32.

140. *The Military Balance 1967-1968* (London: IISS, 1967), p. 4 and *The Military Balance, 1977-1978*, op. cit., pp. 12–15.

141. Milea, op. cit., p. 103.

142. Gheorghe, "Rolui armatei. . . ," op. cit., pp. 29–30.

143. Milea, op. cit., pp. 104–5.

144. Colonel-Lieutenant Mihai Loghiade, "Unitatile Ministerului de Interne," in Cernat and Stanislav, eds., *Apararea Nationala. . .*, op. cit., pp. 171–4.

145. General-Major Ion Geoana, "Apararea Locala Antiaeriana," in Cernat and Stanislav, eds., *Apararea Nationala . . .*, op. cit., pp. 180–7.

146. Gheorghe, "Rolui armatei. . . ," op. cit., p. 33.

147. Colonel Gheorghe Stanciulescu, "Reflectii asupra strategiei rezistantei populare armate," in Cernat and Stanislav, eds., *Politic si Social . . .*, op. cit., pp. 61–6.

148. Nicolae Ceausescu and Joseph Tito, *Sub Steagul Internationalismului Socialist* (speeches, visits) *June 1965-June 1972* (Bucharest, Editura Politica, 1972), pp. 530–35.

149. *Scinteia*, August 25, 1968.

150. Tito, *Sub Steagul . . .*, op. cit., p. 574.

151. Ibid., pp. 615–6.

152. *Scinteia*, November 25, 1971, p. 653.

153. *Lumea*, July 11, 1974, p. 2, and July 18, 1974, p. 3.

154. *Lumea*, September 16, 1976, p. 1.

155. Ibid., p. 2.

156. *Sub semnul prieteniei fratesti romano-iugoslave* (Bucharest: Editura Politica, 1977), p. 292.

157. T. Rakowska-Harmstone, "Socialist Internationalism, Part II," *Survey*, Spring 1976, p. 81.

158. *Economist*, December 17, 1975, p. 6.

159. Gabriel Fischer (Professor, Acadia University), personal communication, October 10, 1975, at McMaster University, Canada.

160. *Lumea*, June 23, 1977, pp. 1–2.

161. *Magyar Hirlap*, October 31, 1976, and *Elet es iradalom*, November 6, 1976.

162. Ceausescu and Jivkov, *Sub Steagul Internationalismului . . .*, op. cit., pp. 21–254.

163. *Scinteia*, July 28, 1976, and October 3, 1976.

164. N. Ceausescu, *Apararea Patriei*, August 15, 1968.

165. *Apararea Patriei*, October 2, 1968.

166. *Scinteia*, May 22, 1969.

167. Ion Ionita, *Apararea Patriei*, May 5, 1971.

168. *Scinteia*, August 21, 1971.

169. *Scinteia*, July 28, 1976, and October 3, 1976.

6

Conclusion:

The Efficacy of Political
and Military Defenses

Ceausescu could claim a considerable degree of sucess for his autonomous policies in foreign affairs, for Romania has successfully pursued policies that were clearly perceived as challenges by the Soviet Union. That such was the case testified to the proposition that Romania did not breach the political and military limits for bloc-state foreign policy autonomy tolerated by Moscow. These limits in turn were not static, conceptually or empirically. They involved a dynamism corollated to actions, views, and elements that cumulatively constituted the active and passive defenses of a defensive network. When this network functioned well, the limits were maintained or expanded, whereas the failure of any of the defenses weakened the network and constricted the limits. The effectiveness of the defense network had empirical reflection in the ability of Romanians to continue policies offensive to Moscow in face of Soviet pressure. With the exception of some tactical retrenchments, Romania did pursue an autonomous foreign policy. Our use of the term "autonomy" itself, though, was designed to indicate that one key element of Romanian defense was the self-imposed limitation on the scope of challenges to the Soviet Union.

The political sphere covered both the political-ideological, and the legal aspects of the limits. In the first chapter, it appeared that the Soviet quest for ideological security required a certain code of behavior on the part of the bloc states that was both restrictive and flexible. It was restrictive in the sense that there were certain types of behavior that were anathema to Moscow, but the fulfillment of such Soviet desiderata worked for greater Soviet flexibility in tolerating bloc-state deviations in other spheres. Moreover, Soviet policy toward the bloc was not per se interventionist, and this passive defense allowed for and could be combined with active Romanian political defenses.

In Romania, Gheorghiu-Dej had established valuable precedents in foreign policy autonomy upon which his successor could build. And Ceausescu did build upon these foundations a foreign policy that insisted upon Romania's right to differ from the Soviet Union in that area, and that rejected supranationality in any form or under any guise. Domestically, however, Ceausescu was content to follow the Soviet model of democratic centralism. The limited domestic reforms that were introduced never strayed far from those current in the Soviet Union.* Domestic and foreign policy, naturally, cannot be completely separated, for they influence and shape each other, but in Romania the manifestation of autonomy occurred through foreign policy.

In the political sphere Romania satisfied one of the key requirements of Soviet policy toward the bloc states, namely it was able to assure the Soviet Union of the security of Communist rule domestically. In essence this entailed control by the Romanian Communist Party of all facets of Romanian life. The Ceausescu leadership has acted with singleminded determination to accomplish this. During times of crisis with the Soviet Union, party control over Romanian life was intensified, at times to what might have appeared as excess in the West, thereby demonstrating to Moscow that an autonomous stance in foreign policy did not entail a weakening of ideological commitment at home.

Furthermore, Romania continued to formulate active political defenses that could help it resist Soviet pressures. Ceausescu, commencing in 1967, began to reorganize, purge, and rotate the country's leadership in order to eliminate all possible sources of challenge to his own leadership. Through these actions he also diminished the Soviet Union's chances of supporting an alternate leadership, or of effectively infiltrating the Romanian decision-making process. Bucharest similarly made great use of its diplomatic skills to avoid sharp confrontations with the Soviet Union. Ceausescu and his lieutenants made frequent use of an esoteric type of communication to express differing views from those emanating from the Kremlin. Furthermore, the Romanians combined an imaginative array of diplomatic tools with tactical concessions to the Soviet Union at times of crisis.

In building bridges to the West, the Ceausescu leadership made use of the passive defenses inherent in Soviet policy toward the bloc that allowed some, albeit limited, contact with the West—in line with the precedent set by Gheorghiu-Dej. In its objections to supranational developments in Comecon, and in the reluctance to participate in joint programs under the aegis of that institution, Romania took advantages of the passive defense inherent in Comecon. Following Khrushchev's failure in 1962 to reorganize Eastern Europe along the line of the "Socialist Division of Labor," the Soviet Union suffered a tremendous setback in its plans to build Comecon into a strong supranational organization through

---

*Romanian reforms in industry, for instance, were on a modest scale compared to Hungary or Yugoslavia and were roughly at the same stage as those in the Soviet Union. See Iancu Spigler, *Economic Reform in Romanian Industry* (London: Oxford University Press, 1973), p. 163. During 1974, however, there were certain retrenchments even from these modest reforms.

which it could achieve important economic and political aims. Neither the "comprehensive" plan of 1971 for Comecon, in which the Soviet Union favored the development of supranational planning as a framework for close coordination of national plans, nor the 1975 follow-up cooperation plan contained sufficient concrete steps for implementation of a truly viable integration plan. Thus Comecon did not become an indispensable institution through which Moscow could assure bloc cohesion. During the 1970s and particularly following the 1973 oil crisis Comecon became more attractive for the bloc states since the Soviet Union provided essential raw materials at lower than world prices and the organization itself provided a market for their industrial goods that could not compete with Western goods in the world markets. Furthermore, indications are that in the near future, despite price readjustments and possible cutbacks in energy sales, the Soviet Union will continue to find Comecon an economic liability. As a result of the benefits to the bloc, then, relations should be more natural. Nevertheless, certain bloc states such as Hungary and Poland have voiced their opposition to full-scale integration and supranationality. Therefore, Romania did not have to shoulder the whole burden of opposition but instead could take advantage of the reservations toward integration of other members. Moreover, Bucharest recognized the economic advantages of cooperation and its actual and projected trade with Poland and the G.D.R., for instance, has been characterized by a dramatic increase. As such Romania opposition to supranationality did not mean an unacceptable challenge to Soviet authority. Furthermore, Moscow could contain these Romanian challenges through the use of strong bilateral links with the other bloc states and through regionalism.

In turning away from Comecon integration to the West and the Third World, Romania was able to establish significant new sources for trade and particularly for importing raw materials, technology, and capital. These alternate sources of supply also gave Romania an important degree of immunity from politically inspired, Soviet economic pressures. Since in the postwar period the trade of the bloc states was limited largely to the Soviet Union and fellow bloc states, trade had been one of Moscow's most effective channels of enforcing bloc-state conformity. In addition to blocking a good part of this channel, the Romanians acquired powerful Western friends, such as De Gaulle, Willi Brandt, Richard Nixon, and Gerald Ford who would (and did) show some concern for Romania's fate in the latter's disagreements with Moscow. This concern, naturally, did not translate itself into a weighty counterbalance to Soviet pressures, but since the Soviet Union wanted to maintain good relations with the West at this time, Moscow would have been influenced, even if minimally at times, by the attitudes of these Western leaders.

The relations with the West, however, had only a limited potential for Romania. Politically, overly close relations could have provoked the Soviet Union. Moreover, in the 1970s detente had largely eliminated Romania's uniqueness among the bloc states in its relations with the Western world. Soviet agreement to the Helsinki document also entailed increased pressure on bloc states to conform to the Soviet line as the danger of ideological "contamination" from the West increased. But perhaps the key limit was in the economic sphere. Romanian industrial goods, despite their low price, could not compete in the Western market. The quality of workmanship and low technological level limited their utility to the highly developed economies of the Western countries. Increased trade deficits placed a heavy burden on the Romanian economy. As well, the West was unable to supply Romania with raw materials, particularly oil. Therefore, Romania had to turn to other sources of supply and to markets where its goods could be sold. The nations of the Third World and the Arab states *had* to be the answer. Here the Romanians could sell their industrial goods for needed raw materials including oil, often on a barter basis. The most remarkable development in Romanian trade in the 1970s has been this large shift toward the Third World and the Arab states.

Politically, Romania, in joining the Group of 77 nonaligned states, enhanced its political and diplomatic prestige throughout the world, since the nonaligned countries comprise the majority of the world states. Diplomatic support from these states at times of friction or crisis with the Soviet Union would have greatly aided the Romanian position. In increasing trade and improving relations with the Arab states, Romania again gained political support from a massive bloc and lost little in assuming an anti-Israeli line. If anything, it was thus able to follow the Soviet line in the Arab-Israeli dispute without having had to pay a cost in a diminution of its foreign policy autonomy.

The Sino-Soviet rift presented both political opportunities and dangers to Romania. The very sensitivity of Moscow to Chinese encroachments upon its own ideological-political fiefdom left Romania with the danger that its contacts with China would act as a provocation to the Kremlin. On the other hand, through skillful use of diplomacy, Romania succeeded in allaying Soviet fears sufficiently to be able to take advantage of Soviet preoccupation with China, and to benefit from Chinese economic help and moral support. Chinese supplies of raw materials which the Soviet leaders were withholding from Romania during the 1960s, and Chinese financial aid following the disastrous floods in 1970, helped Bucharest resist political pressures from Moscow. During the 1970s, as China emerged from isolation, its need for Romania decreased. Relations between the two states remained excellent but at a lower and, for the Soviet Union, less irksome level. Peking's support for Romania's position on its rights of sovereignty constituted at least a moral aid.

In Chapter 2, we looked at the legal-political limits for autonomy. Both in their interventions in Hungary in 1956 and in Czechoslovakia in 1968 the Soviet leadership gave elaborate legal justifications for their acts. While this did not imply that a good defense in international law in itself would have deterred Moscow from intervening in these countries, it does show that the Soviet Union was not immune to arguments in international law. The efficacy of such arguments depended to a considerable extent on Soviet and Romanian interpretation of international law. In both of the approaches there was a heavy infusion of

Marxist-Leninism and of the ambiguities inherent in that doctrine. The Soviet Union agreed that the nation-state would continue to exist in the near future and it professed respect for sovereignty in formal terms. Yet at the same time it viewed the flow of power as moving from the general (that is, the Socialist commonwealth) to the particular (the members). Within the Soviet Union itself, Moscow developed a concept of "double sovereignty" of the republics and the Union that, if extended to the bloc states, would have placed them in a subordinate position in law. Furthermore, there is evidence that Moscow is the latter part of the 1960s increasingly accepted a "socialist international law" in its relations with other Socialist states. The latter included the principle that those things that were held to constitute capitalist inroads in a Socialist society could be legally prevented by the commonwealth. And it was argued by Tunkin and other Soviet jurists that in certain instances in applying general international law, *lex specialis derogat generalis.*

On the other hand, there has been an increased acceptance by the Soviet Union of general international law in the postwar era. Tunkin himself admitted that it no longer contained those principles under which it had earlier (in the Soviet view) supported colonialism. Just as significant, Moscow admitted the supremacy of the principles of jus cogens. These, together with the formal Soviet support for the United Nations, then formed the pivot for Romanian legal defenses, for they represented the gaps in Soviet legal justifications for intervention.

Romania made its arguments both in Marxist-Leninist doctrine and in general international law. In both areas it used a technique of restriction through partial incorporation. With skill and perseverance, Romania pressed forth the argument that since the nation-state was to endure, respect for sovereignty was essential. It also asserted that since general international law, as reflected in the UN Charter, together with the contained principles of jus cogens were supreme, there could be no legal justification for interference with the sovereignty of a nonaggressive state. The Romanians stressed these points both domestically and internationally, thereby formulating an active political-legal defense that they could add to their general defense network.

The military limits for Romanian foreign policy autonomy were set by Soviet considerations of its own security. While the concept of security, we found, incorporates both subjective and objective elements, composed of political-ideological, legal, institutional, as well as military, concerns, the latter did play an important role in Soviet policy toward the bloc. The Soviet Union, a seriously flawed superpower (especially economically), found military considerations particularly compelling. Beginning in the 1950s the Soviet military establishment started to play an important role in the decision-making process of Soviet foreign policy. In examining this process, we found that while the military was indeed a strong influence, it was not the paramount influence. It was clearly subordinate to the political leadership; it had to argue its propositions in both political and military terms and was strongly buffeted by the winds of political change.

We also found that the military in the Soviet Union, as in other states, was far from a homogenous body. It included both those who did not wish to tolerate any deviations from Soviet policy in the bloc states, and those who were willing to accept a modicum of pluralism. Therefore, Romania was not faced with a unified Soviet military that pressed the Brezhnev-Kosygin leadership to force it to conform. The decision-making process within the military itself showed that such commanders as Marshal Zakharov, who showed greater tolerance, wielded considerable power, even if the Minister of Defense and the Commander-in-Chief of the Warsaw Pact were "intolerant." In addition, the top military leadership, until the appointment of Kulikov as Chief of the General Staff in 1971, was made up of older officials who held major commands in World War II. This experience was bound to influence their military thinking to a certain extent. Since Germany had been the main threat, it would follow that these officers would have been more concerned with the northern bloc states which were in the geographical line of that threat, than with Romania in the Balkan area. Kulikov received most of his command experience in East Germany and to the extent to which military experience determines a commander's thinking on strategy, he too should have placed Romania into the lower range of his military concerns. The changes in the Soviet military leadership in 1976 and 1977 placed Kulikov in charge of the WTO, another "new generation" general in charge of the General Staff and a civilian in charge of the Ministry of Defense. All had technical backgrounds and all had previously focused on the East-West axis along the Northern Tier.

Under Ceausescu, Romania took certain steps and made certain demands that could be interpreted either as a threat to Soviet security, or as challenges. Given the general Soviet paranoia about controlling the bloc and ensuring strict cohesion, it was always possible that Moscow would equate the micro level of a challenge with the macro level and therefore take it as a threat. Among these challenges, Bucharest refused to participate in Warsaw Pact maneuvers between 1964 and 1967; it refused to allow Warsaw Pact maneuvers on its soil; it did not participate in the intervention in Czechoslovakia; it began after 1968 to build up strong territorial forces and increased military cooperation with Yugoslavia instead of strengthening its regular forces in line with those of other bloc states; in December 1972 it introduced an "all-horizons" Defense Law; and in 1974 and 1976 it asked for the restructuring of the WTO. There is a prima facie question, of course, whether the Soviet Union did consider these actions to be challenges. An analysis of Soviet statements made in response to, or at the time of, these actions, we submit, did indicate that Moscow perceived these actions as challenges. Nevertheless, this did not demonstrate what kind of counteraction the Soviet Union would take, for the existence of a challenge in itself did not mean Soviet intervention, or even an attempt at intervention. Soviet reaction depended on how seriously it viewed these challenges, which in turn would have been determined by, and reflected in, its military policy.

It is not possible, unfortunately, to determine the precise nature of even past Soviet military policies because of the complexities involved and the limited amount of data available, but it has been possible to detect certain trends in its evolution. It is only by placing Romanian military challenges in the perspective of Soviet military policy that one may gauge Soviet reaction and ascertain the defenses available. Soviet military policy appears to have evolved from the "steamroller" approach of Stalin to Khrushchev's emphasis on nuclear weapons and to the Brezhnev and Kosygin policy resembling a "flexible response." Throughout this period, the role of the bloc states evolved from that of a geographic buffer zone to that of providing modern forces for offensive and defensive operations. Romanian challenges, which amounted to a refusal to participate fully in the new role assigned to the bloc states by Moscow, therefore would appear at first glance to have been very grave.

There were, however, a number of factors which mitigated the gravity of the Romanian challenges. The evolution of general Soviet military policy also brought forth a new approach in Soviet military policy toward the bloc states. Despite a quantum increase of Soviet naval strength in the Mediterranean, Soviet war scenarios during the 1970s considered the greatest likelihood of battle to be on an East-West axis leading to West Germany. The bloc states along this axis would have assumed a greater importance in Soviet strategic thinking as a result of their very location. Furthermore, these northern states had more to fear from a West German attack than the others, a fact which should have enhanced their reliability in Soviet eyes. Moreover, the three states in this area—Czechoslovakia, Poland, and the G.D.R.—had the most highly advanced industrial economies in the bloc and the largest and best trained forces (particularly after 1960). Therefore, beginning in the 1960s, Soviet military policy toward the bloc began to exhibit a regionalism that placed a much greater emphasis on the "Northern Tier" states than those in the southern part. Romania, located in the south, without borders with capitalist states, with a weak industrial base, with a population that had no affinity for the Slavs of the Soviet Union and whose regular army was small and modestly equipped, had a limited importance for Soviet military security. A challenge from Romania, therefore, would not have constituted an immediate threat to Soviet security. Moreover, it could be contained. Should the Soviet Union in the future be able to reimpose itself in Yugoslavia and build naval and air bases there, its whole strategic emphasis would shift. Romanian military challenges then would pose a very real danger to Moscow.

Romanian challenges also struck at that Soviet-dominated institution, the Warsaw Pact. That organization, however, paralleled the evolution of Soviet strategic thinking and as such it incorporated regionalism. It was officially acknowledged by the Soviet Union and the WTO in the 1960s that there was a Southern Tier and a Northern Tier, and, moreover, they referred to the latter as the first strategic echelon of the Warsaw Pact. Second, the Warsaw Pact did not manage to evolve into an effective supranational organization—partly due to

Romanian obstruction. The 1976 addition of a Council of Foreign Ministers enhanced its political role while diluting its military functions. Toward the end of the period under study, the Warsaw Pact became something of an instrument for conflict resolution, in a way channeling Romanian challenges and frustrations into a safe locus. Thus, while useful, the Warsaw Pact did not become an indispensable Soviet tool for military control over the bloc states, and therefore challenges to it by Romania could be contained. In that sense, then, it constituted a passive defense. Moreover, it should be pointed out that the Ceausescu leadership did not pose the ultimate challenge to the Warsaw Pact—Bucharest did not withdraw from the Pact, nor did it threaten to do so.

Therefore, it appears that the evolution of Soviet military policy and the Warsaw Pact provided certain passive defenses to Romania through a flexibility that allowed for containment. In fact, there had been no Soviet or Warsaw Pact military intervention in Romania, and this would tend to indicate that its defenses (both active and passive) had been working and that it did not breach the limits of Soviet tolerance. It is not clear, though, whether there had been attempts at intervention, for these could have shown that Romania had come close to or may even have had briefly breached the limits through its actions or as a result of failures in the defense network.

The method we chose to check for an attempt was to search for a pattern, or at least a tendency, in past Soviet military interventions in bloc states. We could not discern a clear pattern, but we did find certain tendencies that delineated an attempt. The most significant of these involved certain Soviet political and military preparations combined with major military maneuvers. As a result, we analyzed the major Soviet and Warsaw Pact military moves and maneuvers that could have posed a danger to Romania. It appeared that the most dangerous of these for Romania took place in 1969 and 1971. While the major maneuvers in those two years bore some resemblance to previous Soviet interventions in bloc states, they lacked certain key elements that would have constituted an attempt, and furthermore they did not appear capable of fulfilling certain Soviet desiderata in an intervention, such as surprise, speed, and maintenance of troop morale. Therefore, these maneuvers were an attempt to intimidate Romania rather than to intervene militarily. Such pressures were designed to force Romania to conform to Soviet policy. If Romania were to continue an autonomous foreign policy (particularly in the military sphere), it had to ensure that it had strong active defenses.

Chapter 5 attempted to assess these active military defenses. The effectiveness of these were not judged on the basis of *an absolute ability to repulse a Soviet intervention*, but rather on their ability to function jointly with passive military, as well as active and passive political defenses to make a Soviet intervention unprofitable and Soviet military pressures ineffective. Initially, Romania had to express, and then to demonstrate, a willingness to resist, by armed force if necessary, any military intervention. Ceausescu and his leadership proclaimed such a willingness on all possible occasions and reemphasized it at crisis points in Soviet-Romanian relations. This in itself, though, could not establish Romanian credibility, for the large and sophisticated Soviet intelligence network would have detected a pure bluff. Romania had to demonstrate a certain degree of military capacity in order to back up its declared willingness to resist.

Bucharest had to ensure that there was ab initio unity between the party and the armed forces. This, in effect, meant party control of the regular army and of the irregular forces. Among the means used to achieve this was that of structural control. The decision-making process was controlled by the political leadership, and the military leadership had to argue their case in political terms. Ceausescu himself assumed the posts of Chairman of the Defense Council and Supreme Commander of the Armed Forces. In order to retain the loyalty of the troops and officers, the Ceausescu leadership made heavy use of such tools as ideological indoctrination, material incentives, and appeals to patriotism.

Soviet-Romanian crises allowed for proof of the effectiveness of these methods. The armed forces fully supported the Romanian Communist Party and Ceausescu throughout these crises, though in a rather surreptitious manner, following the August 1968 intervention in Czechoslovakia.

As well, Ceausescu moved to assure that there was national support for the territorial integrity of the country. He restricted severely the cultural rights of the large Hungarian minority in Transylvania, abolished the Maghiar Autonomous Region and stressed the process of Romanianization in an attempt to stifle any potential organized irredentism.

The Ceausescu leadership also took concrete measures to enhance the fighting capacity of Romanian armed forces. After 1967, increased emphasis was placed on the domestic production of small arms, of all types of ammunition, transport equipment, some aircraft, of spare parts, and on providing improved services for the maintenance of heavy armaments. As well, Romania cooperated with Yugoslavia in arms production and purchased armaments from the West. All of these lessened, to an extent, Romanian dependence on Soviet arms and increased the capacity of the Romanian forces to put up a prolonged fight.

An even more important development was the institution, after August 1968, of large, armed irregular forces in Romania, and the subsequent change in Romanian strategic thinking. On August 21, 1968, Ceausescu announced the formation of an armed Patriotic Guard of 100,000 taken from representative sections of the population. As well, students and workers were to be given military training. The Defense Law of 1972, in turn, made it illegal to cede any part of Romanian territory to an invader. Equally important after 1968, Romanian war scenarios envisioned resistance by a "people's" (or involving guerrillas) war. The bulk of the regular forces would not bear the brunt of the invasion but rather would have been held in reserve and used only when they could deliver decisive blows. The irregular forces were to meet the invader first, harass him, make use of the local terrain, and if need be continue the fight from the mountains, in conjunction with the regular army.

Furthermore, Romania moved to protect its flanks in order to avoid an all-points-of-the-compass intervention. Ceausescu reached an understanding with Tito that at the minimum ensured Yugoslav neutrality and could conceivably have included a form of military alliance. As well, Ceausescu maintained friendly relations with Bulgaria. He constantly reiterated the need for stability in the Balkans, together with the benefits of Romanian-Bulgarian friendship, in order to minimize any possible contribution that Bulgaria would have made to a Soviet and Warsaw Pact intervention in Romania.

Thus it appears that Romania had the capacity after 1968 to conduct a prolonged "people's" war against a powerful invader. Ceausescu's warnings to the country at times of crises deprived the Soviet Union of the element of surprise, while Romania's capacity to put up a prolonged resistance would have deprived the Soviet Union of speed. The latter, in turn, would have affected the morale of the Soviet troops. Since the Soviet Union had no desire to get bogged down in a Vietnam-type operation in the Balkans, the active Romanian military defenses should have acted as an important deterrent to intervention. In that sense, these defenses enlarged the limits for Romanian foreign policy autonomy.

A source of weakness in these Romanian defenses, however, may be found in the domestic developments in the country. These would relate perhaps more to the future than to the present and past but there has been evidence of strain that could affect the overall defense network. Particularly since the Romanian organization of defense has been geared toward a peoples' war, national morale and support for the leadership is essential. The attempts to modernize Romania, however, have put tremendous strains on the Romanian population. Industrialization especially has been and is being achieved at an extremely high cost to the population. It had been accomplished through vast investments that took away large sums of money from wages and social benefits. As a result, Romanian workers have the lowest wages in all of the bloc states and there is an acute housing crisis in the country. The expansion in industry had been largely labor intensive but it still involved huge capital expenditures. There is evidence of gross inefficiency in the economy and Ceausescu himself admitted in 1977 that one million workers were not doing useful or needed work in the economy.[1]

At the 11th Party Congress in 1974, moreover, the Romanian leadership embarked upon an extremely ambitious industrial growth program that was designed to fulfill Ceausescu's ambition to make Romania into an industrial power. It called for industrial production to increase between six-and-a-half and seven-and-a-half times between 1970 and 1990, including the production of 27 million tons of steel.[2] Previously, industrial growth had been helped by the large movement of peasants to the cities. Romanian agriculture, however, in the 1970s was the most inefficient in the entire Soviet bloc[3] and it could no longer release large numbers of workers because most of the excess had already left for the cities. Ceausescu himself acknowledged that there were shortages of workers in the construction industry, for instance, in 1977,[4] and in an effort to get more workers, the new 1977 penal reforms allowed young convicts to serve their time working at various industrial enterprises instead of being incarcerated. Virtually all of the growth, though, had to come from increased productivity and for this again huge sums of money had to be expended, with the result that wages would continue to remain very low, despite periodic increases. For instance, for 1985 the per-capita income was only projected to be between $2,400 and $2,500, by Bucharest.[5]

Another factor affecting Romania's domestic scene has been Ceausescu's emphasis on patriotism and diplomatic prestige. Both of these were highly valued by the Romanian population and were important in rallying support to the Communist party and to Ceausescu. Appeals to patriotism, however, do suffer in peacetime from a particular form of the law of diminishing returns. As Romania became entrenched upon its course of industrialization, the economic urgency for autonomy decreased, for there was less danger of it being forced to become the "hewer of wood and the drawer of water" in the Soviet bloc. Appeals to patriotism could not substitute indefinitely for better wages or for improved social services. Coupled with intellectual restrictions, these factors have given rise to a number of isolated instances of protest within Romania. The most serious had been strikes by miners, particularly in the Jiu Valley area during 1972 and especially in 1977, when these were well documented by Western sources.[6] There were also some protests from a number of writers when Paul Goma was forced into exile in Paris during 1977. It is conceivable that these strains may well increase in the future, thereby undermining Romanian morale, which already appears to be fairly low and as such present a danger to the functioning of the entire defense network.

There should be a caveat, however, in any analysis of dissent in Romania. The country has a remarkably docile population with an intelligentsia that is by and large much more concerned with the "pecking order" than civil liberties. The strikes in Romania were isolated events and were easily contained, unlike those in Poland. Furthermore, in case of external crisis, populations rally around even unpopular governments. The strains that are evident now are not of the nature that would likely present a danger now, or in the near future. What they point to, however, is that after the mid-1980s if the present trends continue, there may be a domestic development that could undermine the Romanian political military defense network.

During the period under study, then, Romania still had a strong set of active and passive, political and military defenses. It was a very complex set of defenses that had to be coordinated carefully in order to provide an effective defense network that would have allowed the country to pursue its autonomous foreign policy. This coordination was done largely through the figure of Ceausescu, who occupied by the mid-1970s the position of the President of the Republic, the President of the State Council, the President of the Supreme Council of Economic and Social Development, the President of the Defense Council, Supreme Commander of the Romanian Armed Forces, and Secretary General of the Romanian Communist Party. Therefore, he occupied all of the important posts in the country and coupled with the incredibly extensive and intensive personality cult he promoted, he made the phrase *l'état, c'est moi,* quite valid in Romania. He ensured that there were no political rivals left or anyone with a power base of his own. This resulted in the fact that all of his subordinates owed their position to him and sank or swam with him. This in a sense was an additional defense against external pressures. This overcentralization of the command structure, however, presents some problems in itself. There is no provision for a smooth succession in case Ceausescu leaves the scene. No one is powerful enough in the country to take over all or even most of these posts. Therefore, during the succession period there would be an intensive struggle among a collective leadership for supremacy, during which time the efficiency of Romania's political and military defenses would be tremendously weakened. While Ceausescu is still youthful and apparently in excellent health, a fatal accident could leave the country in turmoil.

Nevertheless during the period of this study Ceausescu was in office and was able to provide the necessary and delicate coordination of Romania's defenses. To this job he brought the chauvinistic prejudices that he developed from an early age* and a considerable organizational experience. This included supervision of the collectivization of agriculture[8] and service as Deputy Minister of the Armed Forces and Chief of the Higher Political Directorate of the Army, with the rank of General-Lieutenant.[9] Thus Romania had a capable if somewhat ruthless coordinator of its defense network.

Since this network functioned well, Romania has been able to pursue an autonomous foreign policy despite Soviet pressures to conform to its policy line. The effectiveness of the defense network helped to maintain or expand the limits. As the scope of Romanian foreign policy autonomy itself was modest, containable, and quintessentially Romanian, Bucharest acted within a considerable safety margin of the Soviet military and political limits of tolerance.

NOTES

1. N. Ceausescu, *Cuvintare la plenara Comitetului Central al Partidului Comunist Roman 29 Junie 1977* (Bucharest: Editura Politica, 1977), p. 11.

2. "Directivele Congresului al XI al Parditului Comunist Roman," *Scinteia*, August 3, 1974.

3. *Anuarul Statistic al R.S.R. 1977*, Bucharest, 1977, p. 219.

4. Ceausescu, op. cit., p. 11.

5. *Romania Libera*, December 8, 1977, p. 9.

6. *The Globe and Mail* (Toronto), November 28, 1977.

7. Michel P. Hamelet, *Nicolae Ceausescu* (Bucharest: Editura Politica, 1971), p. 10.

8. Ibid., p. 62.

9. Ibid.

---

*His home village, Scornicesti, had provided four captains for Mihai Viteazu in the 16th century, when he briefly united the Romanian principalities.[7]

Bibliography

BOOKS: GENERAL

Admoeit, Hannes. 1973. *Soviet Risk-Taking and Crisis Behaviour: From Confrontation to Coexistence*. Adelphi Paper No. 101. London: International Institute for Strategic Studies.

Antip, Colonel C., and Colonel G. Bejancu. 1966. *The Armed Forces of the Socialist Republic of Romania*. Bucharest: Military Publishing House.

Aron, Raymond. 1966. *Peace and War*. Garden City, New York: Doubleday & Co.

Art, R. J., and K. N. Waltz. 1971. *The Use of Force*. Boston: Little, Brown & Co.

Aspaturian, Vernon V., ed. 1971. *Process and Power in Soviet Foreign Policy*. Boston: Little, Brown & Co.

Bender, Peter. 1972. *East Europe in Search of Security*. London: Chatto and Windus.

Brant, Stefan. 1955. *The East German Rising*. London: Thames and Hudson.

Brown, J. F. 1966. *The New Eastern Europe*. New York: Praeger.

Brzezinski, Zbigniew. 1967. *The Soviet Bloc: Unity and Conflict*. Cambridge, Mass.: Harvard University Press.

Buchan, Alastair, and Philip Windsor. 1963. *Arms and Stability in Europe*. New York: F. A. Praeger.

Capatina, Dan, and Sergiu Iosipescu. 1973. *File Din Cronici*. Bucharest: Editura Militara.

Cernat, I. S., & E. J. Stanislav., eds. 1974. *Doctrina Militara a Romaniei Socialiste*. Bucharest: Editura Politica.

——. 1974. *Apararea Nationala a Romaniei Socialiste*. Bucharest: Editura Militara.

Cernea, Mihail. 1964. *Dialectica Construiri Socialismului*. Bucharest: Editura Stiintifica.

Ceterchi, Ioan. 1975. *Socialist Democracy*. Bucharest: Meridiane Publishing House.

Constantinescu, G. 1970. *Romania's Economy*. Bucharest: Meridiane Publishing House.

Dallin, David J. 1962. *Soviet Foreign Policy After Stalin*. London: Methuen & Co.

Dinerstein, H. S. 1959. *War and the Soviet Union*. London: Atlantic Books, Stevens and Sons.

Djilas, M. 1962. *Conversations with Stalin*. London: Rupert, Hart, Davis.

Doolin, Dennis J. 1965. *Territorial Claims in the Sino-Soviet Conflict*. Stanford, California: The Hoover Institute.

Ecobescu, Nicolae, ed. 1976. *Catre O Noua Ordine Internationala*. Bucharest: Editura Politica.

Ecobescu, N., and S. Celac. 1975. *Politica externa a Romaniei Socialiste*. Bucharest: Editura Politica.

Erickson, John. 1971. *Soviet Military Power*. London: RUSI.

——. 1962. *The Soviet High Command 1918-1941*. London: Macmillan & Co. Ltd.

——. 1976. *Soviet-Warsaw Pact Force Levels*. Washington: USSI Report 76–2.

Fischer-Galati, S. 1967. *The New Rumania: From People's Democracy to a Socialist Republic*. Cambridge, Mass.: M.I.T. Press.

——. 1970. *Twentieth Century Rumania*. New York: Praeger.

Floyd, David. 1965. *Rumania: Russia's Dissident Ally*. New York: F. A. Praeger.

Frankel, Joseph. 1963. *The Making of Foreign Policy*. London: Oxford University Press.

Gallagher, M., and R. Kolkowicz, et al. 1970. *The Soviet Union and Arms Control*. Baltimore: Johns Hopkins Press.

Gallagher, M. P., and K. F. Spielmann, Jr. 1972. *Soviet Decision-Making for Defense*. New York: Praeger.

Garder, Micel. 1966. *A History of the Soviet Army*. London: Pall Mall Press.

Garthoff, R. L. 1954. *How Russia Makes War*. London: George Allen & Unwin Ltd.

——, ed. 1966. *Sino-Soviet Military Relations*. New York: Praeger.

——. 1966. *Soviet Military Policy*. London: Faber and Faber.

——. 1958. *Soviet Strategy in the Nuclear Age*. New York: Praeger.

——. 1959. *The Soviet Image of Future War*. Washington: Public Affairs Press.

Goure, L., F. D. Kohler, and M. L. Harvey. 1974. *The Role of Nuclear Forces in Current Soviet Strategy*. Coral Gables, Fla.: Center of Advanced International Studies, University of Miami.

Griffith, W. E. 1971. *The Great Globe Transformed*. Cambridge, Mass.: M.I.T. Press.

——. 1964. *The Sino-Soviet Rift*. London: Allen & Unwin.

Hale, Julian. 1971. *Ceausescu's Romania*. London: George G. Harrap & Co.

Hamelet, Michel P. 1971. *Nicolai Ceausescu*. Bucharest: Editura Politica.

Hanak, H. 1972. *Soviet Foreign Policy Since the Death of Stalin*. London: Routledge & Kegan Paul.

Hartmann, R. H. 1967. *The Relations of Nations*. New York: The Macmillan Co.

Harvey, M. L., L. Goure, and W. Prokofieff. 1972. *Science and Technology as an Instrument of Soviet Policy*. Coral Gables, Fla.: Center for Advanced Studies, University of Miami.

Holsti, K. J. 1967. *International Politics*. Englewood Cliffs, N.J.: Prentice-Hall.

Horelick, A. L. and M. Rush. 1966. *Strategic Power and Soviet Foreign Policy*. Chicago: University of Chicago Press.

Horton, F. B., A. C. Rogerson, and E. W. Warner, eds. 1974. *Comparative Defense Policy*. Baltimore: Johns Hopkins Press.

Ionescu, Ghita. 1964. *Communism in Rumania 1944-1962*. London: Oxford University Press.

——. 1965. *The Breakup of the Soviet Empire in Eastern Europe*. Baltimore, Md.: Penguin Special.

——, ed. 1972. *The New Politics of European Integration*. London: Weidenfeld and Nicholson.

——. 1967. *The Politics of the European Communist States*. London: Weidenfeld and Nicholson.

Jacobsen, Carl G. 1972. *Soviet-Strategy-Soviet Foreign Policy*. Glasgow: Robert Mackenzie & Co.

James, Alan. 1969. *The Role of Force in International and U.N. Peace Keeping*. Enstone, Oxford: The Ditchley Foundation.

Jamgotch, Nish. 1968. *Soviet-East European Dialogue*. Stanford: Stanford University Press.

Jowitt, Kenneth. 1971. *Revolutionary Breakthrough and National Development: The Case of Romania 1944-1965*. Berkeley: University of California Press.

Jukes, Geoffrey. 1972. *The Development of Soviet Strategic Thinking Since 1945*. Canberra: Australian National University Press.

Kaser, Michael. 1967. *Comecon: Integration Problems of the Planned Economies*. 2nd ed. London: Oxford University Press for RIIA.

Kaufman, W. W., ed. 1956. *Military Policy and National Security*. London: Oxford University Press.

Kennedy, R. F. 1969. *Thirteen Days: The Cuban Missile Crisis, October 1962*. New York: W. W. Norton & Co.

King, Robert R., and R. W. Dean. 1974. *East European Perspectives on European Security and Co-operation*. New York: Praeger.

Kintner, W. R., and R. L. Pfaltzgraff, Jr. 1971. *Soviet Military Trends: Implications for U.S. Security*. Washington: American Enterprise Institute for Public Policy Research.

Kintner, W. R., and H. F. Scott. 1968. *The Nuclear Revolution in Soviet Military Affairs*. Norman: University of Oklahoma Press.

Knorr, Klaus. 1966. *On the Uses of Military Power in the Nuclear Age*. Princeton, N.J.: Princeton University Press.

Kolkowicz, Roman. 1967. *The Soviet Military and Communist Party*. Princeton, N.J.: Princeton University Press.

Labedz, L., and C. R. Urban. 1965. *The Sino-Soviet Conflict*. London: The Bodley Head.

Lendvai, Emil. 1965. *Eagles in Cobwebs*. New York: Praeger.

Mackintosh, M. 1967. *Juggernaut: A History of the Soviet Armed Forces*. London: Secker and Warburg.

——. 1962. *Strategy and Tactics of Soviet Foreign Policy.* London: Oxford University Press.

Merglen, Albert. 1968. *Surprise Warfare.* London: Allen & Unwin.

Merriam, C. 1934. *Political Power: Its Composition and Incidence.* New York: McGraw-Hill.

Moca, G. 1973. *Suveranitatea de Stat: Teorii Burgheze Studii Critic.* Bucharest: Editura Politica.

Montias, J. M. 1967. *Economic Development in Communist Rumania.* Cambridge, Mass.: M.I.T. Press.

Morgenthau, Hans. 1965. *Politics Among Nations.* New York: Alfred A. Knopf.

Murgescu, Costin. 1974. *Romania's Socialist Economy.* Bucharest: Meridiane Publishing House.

Nagy, Imre. 1957. *On Communism.* London: Thames and Hudson.

Northedge, F. S. 1974. *The Use of Force in International Relations.* London: Faber and Faber.

O'Ballance, Edgar. 1964. *The Red Army.* London: Faber and Faber.

Onescu, Colonel V. 1964. *Efortul Economic al Poporului Roman in Razboiul Antihitlerist.* Bucharest: Editura Politica.

Osanka, Mark Franklin. 1962. *Modern Guerrilla Warfare.* New York: The Free Press of Glencoe.

Pitea, Simion. 1976. *Economia si apararea nationala.* Bucharest: Editura Militara.

Remington, Robin Alison. 1971. *The Warsaw Pact: Case Studies in Communist Conflict Resolution.* Cambridge, Mass.: M.I.T. Press.

Roberts, Henry L. 1970. *Eastern Europe: Politics Revolution and Diplomacy.* New York: Harper.

Schapiro, Leonard. 1970. *The Communist Party of the Soviet Union.* 2nd ed. London: Eyre & Spottiswoode.

Schelling, Thomas C. 1960. *The Strategy of Conflict.* Cambridge, Mass.: Harvard University Press.

Schopflin, G. 1970. *The Soviet Union and Eastern Europe.* London: A. Bond.

Seton–Watson, Hugh. 1961. *The New Imperialism*. London: The Bodley Head.

Skilling, H. Gordon. 1966. *The Governments of Communist East Europe*. New York: Crowell.

Snyder, Glenn H. 1961. *Deterrence and Defense*. Princeton, N.J.: Princeton University Press.

Sokolovsky, Marshal V. D., ed. 1963. *Military Strategy: Soviet Doctrine and Concepts*. London: Pall Mall Press.

Spigler, Iancu. 1973. *Economic Reform in Rumanian Industry*. London: Oxford University Press.

Staar, Richard F. 1967. *The Communist Regimes of Eastern Europe: An Introduction*. Stanford, California: Hoover Institute.

Tai, Sung An. 1973. *The Sino-Soviet Territorial Dispute*. Philadelphia: The Westminster Press.

Tanasescu, G. 1976. *Rolul Statului in Dezvolarea Agriculturii Socialiste*. Bucharest: Editura Politica.

Tatu, Michel. 1969. *Power in the Kremlin*. London: William Collins Sons & Co.

Toma, P. A., ed. 1970. *The Changing Face of Communism in Eastern Europe*. Tucson: University of Arizona Press.

Twitchell, K. H., ed. 1971. *International Security*. London: Oxford University Press.

Ulam, Adam B. 1968. *Expansion and Coexistence*. London: Secker & Warburg.

Wolfe, T. W. 1964. *Soviet Strategy at the Crossroads*. Cambridge, Mass.: Harvard University Press.

——. 1970. *Soviet Power and Europe 1945–1970*. Baltimore: Johns Hopkins Press.

——. 1966. *The Soviet Military Scene: Institutional and Defense Policy Considerations*. Rand Corporation Memorandum, RM-4913-PR June 1966.

——. 1961. *Trends in Soviet Thinking on Theater Warfare, Conventional Preparations and Limited War*. Rand Corporation Memorandum RM-4305-PR.

SELECTED ROMANIAN PERIODICAL ARTICLES

Belli, N., and M. Chirita. 1971. "Aspete Economice ale Infaptuirii Securitatii Europeene." *Rivista Romana de Studii Internationale*, Bucharest: ADIRI, Anul V(4/14).

Berar, P., and Ioan Mitran. 1971. "The Unity of Theory and Practice in Party Activity." *Lupta de Clasa*, Bucharest: June.

Bogdan, Cornelui. 1977. "Europe in a Changing World." *Revue Roumaine d'Etudes Internationales*, 2(36).

Bogdan, Radu. 1968. "The Codification of the Contemporary International Law—a Stringent Necessity." *Lupta de Clasa*, Bucharest: October.

Ceausescu, N. 1965. "Report to the Grand National Assembly." *Lupta de Clasa*, Bucharest: September.

Celac, Sergiu. 1970. "Securitatea si colaborarea in Europa." *Lupta de Clasa*, Bucharest: May.

Closca, I. 1969. "The Necessity for a Negotiated Settlement of International Issues." *Lupta de Clasa*, Bucharest: February.

Csik, Nedelea. 1970. "The Dialectics of the National and International in the Development of Socialist Society." *Lupta de Clasa*, Bucharest: January.

Duculescu, V. 1973. "The Sovereign State in International Relations." *Era Socialista*, Bucharest: July 13.

Ecobescu, N., and D. I. Mazilu. 1970. "Securitatea si Colaborarea in Europa." *Lupta de Clasa*, Bucharest: June.

Fintinaru, I. 1965. "Criza de N.A.T.O." *Lupta de Clasa*, Bucharest: February.

Florian, Radu. 1972. "Cu Privire la Contradictiile Societatii Socialiste." *Lupta de Clasa*, Bucharest: May.

Hutima, E., and Ion Dinu. 1965. "Industrializarea Socialista—Obiectul Central al Partidului." *Lupta de Clasa*, Bucharest: December.

Ionescu-Guilian, C. 1964. "Marxismul si Antropologia Filozofica." *Lupta de Clasa*, Bucharest: September.

Lazarescu, C. 1970. "Suveranitatea." *Lupta de Clasa*, Bucharest: April.

———. 1967. "The Evolution of the Contemporary World and the Principles of International Relations." *Lupta de Clasa*, Bucharest: September.

Macovescu, Gheorghe. 1967. "International Relations and the Struggle for Peace." *Lupta de Clasa*, Bucharest: December.

Mazilu, D. 1971. "In Full Accord with the Fundamental Decisions of the Epoch." *Lupta de Clasa*, Bucharest: October.

Mitea, C. 1972. "Idea de Securitatea Europeana." *Lupta de Clasa*, Bucharest: February.

Mitran, Ion. 1968. "Unitate Trainica intre poper si partid." *Lupta de Clasa*, Bucharest: September.

Moldovan, R. 1970. "Colaborarea economica intre statele socialiste." *Lupta de Clasa*, Bucharest: April.

Pana, Gheorghe. 1971. "Leadership by the Romanian Communist Party in the Entire Activity of Building the Multilaterally Developed Socialist Society." *Lupta de Clasa*, Bucharest: December.

Papadopol, Vasile. 1968. "Codul Penal Nou." *Lupta de Clasa*, Bucharest: May.

Paruta, Mihai. 1973. "Setting International Economic Relations on a New Basis." *Viata Economica*, Bucharest: October 12.

Popescu, Dumitru. 1972. "Implications of the Party's Ideological Program in the Literary Output." *Lupta de Clasa*, Bucharest: February.

Popescu, Nicolae Atin. 1969. "Securitatea si colaborarea in Europa." *Lupta de Clasa*, Bucharest: June.

Radulescu, Ilie. 1966. "Rolul Conducator al statului nostru socialist." *Lupta de Clasa*, Bucharest: March.

——. 1973. "The National and the International Aspects of Contemporary Economic Collaboration." *Probleme Economice*, Bucharest: August.

Voicu, Ion. 1973. "National Sovereignty and the Doctrine of International Law." *Era Socialista*, Bucharest: September 18.

SELECTED ROMANIAN DOCUMENTS

Bill on the Organization of National Defense of the Socialist Republic of Romania. *Scinteia*, December 29, 1972.

Central Statistical Bureau. 1971. *Statistical Pocket Book of the Socialist Republic of Romania 1971*, Bucharest.

Codul de Procedura Penala. 1969. *Buletinul Oficial al R.S.R.* No. 145–146. Bucharest.

Codul Penal al Republicii Socialiste Romana. 1968. Bucharest: Editura Politica.

Conferinta Nationala a Partidului Communist Roman 19-21 Iulie. 1972. Bucharest: Editura Politica.

Consiliul de Stat. 1976. *Constitutia Republicii Socialiste Romania.*

Constitution of the Socialist Republic of Romania. 1969. Bucharest: Meridiane Publishing House.

Cuvintare la Consfatuirea Cadrelor din Ministerul Fortelor Armate. 1970. Bucharest: Editura Politica, February.

Decree on Organization and Operation of the Ministry of National Defense. 1972. *Buletinul Oficial al Republicii Socialiste Romana,* Pt. I, No. 130, November 21, pp. 1048–1051.

Digest of General Laws of Romania, Vol. 1-4. 1976. Bucharest: Editura Stiintifica si Enciclopedica.

Directia Central de Statistica. 1965–1977. *Anuarul Statistic al R.S.R.* Bucharest.

Directives of the Eleventh Congress of the R.C.P. 1975. Bucharest: Meridiane Publishing House.

Raport la cel de-al XI-lea Congres al P.C.R. 1974. Bucharest: Editura Politica.

Romania pe Drumul Construirii Societatii Socialiste Multilateral Dezvoltate (N. Ceausescu speeches) Vols. 1–11. 1965–1977. Bucharest: Editura Politica.

Sub semnul prienteniei fratesti romane-bulgare. 1977. Bucharest: Editura Politica.

Sub semnul prieteniei fratesti roman-iugoslave. 1977. Bucharest: Editura Politica.

Sub Steagul Internationalismului Socialist June 1965–June 1972. 1972. Bucharest: Editura Politica.

Tratatul de Varsovie. 1955. *Scinteia,* May 15.

SELECTED PERIODICALS AND NEWSPAPERS

Apararea Patriei. Central Organ of the Ministry of the Armed Forces, 137 Str Izvor, Bucharest.

Buletinul Oficial al Republicii Socialiste Romana. Bucharest.

Contemporanul. Saptaminal Politic, Social, Cultural. Bucharest.

Gazeta Literara. Organ saptaminal al uniunii Scriitoritor din Republica Socialista Romana.

Luceafarul. Revista de uniunea de scriitori din Republica Socialista Romana.

Lupta de Clasa. Theoretical Organ of the Central Committee of the Romanian Communist Party. Bucharest to August 1972, thereafter changed to *Era Socialista.*

Nepszabadsag. Daily organ of the Hungarian Communist Party. Budapest.

Probleme Economice. Societatea de Stiinte Economice din R.S.R., Academia R.S.R., Bucharest.

Revista Economica. Consiliul Suprem al Dezvoltarii economice si sociale. Bucharest.

Revue Roumaine D'Etudes Internationales. À.D.I.R.I. Bucharest.

Romania libera. Cotidian Politic de Informatie, Reportaj si Comentariu—after 1968—Cotidianul Consiului National al Frontului Unitatii Socialiste.

Romania literara. Saptaminal al Uniunea Scriitorilor din R.S.R. Bucharest.

Scinteia. Daily organ of the Central Committee of the Romanian Communist Party. Bucharest.

Sovetskoe Gosudarstvo i Pravo. Moscow.

Studii. Academia de stiinte sociale si politice din R.S.R. Bucharest.

Viata Militara. Editura Militara. Bucharest.

Index

About the Author

AUREL BRAUN is assistant professor of international relations at the University of Western Ontario and a research associate of the Centre for International Relations at Queen's University.

Dr. Braun is the author of several articles on Eastern Europe and strategic studies.

He holds a B.A. and M.A. from the University of Toronto and a Ph.D. in international relations from the London School of Economics, London, England.

Related Titles
Published by
Praeger Special Studies

THE FRENCH COMMUNIST PARTY IN TRANSITION:
PCF-CPSU Relations and the Challenge to Soviet
Authority

Annette Eisenberg Stiefbold

*THE INTERNATIONAL POLITICS OF EASTERN EUROPE
edited by
Charles Gati

**NATIONS IN ARMS: The Theory and Practice
of Territorial Defense

Adam Roberts

*POLITICAL DEVELOPMENT IN EASTERN EUROPE
edited by
Jan F. Triska and
Paul M. Cocks

YUGOSLAVIA AFTER TITO

Andrew Borowiec

*Also available in paperback.
**For sale in U.S. and Phillipines

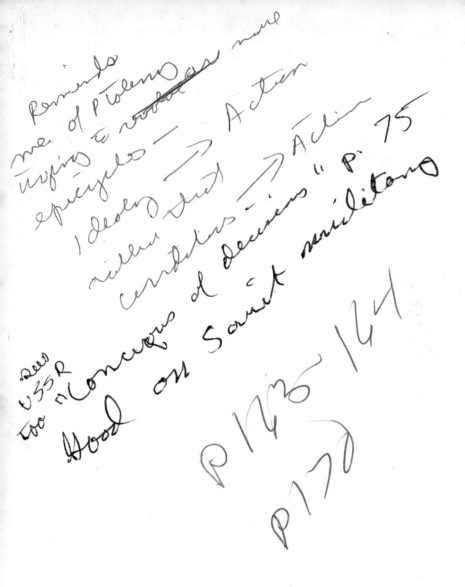